fire season

GARY INDIANA
fire season
selected essays 1984-2021

introduction by
CHRISTIAN LORENTZEN

SEVEN STORIES PRESS UK
London

Copyright © 1984, 1992, 1993, 1996, 1999, 2000, 2002, 2004, 2006, 2008, 2009, 2010, 2011, 2012, 2013, 2015, 2018, 2020, 2021 by Gary Indiana.

Many of the earlier essays in this book
were published in a previous collection entitled Let It Bleed.

All rights reserved. No part of this book may be reproduced, stored in a retrieval system, or transmitted in any form or by any means, including mechanical, electronic, photocopying, recording, or otherwise, without the prior written permission of the publisher.

Seven Stories Press UK
8 Blackstock Mews, Islington
London N4 2BT
United Kingdom

ISBN: 978-1-838415-95-2 (paperback)

9 8 7 6 5 4 3 2 1

For Susan Willmarth

CONTENTS

Introduction by Christian Lorentzen   xi

I Did Not Know Anna Politkovskaya   1

Barbara Kruger: The War at Home   8

The Steilneset Memorial   15

Northern Exposure   20

The Brothers   45

Romanian Notes   58

Being and Nothingness American Style   68

Weiner's Dong, and Other Products of the Perfected Civilization   79

Pasolini, *Mamma Roma*, and *La Ricotta*   89

The Sadean Cinema   94

Murdering the Dead   99

Hazards of a Snowball Fight   106

Missive Impossible   115

Peak Attitude: The Novels of Renata Adler   119

Parade's End: Echenoz's *1914*   130

Don't Buy Us with Sorry After Burning Down the Barn   134

The P and I   140

Town of the Living Dead   148

LA Plays Itself   167

Pierre Guyotat's *Coma*	197
Barbet and Koko: An Equivocal Love Affair	201
Mastering the Art of Soviet Cooking, by Anya von Bremzen	207
Paul Scheerbart, or The Eccentricities of a Nightingale	217
Unica Zürn	224
Munch's Telephone	231
A Coney Island of the Viscera	236
Tough Love and Carbon Monoxide in Detroit	247
And Rats in All the Palm Trees, Too	260
Always Leave Them Wanting Less	264
Hidden in Plain Sight: Robert Bresson's *Pickpocket*	276
Movie Rites	281
Disneyland Burns	284
Daniel Schmid's *La Paloma*	308
Caviani's Ripley	311
The Serpentine Movements of Chance	314
Notes on Sam	319
Hannah and Her Sister	325
Somewhat Slightly Dazed: On the Art of Roni Horn	334
Viva Manchette!	345

Have you made any plans?
Take an overdose, slash my wrists then hang myself.
All those together?
It couldn't possibly be misconstrued as a cry for help.

SARAH KANE, *4:48 Psychosis*

INTRODUCTION

CHRISTIAN LORENTZEN

"Up close, Bill Clinton looks like he's covered in fresh fetal tissue." So begins Gary Indiana's report on the 1992 New Hampshire primaries. Right away an aspect of Indiana's genius is present: the phrase, profane yet precise, that transforms an oversaturated image, the face of an all-too-familiar figure, and remains burned in your mind for good. Then the overtones: the abortion debate, the notion of an experimental Frankenstein politics mixing right and left, and the overgrown baby who was soon to be elevated to the White House. We know how that turned out and that there was worse to come. This is what Clinton sounded like at the time: "The platitudinous verbal droppings, more like noises one makes to stimulate horses than actual thoughts, also resemble bromides from a soothing commercial for Preparation H: the proctologist, on close examination, has ruled against radical surgery in favor of something smooth and greasy and easy to dissolve in the collective rectum." The recourse to the scatological, to find the disgust in a political style that runs cover for corporate greed, jetset plundering, and the heartland immiserations of globalization. It still holds in the Democratic Party today. What are the words of Biden, Harris, and Buttigieg but balms against their obviously hemorrhoidal GOP opponents?

Political assassinations, witch trials, episodes of torture, videotaped police beatings, bloody foreign invasions, crudely administered if humane assisted suicides, seedy crimes of passion and revenge—these are some of the forms of violence that are the backdrop of *Fire Season*. A cliché much repeated these days is that "the end of history" was reached with the dismantling of the Berlin Wall in 1989 or the dissolution of the Soviet Union in 1991, and that Clinton presided over a temporal interzone that was either an affluent coma or simply a long party accompanied by blackout, until history resumed with the attacks of 9/11 or the financial crash of 2008 or the Brexit referendum and the election of Donald Trump in 2016. That was never true—it never seemed true at the time—and the essays in this volume prove it. Gary Indiana was born in 1950 in Derry, New Hampshire. He had lived a dozen lives already, in Berkeley, Los Angeles, and New York City, writing poems, stories, and plays, and acting in films around the world, before he published his first novel, *Horse Crazy*, in 1988. His work connects the twentieth and the twenty-first centuries in ways readers and critics are only beginning to apprehend.

The essays in *Fire Season* span from 1985 to 2020. Their geographic reach is roughly from Moscow (the meagre wonders of cooking in Soviet times; the murder of the journalist Anna Politkovskaya under the Putin kleptocracy) to Los Angeles (the murder of the Black Dahlia; the trial of the cops who thrashed Rodney King). Psychically, *Fire Season*'s center of gravity might be the 1960s. A trio of essays take up its rippling hangovers: there is the Kennedy assassination, which Indiana identifies as ground zero of America's "violated innocence" and therefore its subsequent apparent derangement; there is Branson, Mississippi, a landlocked resort where he inspects washed-up refugees from the *Lawrence Welk Show* who dance and sing to make a few dollars before their date with the embalmer; and there is Andy Warhol, subject of the latest essay collected here, from 2020, a virtuoso exercise in correcting a biographer's philistine misremembering performed by an eye witness.

Indiana is often associated in the popular mind or the minds of magazine editors with the "Downtown" Manhattan of the 1980s, and while this is not wrong—he was living as he does still, some of the time, in the East Village, was present at the Mudd Club, and so on—it is not enough. The vision of his novels, especially his true crime trilogy (*Resentment, Three Month Fever, Depraved Indifference*) spans the whole of America, and his literary sensibility is rooted in Europe. He was art critic for the *Village Voice* from 1985 to 1988 (those columns are collected in the recent volume *Vile Days*), and the criticism that has followed, much of which is in this book, demonstrates a corollary to Renata Adler's judgment that regular critics usually go "shrill" or "stale" or "shrill and stale" and become "hacks" after prolonged exposure to reviewing works that are neither masterpieces nor atrocities but merely the stuff that's around in a given week when the deadline comes: the risk of hackdom (Indiana quit the art critic job out of boredom) is a necessary one for the serious critic to become great.

Most of the writers, artists, and filmmakers Indiana scrutinizes in these pages are geniuses, and his criticism meets them at their level. From the fictions of Paul Scheerbart to the paintings of the young artist Sam McKinniss (one of which is on the cover of this book), through Samuel Beckett, Unica Zürn, Robert Bresson, Jean-Pierre Melville, Pier Paolo Pasolini, Louise Bourgeois, Adler herself, Jean-Patrick Manchette, Barbet Schroeder, Barbara Kruger, Tracey Emin, Roni Horn, and so on—Indiana's subjects, yoked together, take on the quality of a personal cannon. Not entirely alternate (there's a Nobel winner in there) but far from obvious, their grouping here, an act of haphazard curation on Indiana's part, is a welcome tonic in an age when the concept of the lasting has been evacuated in favor of the metrics of hype. Our only hope in such a world is a critic as sophisticated and independent as Indiana to inform our own judgments and reactions. There is acid in everything Indiana writes, but it is of the sort that acts as a purifying agent, eliminating adulterants, euphemisms, phony received wisdom. His essays are humane to the core.

Like the Clintons, George W. Bush, Donald Trump, Martha Stewart, Steven Spielberg, Oprah Winfrey, and Bruce Springsteen, Gary Indiana is a member of the Baby Boom generation. But as he writes of Pasolini, he is "unique in his degree of loathing" of the corporate culture his cohort have fostered, of the political cowardice they've perpetuated, and of the degradations the American language has suffered on the way from the typewriter to Twitter. There are notes of political despair in Fire Season—how could there not be? Of the Tsarnaev brothers and the Boston Marathon bombing: "Why did they do it? How could they? In the world we live in now, the better questions are: Why not? Why wouldn't they?" Perhaps we do live in a fallen world, one of darkness, violence, and superficiality—that much is obvious to anyone with a television or a cellphone. In these essays Gary Indiana shows us over and over that the fallen world can't be the only one.

I DID NOT KNOW ANNA POLITKOVSKAYA

Yesterday, I saw a YouTube video of Grozny today, when the showplace part of it, thrown up fast as a bank heist with massive infusions of Russian aid, resembles a Martian colony from the cover of an old science-fiction novel: marble esplanades, Moorish waterworks, winding veils of novelty lighting crawling over Ali Baba spires and minarets, "playful" high-rise slabs from the desk of Philip Johnson, Coney Island knockoffs of the Taj Mahal, the Blue Mosque, the Transamerica building.... A Potemkin village for the 1 percent of the 1 percent. And then the glorious new sports stadium, which can probably be rented out for honor killings and executions... the camera spots Ramzan Kadyrov nuzzling Mike Tyson, while nearby, on stage, Hilary Swank wishes the Little Stalin of the Northern Caucasus a happy birthday.

I wonder: Do vicious children attach more sentimental import to their birthdays than normal people do? I ask because this Kadyrov, this torturer, this pie-faced emblem of human filth, is having the time of his life, frugging with himself onstage like a drunken Mayfair date rapist, dodging Jean-Claude Van Damme's karate kicks, gleeful as a six-year-old tearing ribbons and giftwrap off a Kalashnikov. And it is said that the person who contracted the murder of Anna Politkovskaya, probably someone high in the FSB, intended it as a gift to the Moscow dictator, who turned fifty-four that very day. Some people think Kadyrov sponsored the murder ("also as a birthday gift for Putin," they always note with a certain black humor), though here, I think, the better wisdom belongs to Alexander Litvinenko: "Only one person in Russia can kill someone like Anna Politkovskaya, with her standing, her fame, and that is Putin." A present Putin gave himself, then.

Killed why? Because a truly insensible gangster kills the witnesses even if they've already spilled. For revenge, the thrill of impunity, the joy of killing that Ramzan Kadyrov and Vladimir Putin know so well. Because no one like myself, who has never been to Chechnya, knowing whatever I know about it because of Politkovskaya, can look at this spun-sugar Neuva Grozny without seeing mangled corpses tossed from army trucks, mothers picking over body dumps for a son's jawbone or a husband's arm, mile upon mile of slaughtered livestock, looted farmhouses, incinerated villages. What is that expression? You can't make a silk purse from a sow's ear.

> The lives of hundreds of thousands of people, people who wanted to live, enjoy themselves and raise their children, their lives will no longer exist, they will be killed, waiting in vain for our mercy. But do not think that we will get away with this, that we will be able to continue our careless, happy lives.
> —Anna Politskovskaya, January 3, 2000, *Novaya Gazeta*

It is all too bad if we pretend a happy end will come anybody's way if one person's happy end is someone else's catastrophe. "This is a very old fairy tale like many others before," Politkovskaya wrote. And later, speaking of Kadyrov in his father-of-the-country costume: "I think that the new Kadyrov is the one who gives a ride in his car to Moscow ladies who long for more brutality... Many of our colleagues have gone out of their way to make us believe... that absolute evil can triumph today so that in some hypothetical future this evil can become good. This is absolutely not true."

In French there is a special word for the sensation roused by the sight of a happy murderer, who has seemingly gotten away with everything and wants the world to know it: *abrutir* is the verb form. *Abrutissement* is the visceral feeling of being turned into an animal, of being made crazy enough to kill. Something to be gleaned from Politkovskaya's writings, if we do not already know it, is that people in the wrong experience *abrutissement* as readily as those who are, demonstrably, in the right. *Abrutissement*, implicitly the absence of thought, may be precisely what enables people to do evil, as Hannah Arendt speculated: "Could the activity of thinking as such, the habit of examining whatever happens to come to pass or to attract attention... be among the conditions that make men abstain from evil-doing, or even actually 'condition' them against it?" I would say that those with great heart are invariably in the right, in some sense, but that isn't enough. Or at least it's a question.

Surely one day an opera will be written, in the spirit of *The Death of Klinghoffer* or Rautavaara's *Rasputin*, about the Nord-Ost hostage crisis of 2002. Nord-Ost is *Coriolanus* and the Brothers Grimm, *Antigone* and Pirandello—in truth, Nord-Ost is a lot about *Antigone*. And even more about *The Revenger's Tragedy*. A nested doll kind of opera: make-believe soldiers singing and dancing onstage; the audience an eclectic mixture of 850 souls, many of whom believe at first that the terrorist attack is part of the musical; Chechens in ski masks and burqas—forty-five, fifty? it's never been known exactly how many, and at least a few are thought to have slipped away before the end— promising to kill everyone in the theater unless Putin withdraws all Russian troops from Chechnya, immediately.

At a potentially crucial moment, Politkovskaya, who knows this demand won't even be considered by Putin, knows Putin's style of crisis management is such that rescuing live hostages is not a priority. This is a grim and finally thankless duty she accepts despite the fact that the Chechens who've asked for her act like she owes it to them, and the Russians on the other side of this have tried to kill her at least once.

Anna is not an operatic character at all, even if her role in print is that of a premonitory chorus, or the Nurse in *Medea*, or Cassandra—all the same, she is the only mediator the terrorists will speak to. But it does not go smoothly. It doesn't go at all. Other negotiators arrive and leave with equally empty hands. (Conspicuous by his absence is Kadyrov senior, still president of Chechnya at this time. The terrorists will release fifty hostages if he meets with them; with congenital cowardice, he later claims he was never told of the offer.)

Finally the gas, still unidentified, some mixture of fentanyl and a special KGB ingredient no doubt, wafting in filmy layers from the ventilation system. This moment when the gas spreads through the theater, inducing lethal sleep—there is a fable here, surely, about the Russian public and their wish to know nothing about what their army is doing in Chechnya (just as Americans don't want to know what their drones do in Iraq and Afghanistan); the press blackout of this Second Chechen War; the theatrical illusion of "consumer's democracy," and this place where it collides with the unforgivable reality behind the curtain. And something about the witch's poisoned apple too, and the Potemkin mutiny, and Alaric the evil dwarf counting the Rhine gold in the Kremlin.

Politkovskaya was much loved, but not an easy person, abrasive with colleagues, prone to insult the wrong people to their faces, and, while it says nothing about whether she was right, self-righteous; her flaws as well as her virtues (talent, compassion, indefatigable persistence) made her an exemplary witness to barbarism in Chechnya. She wrote droll, finely observed, occasional pieces on her travels abroad, the Paris launch of one of her books, the life and times of her dog, press corps meet-and-greets and tête-à-têtes, of variable absurdity, with various exiles and world leaders; in Denmark, she is pleasantly startled by the humane treatment of prisoners; in Australia, amazed to get on a naval base by simply flashing her passport. It shouldn't really be surprising that she could enjoy having a good time, but it is, a bit, because the great majority of her writings record unbearable events and circumstances. One wishes she had had more time for selfish pleasure, less responsibility. An abiding theme of her peregrinations is her stupendous relief at not being in Russia. Even though we know her fate, only one of these pieces is sad-making—the one about going to Tango Por Dos in London. Sad because it was thrilling to watch, and a stabbing reminder that the passions of the tango were probably not in the cards for her any longer. Not because she was too old for them, but because she saw intimate relationships in Russia as generally brutish and stupid, conducted in apartments that were too small, squalidly troubled by money problems, and too likely to carry on past their expiration date.

And besides, there was Chechnya.

There's this, I would say: for a person who sets off on a difficult road, at first the pleasant, crooked country lanes and rustic byways branching off in all directions remind him that he can change his course at any time. "If I get tired, I will take the next one to the right, or to the left, or go down some road that comes after that." But if this person keeps following the same route, eventually these intersecting forks and branches become unwanted distractions, and after a while he doesn't even take account of them. Sooner or later, he reaches a point of no return. After that he cannot turn away from what his particular, chosen road presents him with without losing his sense of who he is. Because he now understands that he has chosen it, and, in a mysterious way, the road has also chosen him.

People say Politkovskaya changed after Nord-Ost. Or after she was tortured and put through a mock execution in Chechnya. Or after being poisoned on a flight to Beslan during *that* hostage crisis. Whatever the case, you can see a change, nothing exactly alarming, a small tear in the scanning pattern, in her later interviews: something like a shadow, or a wash of gray watercolor, clouding her skin; she is probably just exhausted. Her voice level, measured, almost without inflection, like that of a person who has removed some vital part of herself to a safe, distant place.

"She wasn't charismatic, she didn't fill lecture halls, and she wasn't much good at talk shows either." (Anne Applebaum, foreword to *Putin's Russia* by Anna Politkovskaya) Well, all this is partly why we trust her. Even among the few outstanding journalists of our time, there is no one quite as indifferent to the circus of renown as she was.

"There is no need for truth today." A Chechen widow who has seen all her relatives slaughtered tells this to the camera in Masha Novikova's documentary, *Anna: Seven Years on the Frontline.* "That's why they killed her." Politkovskaya was believed, even by some who despised her, because she really did write only what was true. Not just reporting parts of the truth that happened to serve her parti pris, but also complicating facts, mitigating causalities, the "yes, but . . ." that even well-intentioned people quite often omit from their account of things. What happens when your idea of the truth is whatever evidence fits is this: inevitably, the little thing you left out to sound more convincing will eventually surface, and even though it is a small thing, your decision to leave it out will make this little thing bigger than the big thing you were trying to reveal. The same is true of exaggerations: the fudged figure, the inflated injury, the overdrawn malfeasance inevitably makes the world a little worse.

Whether we admit it or not, we expect journalists to be magically immune to real danger, in part because they are, technically, "civilians," like us, and even though civilians are killed in far greater numbers than soldiers in all modern wars, some originary concept of war as a contest between specially trained, armed men in uniform makes the kind of wars we have today bewilderingly muzzy and shockingly without boundaries or respect for persons.

It is, in reality, all the same war, everywhere and endless, subsiding in one place as it flares in another. There is no special category of noncombatant equivalent to the white flag or the red cross: even those universally recognized symbols mean nothing to most people in the "conflict areas" of 2014. The savagery of the Second Chechen War was more extreme than anything seen in Europe since the days of Vlad the Impaler. Anna Politskovskaya understood that she had nothing protecting her. "Risk is part of our job. It's not part of a teacher's job or a doctor's job but it is of our job. I think a journalist has to be prepared and understand that it can happen, so no tears and no fears. The important question is, what change has our article brought? Has something changed for the better in our society?"

(2014)

BARBARA KRUGER: THE WAR AT HOME

War has broken out. Where or how, nobody knows any longer. But the fact remains. By now it is behind each person's head, its mouth agape and panting. War of crimes and insults, of hate-filled eyes, of thoughts exploding from skulls. It is there, reared up over the world, casting its network of electric wires over the earth's surface. Each second, as it rolls on, it uproots all things in its path, reduces them to dust. It strikes indiscriminately with its bristling array of hooks, claws, beaks. Nobody will survive unscathed. Nobody will be spared. That is what war is: the eye of truth.

—J. M. G. LE CLÉZIO

Technically speaking, "we" know almost nothing about Barbara Kruger. The bits of biography that emerge in scattered fashion from her inter-views are carefully circumscribed, illu-minating in a general way, withhold-ing in another way. She has pretty much refused to be overly "expressive" about herself-as-art-ist, and her work, though each example of it is distinctly a signa-ture piece, has something of the impersonal lucidity we find in Marcel Duchamp's work.

Duchamp's subject was art and life, or art-in-life. Kruger's work is about the war at home, in each of us: between good and bad, men and women, black and white, losers and winners, creeps and assholes, all the sociocultural dissonances that make the world so tweaked. It seems to issue from an angrily saturnine clarity about how things go wrong between people, how affection subtly modulates into rage, how the brightest moment can turn to shit on a dime. Less abstract subjects than Duchamp's, let's say. Less parochial in its assumption that the art object is a commodity and a medium of exchange and enough said.

The physicality of Kruger's objects is often surprising because, in a way, their "objectness" seems simply the right thing for that idea in that place at that time, and her ideas translate easily from medium to medium. Transparence is the ideal condition of her work, as in an installation like *Power Pleasure Desire Disgust*, where virtually everything is a verbally seething skin projected onto architectural volumes—because, in a sense, the condition of consciousness this work recommends is something with sharp, clear lines and a lot of empty space to reflect in.

An art of ideas, in other words, yes, but if conceptual art, say, often reflects a fundamental disjunction between the pleasure the artist took in using materials and the message that comes across, proposes that we locate meaning and pleasure outside the physical, as if the "art" were trapped in expediently attractive containers, and regard aesthetics as a sort of secondary concession to decoratively severe appetites, Kruger in contrast is the least metaphysical and mystifying of artists. An existentialist artist, in a sense. The pleasure in the well-made product, something visually arresting and sometimes horrific, is less distant from our regular menu of pleasures and provocations than a spiral jetty or a field of lightning rods somewhere in New Mexico that we're never going to visit. This work is subtle and blunt at the same time, blunt language with subtle implications, and participates in many strategies of commercial media, since these are, in fact, more persuasive and more authentically gratifying than a lot of contemporary "fine art"—the commercial media comprise the vernacular of our time, and they're what resonate for us in our actual lives. Kruger targets the ego and libido of things, rather than nu-ances of art history, or intellectual conundrums, though you can read "art issues" into her works as readily as "life issues," and you wouldn't be wrong.

Kruger compresses the telling exchanges of lived experience that betray how skewed our lives are: epigrammatically, slashed across strangely power-ful, recuperated iconography. The varying scale of this work has a nice clean "just enough" and sometimes "let's give this icky emotion real grandeur." What I like best are startling incongruities of scale, as in a huge riot of pretty flowers with the simple, small, square kicker in the center: JAM LIFE INTO DEATH. It's the agenda of all advertising and all television, all media all the time.

Kruger's rich raw material is this bizarro world of media that surrounds us and gurgles in our living rooms, that makes our choices for us, shows and tells us what reality's supposed to be, *according to what, we might ask, but fewer and fewer of us do ask, if you want to be clear-minded about it*—a theater of death, where the shadows of the dead—us—flicker in Plato's cave; a theater of unceasing electronic fizz that creates and nurtures the desire to be-come discorporate, to become a floating, bodyless replica of oneself in a world that's no longer entirely a world, a figure instead of a body, something ME and NOT ME, YOU and NOT YOU in the same collapsed moment.

Mental notes in the housewares department of Walmart. Yes, Walmart. You can get anything you want at Walmart. The fact that you want it means you are already dead. Last Christmas I had an epiphany at Walmart. No, that's a little grand. If you want the epiphanic version, take a look at Kruger's sculpture of Santa Claus molesting a little girl with Jesus Christ on the verso side, suffering in the extravagant way that Jesus is wont to do. (Incidentally, I wanted to title this "Why I Am Not a Christian, by Bertrand Russell.") It was two weeks before Christmas. Each department in Walmart had its own Muzak system blaring Christ-mas carols, and each department manager, apparently, had decided to program a different medley of joyfully moronic carols. And, as you walked through Walmart, these competing festive audios melted together into a completely disso-nant, sour, even terrifying mélange, as if Stockhausen had decided to do a Christ-mas album, and you know something, it was perfect, it was almost art, and no one in Walmart seemed to notice they were being subtly encouraged to go home and commit suicide. This has something to do with Barbara Kruger's work, I think. The ruin of certain smug and reassuring representations, the defacement of delusion, with just enough melody left in to seize your attention.

There are moments when some of Kruger's images just paste themselves over reality. It's their precision, their abstemious lack of digressiveness that gives them this force, a concentrated quality, a quality of "here's the issue and here's what it looks like," and people writing about this work have frequently become entangled, tripped all over themselves puzzling out who "I" am and who "we" are and who "you" are, as if the work were "embodied" in the artist and the spectator, the way Jackson Pollock is embedded in his wild and crazy semenoid drips and splatters, but something almost opposite is at work in Kruger's activity, which resists the idea of the self-heroicizing gesture, but more importantly repudiates the fixing of the subject in the conventional artist/spectator relation.

You don't have to read Lacan to appreciate this work, but Lacan is helpful if you want to take the work in without miring yourself in direct, frontal re-lation to what it's saying at the moment you're looking at it. For one thing, the moment concretized in a Kruger piece is going to connect with a different moment in your life, in fact the "meaning" you perceive in it is bound to be different when it does fold into your biography—you can save the per-sonal part of your eureka, in other words, for some dark night of the soul, some appropriately hideous moment with a special someone whose mask just fell off. I am always urging people to read Lacan. In a Lacanian sense, I and we and you are floating signifiers of a paradigm, the elements of a model of consciousness in a particular scenario of crisis. "I" is an idea of "I," "you" a construct of "you," as in, this is how "we" manage a crisis, how "we" negotiate sex and money and politics, here's a map of "our" habitual re-sponses, here's a diagram of "our" dynamic, and if you look at it head-on, look at the naked lunch at the end of your fork, you can figure out what's wrong with it, why the mechanisms of transpersonal exchange that domi-nate our society leave you feeling like a turned trick, why it's killing you softly with its dumb song, because it hurts so good.

Your comfort is my silence. Your money talks. Buy me, I'll change your life. These are propositions, albeit more visceral than logical propositions—though they are logical too, and follow the equation of democracy = capitalism = demolition of utopia. The logic of a system in which anybody's loss is someone else's gain. Where commodities substitute emotions, products replace empa-thy, only the externalized manifests existence, and life no longer lives, its im-personation enacted, instead, upon a labyrinth of screens. It becomes possible to watch life turn into death from the passive spectatorship of the post-humous. It becomes impossible to intervene in time and space, impossible to occupy a concrete reality, impossible to change the movie of virtual chimera and actual absence.

How do we verify a proposition? If you're Wittgenstein, you follow the thread to the place where it runs out short of the punctum. If you're Kruger, you picture how the proposition seals itself, how it might incarnate as a metaphor, what the shorthand way of showing it is. And often this has a narrative teaser going on, the suggestion of a B-movie or film noir exten-sion at either end of it, carrying both a sense of its punishing absurdity and a tacit bow to its seductiveness. Kruger is more the frame-by-frame analysis of *Laura* or *Where the Sidewalk Ends*, perhaps, than the semiotic autopsy of *Cat People* or *I Walked with a Zombie*. But *I Walked with a Zombie, the Musical* wouldn't be an implausible Kruger installation. In a way, she's already done that.

Much of her iconography is drawn from the 1940s and 1950s, and from reconstituted later images that carry traces of the slightly *recherché* quality associated with the 1940s and 1950s, when American imperial clichés were minted and permeated the visual style of magazines, newspapers, movies, and early TV. The look is eo ipso "ironic," because we're all several decades beyond the look. But all culture has done with what the look signifies is translate it into more bedazzling, "modern" pictorialism that fools us better and makes the imaginary payoff even more imaginary. You won't have bet-ter sex in a Lexus than you did in your father's Oldsmobile. You might have better-*looking* sex, more *modern* sex, sex in a glistening world where every-thing's a throbbing penis and every-thing's a moist vagina and every second is an orgasm as explosive as a hydrogen bomb, if indeed you were going to have sex, but the truth is you aren't going to have sex at all, you're just going to spend a lot of money on a car, and that car isn't even going to be a nipple ring. That car is going to be the cradle for your cell phone. And you're not going to be young again, so the car will look great but you're going to look really old. So what we have, looking at the Oldsmobile, is the memory of sex—in other words, what sex really is.

Radio: This is Calypso Debbi (I swear), now you know when you go to Car-nival in Peru, stock up on water balloons, and skip the manure.

A lot of people get freaked by Barbara Kruger's art. Uptight around it, de-fensive, hostile, threatened, as if it were a person telling them things, which it is, of course, but then a certain number of people never get the joke, and don't want to get the joke: that they're telling it while it's telling them.

Or it's not their mode of amusement. They'd like a *New Yorker* cartoon instead. And of course there will always be times when a *New Yorker* cartoon is more welcome than something darker and smarter.

It can be troubling, perplexing, irritating, whatever, when an artist goes for an extreme purity of diction, as Kruger does, because we often crave a certain messiness, a bit of throw-away, some superfluous oxygen, an aria of the asshole-ism Kruger has frequently lauded in her writing: her visual work doesn't provide those types of escape. It's a distillation, a type of essence, and not to get the joke is to miss the only relief it offers. If you get the joke—better still, if you adopt the joke, take it over as your joke, put yourself in whichever "I" or "you" or "us" seems to be winning here, on the side of the angels—the work becomes conversational, even relaxed, an ef-fort to break through the reciprocal deafness that modern life has wreaked on our ears and nervous systems.

The implicit faith of this work is that we can, now and then, find our way out of our delusions and the infantilization our culture prescribes as a placebo utopia, to something like an authentic adulthood, reason, and the golden rule, and that the effort to do this is worth the mental anguish it en-tails, and could even make us happier, in many ways, than the gladiatorial fantasies we're trained to apply in every social arena. This is the subtext: the conviction that empathy can, in fact, change the world—a little at a time, and not always, and you will only improve things a little bit, anyway, but if you don't even try, the incurably ugly side of human nature has already won the war inside us all.

When he was still LeRoi Jones, Amiri Baraka wrote a novel called The System of Dante's Hell, *where I found the following lines: "And it seemed a world for Aztecs on the bone side of mountains. A world, even strange, sat in that leavening light & we had come in raw from the elements. From the cardboard moonless world of ourselves . . . to whatever. To grasp at straws."*

(1999)

THE STEILNESET MEMORIAL

In Finnmark, at the Arctic tail end of Norway that lops over Sweden and Finland, American artist Louise Bourgeois and Swiss architect Peter Zumthor collaborated on a monument to the ninety-one persons burned there as witches in the seventeenth century. On June 23, a year after Bourgeois's death, the Steilneset Memorial was opened to the public by Queen Sonja of Norway (that rare thing, a monarch people actually like) in a dedication ceremony that drew what appeared to be most if not all of the surrounding population.

The witch trials, tortures, and executions that took place at Steilneset, on the island of Vardø, were inspired in part by a post-Reformation mania to impose Lutheranism as the state religion of the then-combined kingdom of Denmark-Norway, in part to assert the sovereignty of the aptly named King Christian IV, who wanted to rid his demesne of "ungodly persons" and impress upon Russia—on a clear day, just visible across a swath of the Barents Sea—the presence on Vardø of a military fortress replete with troops and many cannons.

The victims of the witch hunts were mainly women, many employed as domestic servants, though a fair number of men from the Indigenous Sami people, long regarded throughout Europe as sorcerers adept at "wind magic," met the same horrible fate. The Devil was believed to inhabit the far north and to pass into people by means of enchanted bread, direct satanic contact, or various spells and incantations. The possessed assumed the form of animals, caused storms at sea that threatened fishermen, made sheep and other livestock explode. They inflicted injuries and illnesses on neighbors. Everyday calamities were ascribed to the sinister workings of the Adversary and his largely penurious minions, who confessed they had been offered anything they wished for. The scope of their wishes seldom extended beyond the acquisition of a cow or a goat, but witches were witches and they all had to burn. As happened across Europe and in Massachusetts during this period, the accused, once denounced and put on trial, confessed under torture and implicated others, who were tried in turn.

Guilt was established by tossing these hapless persons into the sea. Water was thought to repel evil. If they sank they were innocent, if they floated, guilty. An inquisitor was imported from Scotland, where witch hunts had enjoyed great success. Of the 135 people of Finnmark accused of witchcraft, two-thirds were condemned to death, the majority of them burned at the stake in Steilneset.

Religious manias no longer feature in Norwegian life, unless you include the church burnings committed throughout the country by satanist death-metal cultists between 1992 and 1996. Poverty, which greatly factored into the witch hunts—not only in Norway but across Europe and colonial America as well; virtually no person of substantial wealth was ever burned as a witch—is likewise not a big Norwegian problem at the present time. Thanks to North Sea oil, Norway is one of the world's richest countries, and an underpopulated one. Its citizens enjoy the most generous social-welfare system to be found in Europe and probably anywhere else. Norway currently invests millions in cultural and other projects in the public interest. The witches' memorial in Vardø is one of two hundred ventures designed to enliven Norway's eighteen national tourist routes with structures and installations by architects and artists. These include rest areas, ferry landings, bridges for fishing, and hiking paths and lookouts sited in ravishing natural locations, of which Norway is unusually full.

Vardø is more austere and desolate than beautiful, an outcrop of bleariness where the sun never sets through the summer and then disappears for the winter. There's the frigid sea and endless sky and dark stunted hills across the water. That's about it. Like much of Finnmark, Norway's northernmost county, Vardø once flourished as a hub of the fishing industry. In recent decades, factory vessels depleted the catches. People migrated south to Oslo and Bergen. What remains are reindeer and sheepherders, a deliquescent service industry, people with second homes and others whose occupations one can only guess at. It would have made a perfect setting for a Chabrol film or a Simenon novel.

While other completed tourist-route projects in Norway are elegant, utilitarian interventions into spectacular vistas, the Bourgeois-Zumthor collaboration has a different resonance of historical excavation. Public memorial objects often lack visual and tactile appeal and most frequently honor soldiers lost during wartime; the Vardø memorial is, by contrast, an active sensory experience, recalling an ignominious fold of history instead of a heroic one—an improbable, cautionary monument to an abuse of power.

The Steilneset Memorial occupies the same site where the Finnmark victims were incinerated, a quick walk from the Vardøhus fortress past the village church. It consists of two structures designed by Zumthor, one of which, the Glass Pavilion, houses Bourgeois's installation *The Damned, The Possessed, and The Beloved*, 2007–10. The other, Memory Hall, is a lengthy enclosure shaped something like an anchovy fillet, supported by a complex pinewood frame inspired by the fish-drying racks that stand abandoned in nearby fields and farmyards. Its walls, white on the outside, consist of stiff fabric stretched by wires into a regular wavelike pattern, suggestive of a ship's tethered sails.

Ninety-one small, square windows recessed in metal frames punctuate the walls at irregular heights determined by casting a die. Entered via a wooden ramp, the structure yields to the touch—its inner walls are fabric too, a black fiberglass textile coated in Teflon—and it shudders in the wind. Each window represents a victim of the witch trials, identified, along with details of the individual's ordeal, by a legend in white letters on a black-silk hanging plaque. Small, bell-shaped lightbulbs suspended in the windows give the long passage through the space a feeling of weightless movement along a torchlit corridor, a sensation enhanced by the raised catwalk underfoot.

The effect of slightly altered gravity produced by the varying heights of the windows and lights, the elevated walkway, and the square, recessed views of the outer world suggests a theater in which the curtain is about to come up (or has just come down) on the bleak events described on the fabric plaques. The sensual immediacy of Zumthor's materials is offset by an overall intellectual precision of design. The architect finds the cleanest, least obstreperous solutions to the shaping of spaces; the Vardø memorial has exactly enough solidity to occupy a stark, weather-ravaged coastal terrain without collapsing, like a small craft navigating a tempest.

The long room ends at the door to an exit ramp. A few yards away, a cubical pavilion of black glass, like the dot at the end of an exclamation point, encloses Bourgeois's installation, a terminus of high drama after the studied quiet of the larger building. *The Damned, The Possessed, and The Beloved* is an unforgettable vision in this ragged, elemental patch of ultima Thule. A steel chair, centered inside a thin, sloped ring of cement—something like the mouth of a volcano—shoots perpetual flames from its seat. Seven huge oval mirrors, angled above the chair on slender pylons, twist the flames into sinister shapes, compress and bloat the cement and metal ensemble, and suggest the varied psychological distortions that spectacles like witch burning produce in their witnesses.

The fire's contorted reflections bring to mind the misshapen bodies in certain Francis Bacon paintings; the evocation of torture is immediate and unmistakable; the coils and stuttering tendrils of mirrored flame echo the shape-shifting transmigrations of humans into wolves and foxes and birds that the Vardø victims often confessed to.

The chair as stand-in for a human figure, "viewed" by flanking or overhanging mirrors, appears in many late Bourgeois works, sometimes dwarfed by surrounding elements that transform it into an emblem of pathos and isolation, the individual misread by the eyes of others. Something stubborn and brave in this solitary being confounds its own powerlessness. It is, after all, the true subject of the work, the cynosure reached by an arduous spiral staircase or sealed under a bell jar, the thing reflected and pondered. The cage of social forms—in this case a thicket of lethal demonological laws—has no meaning without the monadic subject trapped inside it.

The Damned, The Possessed, and The Beloved is a fantastic restaging of the central drama in Bourgeois's work: the plight and glory of the individual shaped and oppressed by the configurations of families and larger social structures. It bears witness to a wretched episode in human history—and, implicitly, to the myriad such episodes that have continued into the present, in various guises, in the name of various causes and gods and ideologies. In reenacting the repressed crimes that happened in Vardø, Bourgeois's installation, coupled with Zumthor's understated architecture, is a compelling plea for empathy with people destroyed by the fires of collective madness.

(2011)

NORTHERN EXPOSURE

FUNNY MR. BILL

Up close, Bill Clinton looks like he's covered in fresh fetal tissue. His skin is virtually poreless. The high, ample hair (a premium commodity in this race of semiskinheads), the trim, pneumatic body, the tasteful but not unduly elegant suit, everything has been processed into movie star perfection. He could be a retired sports figure in an infomercial, endorsing a small kitchen appliance or a home treadmill. Something in the grooming suggests one of those miniature species bred to win show ribbons, a Shetland pony or a toy terrier.

Here amid the authentic wood-grain paneling of the American Legion Henry J. Sweeney Post 2 on Maple Street, in Manchester, a large and not unduly elegant crowd of Clinton people has wedged itself between the floor-level microphone and the cash bar. Someone, I'm not sure who, introduces Legion Post Commander Tom Murphy, "who is gonna do the pleasure of introducing Governor Clinton."

The locutions are pure Main Street New Hampshire. Regarding the candidate, Murphy says, "I have read much of what he stands for and espouses to." "It's my distinguished pleasure to honor and introduce to you"—and perhaps he really does say—"the next president of the United States," though the ante here is simply getting the numbers back to where they were before Gennifer Flowers. The will to believe is palpable in the room, if hardly overwhelming. There's a certain mild tension skimming off the synthetic fabrics and plastic cocktail glasses, roughly the voltage of a joy buzzer.

This is a grown-up crowd. There are infants and small kids and grandmothers swaddled in bright ski parkas, and knitted beanies, but the main energy emits from men and women of a certain age who buy their clothes out of state and are no strangers to the cash bar of the American Legion Henry J. Sweeney Post 2. I mean that, as Nixon would say, in the best sense of cash bar. Here you have your conservative machine Democrats (what used to be called savings and loan Democrats), mingling with plumbing contractors and Goodyear franchise managers and district assembly-persons, the types that strike all sorts of sweet little deals in places like this on a normal weekday, many 100 percent behind the candidate but ready to switch horses if the numbers today and tomorrow and next week don't play out as expected.

Clinton doesn't wait on too much fanfare. This is an earnest, flesh-pressing, I'm-not-there-yet-and-I-need-each-and-every-one-of-you speech. The point of the exercise is to find a credible way of projecting "concern" that these people are "hurting," Bush's euphemism for "broke." What's Clinton's campaign all about? Three words: "fairness, responsibility, and unity." Where do Republicans make their mistake? Well, for one thing, "most poor people get up in the morning and work" and therefore deserve government help. But let's not slip into socialism. This guy wants "to make more millionaires than Reagan and Bush, but the old-fashioned way." Empower those local governments. Crack down on corporations moving jobs out of the country. And let's have boot camps, military style, for some of our less hardened, first-time-felony criminals. While we're at it, let's enforce child support.

The platitudinous verbal droppings, more like noises one makes to stimulate horses than actual thoughts, also resemble bromides from a soothing commercial for Preparation H: the proctologist, on close examination, has ruled against radical surgery in favor of something smooth and greasy and easy to dissolve in the collective rectum. In case anybody thought he was some woolly-haired tax-and-spend liberal, Funny Mister Bill throws in enough hard talk about welfare recipients and crime to make you forget he's a Democrat. For this particular crowd, he's already demonstrated his Americanism by letting a lobotomized Death Row inmate go to his end by lethal injection—one of three hideously bungled, "painless" executions the same week in America. And if a fair number of conservatives, even New Hampshire conservatives, wince at the stark realities of capital punishment, quite a few think it ought to be as painful as possible.

If Clinton cares jack shit about anything besides getting elected, it doesn't show on that eerily symmetrical face, a visage of pure incipience: soon-to-be-jowly and exophthalmic, a fraction past really sexy, but warmingly cocky, clear-eyed, with an honorary, twinkling pinch of humility. The accent has just enough grain, enough slow roll in it for people to recognize a Good Old Boy with decent values and bootstraps pulled all the way up. His ideas are so lacking in genuine nuance or arresting detail that he might very well pass, if not now then later, as the statistically ideal mediocrity New Hampshire often favors, when it isn't worshipping some pathologically unpleasant, penny-ante fixer like John Sununu. Apart from bland-as-buckwheat officials with no fixed opinions on anything, the Granite State likes pissy, preening, patently empty wastebaskets à la Sununu to push its citizens around from time to time, exploiting them in sadistically unprofitable ways.

There is real social masochism in New Hampshire among the blue-collar immigrant stock of the southland. ("Southland" is my own term for south of Concord, east of Keene, not a New Hampshire term.) Those for whom "Live Free or Die" has traditionally meant dropping out of tenth grade and heading straight for Kiev Bros, and Jody shoe shops, Raytheon, or the mills, feel such depths of cultural inferiority that truly abusive public figures often resonate more winningly with them than reformers and do-gooders. And that's the target constituency, despite today's preponderance of the class three notches above trash. New Hampshirites respect cunning over noble intentions. The Bavarians of New England have never cottoned to obligatory self-improvement or any too reachy sense of community, since these concepts involve sales tax and state tax and the dreaded welfare, which would bring hordes of shiftless coloreds swarming over the border from Massachusetts. New Hampshire makes its money on state liquor stores and highway tolls. Not coincidentally, the state has ranked, for decades, fiftieth in the nation in support of higher education.

Aside from the daily dose of social Darwinism provided by the *Manchester Union Leader*, New Hampshire's only statewide daily paper, the paradigm of "Ignorance in defense of intolerance is no vice" has been held in place for decades by the Catholic Church, though the south is full of Catholics who stopped attending mass after Vatican II, when the transubstantial rites of cannibalism switched from Latin to English. (One woman in Derry told me the secularization of the mass was an egregious example of "coddling the young," like the local Rock the Vote registration drive, which unsuccessfully tried to force the Supervisor of the Checklist to register students at the local high school instead of at the town hall. When the Democratic candidates moan about "the first generation of Americans to do worse than their parents," they're waving a blank rhetorical flag. Among working-class parents in this neck of the woods, what was good enough for them is good enough for their brats, and if their brats do a little worse, boo hoo.)

Resentment is running high at the American Legion Henry J. Sweeney Post 2. One woman in a beige parka steps up to the microphone to denounce the State of the Union Address, specifically the Marie Antoinette capital gains passage about Puritans lying awake at night, obsessed with the idea that somebody somewhere might be having a good time. (Our Halcion-sedated chief executive should've recognized Peggy Noonan's winsome hen tracks as relics of the good old days, when people without trust funds didn't realize they were "hurting.")

It takes a member of the press corps, the *Village Voice*'s Alisa Solomon, to mention the A-word: for this bunch, apparently, "health care" doesn't necessarily extend to the politically charged issue of AIDS. Or perhaps it does, but they'd really rather not discuss it. Clinton exudes a pat, uninterested answer about more money for research, etc., adding that "President Bush has only mentioned the word AIDS about three times since he's been president." Alisa later notes that this is the first time Clinton has mentioned it at all.

CALIBAN

The Buchanan crowd is something else again. The Palace Theatre, a porn movie house throughout my teens and later boarded up like most Manchester businesses off Elm Street, has reopened as a legitimate theater. And a grand-looking place it is, with raked seats and ormolu sconces and delicate chandeliers, like a vintage Keith Circuit vaudeville hall.

There is one Black man in the cream-white audience, wearing a tight black suit, applauding feverishly, a true believer who will gladly salt himself when they throw him into the stew pot, as long as he can be the last one in. Onstage, former Manchester mayor Bob Shaw lectures us about "a little tea party we threw down in Boston a few years ago," flanked by another local hack, the city chairman of Buchanan for President. While the candidate speaks, these two mavens perch on folding chairs nearby, in badly tailored gray suits, one porcine, gangling, and rabid looking, the other scrunched up like some demented antique dealer with dreams of world domination, Tweedledum and Tweedledee, cackling and stomping their feet. A tableau of jolly idiocy. Potent ecstasy from the audience of functional dipsomaniacs and blue rinse jobs with ropes of synthetic pearls and minks woven circa 1970, LaRouche defectors, Chamber of Commerce ghouls, and assorted bits of space debris. An extremely fat man with inflamed pimples rocks in his seat behind me, muttering "Right on!" every time Pat scores some soaring polemical eureka.

The thrust of The Speech is that America has to be Number One. Not simply Number One in standard of living and capitalization and investments and technology and aircraft construction and car sales, but Number One in unbridled odiousness. The tautological form of The Speech presents a self-evident case that the US is not simply part of the world, but superior to everything in it. Like anyone else from Rockingham and Hillsborough counties, I am able to instantly translate The Speech from its slightly euphemistic idioms into plain English:

We must show these sordid fuckers, the Japs, that we are better than they are because, goddamn it, we're Americans, we're white, we're the greatest nation the world has ever known, and we invented everything. Flat screens and chips and VCRs and semiconductors and the Waring blender. And it's all being taken away from us by a bunch of satanic Nips and totalitarian Chinks and ingrate Koreans and devious wetbacks who've tilted the playing field and by Christ a level playing field isn't the point anyway, we've got to win!

The Europeans—whose gene stock, granted, is the only one worth preserving—are evilly attempting to wrest Boeing and Burger King from America's grasp. Race filth from Taiwan is gobbling up McDonnell Douglas. My god, the bastards will be seizing control of Disneyland unless this belligerent turd at the podium with his socks falling down isn't listened to, and then the residents of Manchester, New Hampshire, can kiss the eternal glory of being an American goodbye. Poor little Mickey Mouse is gonna wind up a squalid, syphilitic frog, or a sex-crazed wop, or a stinking guinea, or a bloody wog, or, god help the little rodent, a flaming African jigaboo.

"I've heard about parts of New Hampshire emptying out, the way you used to read about it in the Dust Bowl . . . eight years of Reagan, whatever good things he did have been wiped out in these three years . . . the World Bank in the last three years has given three and a half billion dollars to Communist China . . . at zero interest . . . those loans are guaranteed by you . . . the Export Import Bank is helping American business locate a new paper mill in Mexico . . . has anybody been up to the James River Paper Mill in Berlin? I was up there yesterday . . . they're holding on . . . they don't know what's going to happen . . . they're responsible for twenty percent of the economy of the North Country . . . what are we doing financing paper mills in Mexico when paper mills in New Hampshire are teetering on the brink of going under? [Thunderous applause.] We were the world's leaders in textiles. Number one in steel. These industries are going, going, some of them are gone . . . I've been up in the North Country of your home state . . . Mr. Bush just had a new guest visiting him, Lee Pong I think is how you pronounce his name . . . he's the fellow who ordered the tanks in Tiananmen Square . . . that Chinese Communist regime is right now selling missile technology . . . to our enemies in Tehran . . . they dumped all their sweater products in the United States and killed Pandora Mills . . ."

Never mind that most of New Hampshire has always been thinly populated. Never mind that the former Brown Co. Mills have been in decline for thirty years—in steeper decline since their purchase, in 1980, by the Virginia-based James River Corporation, which failed to refurbish the industrial plant when the capital was there. That the population of Berlin has been dropping steadily since 1960, precipitously so since the departure of the Converse Shoe Company in 1979, or that absolutely nobody in New Hampshire refers to Coos County and the wasteland near the Canadian border as "the North Country."

As it happens, Pandora Mills was not ruined by Chinese sweaters being dumped on the American market. Pandora was ruined by a leveraged buyout of its clothing division following the company's 1983 acquisition by Gulf + Western; as the former president of Pandora Knitwear, May Gruber, informs me after the Palace Theatre loathe-in has dispersed into gelid evening, trailing acrid vapors of Nissan and Honda exhaust. Admit nothing, blame everybody, be bitter—this could easily be Pat Buchanan's campaign slogan, as well the state motto.

Perhaps the sorriest aspect of the Buchanan campaign is the obligation most mainstream journalists feel to declare this boor "interesting," mainly because he customarily feeds at the same trough they do. Yes, he will get 30 percent of the New Hampshire Republican vote, and so would Adolf Hitler or General Franco. I'm from here, and I've seen this movie before. Buchanan is scary, yes, but so is the more congenial, saner fringe candidate, Chip Woods, an air crash survivor whose reconstructed face at least confronts us with the useful paradox that appearances, which all philosophy since Plato shows us to be false, absolutely dictate the selection of rulers in a televised democracy. By contrast Buchanan is, tediously, exactly what he looks like, a bigoted mick whose pathology runs to fag bashing and other symptoms of sexual hysteria.

And what of these bullying, cowardly people, stewing in the bilious sweats of their own zeal, bursting into rapturous applause—the heartiest applause of the evening—when Buchanan sneers that AIDS is "still a disease of homosexuals" and "addicts," or vows to rid the NEA of every piece of "scandalous, filthy, or antireligious art"? What about these jumped-up hillbillies, frothing at the dentures to beat up people with AIDS, single mothers on assistance, the homeless, anybody weaker than they? Who regard themselves as the only true victims of history, as "hurting" just because the world is larger than they are, more complex than the country they live in, and not, for the most part, white?

It's standard among the Buchanan set to begrudge any minority the status of victim, to bewail "reverse discrimination" in any attempt at social reparation, so it's no surprise that the *Union Leader*, Buchanan's principal endorser in the state, has taken up several of Pat's pet peeves. In a January 30 editorial, staffer Leonard Larson attacks "the annual guilt trip over Hiroshima" and complains that "the popular media history ... will probably define World War II in just two events." And guess what the other one is.

"It's already part of revisionist history that Americans could have—should have—stopped the Nazi slaughter of six million Jews while twenty million other people were also dying in Europe.

"... So that wasn't a war we were in. There was the Holocaust and everything else was incidental. The revisionists would make it a fact."

I should stress that the *Union Leader* is perfectly capable of going much further than this, of denying that the Holocaust even happened one week, and using the same fictional Holocaust the next week to attack Louis Farrakhan or some other anti-Semite of color, depending on which minority its editrix, Mrs. Nackey Scripps Gallowhur Loeb, widow of the odious William, feels like bashing when she staggers out of bed in the morning.

On other matters too the paper has the mercurial temper of a pit viper. It detested Jimmy Hoffa until Jimmy Hoffa became the enemy of Robert Kennedy, and then ran a decade of editorials lauding Hoffa as the savior of organized labor. (The paper threatened to withhold its endorsement of Richard Nixon in '72 unless Tricky Dick sprung Hoffa from the federal penitentiary; Nixon grudgingly obliged.) It devoted eight years of deifying editorials to then governor John Sununu and his albatross reactor in Seabrook, yet currently refers to him as Bush's "pimp," because Sununu refuses to endorse Buchanan. Like the Stalinist-era *Pravda*, the *Union Leader* never simply changes its mind; it "discovers" a pattern of ideological error or flawed character in its former allies, admits to having been "duped," and busily retracts every positive thing it's printed about the latest charlatan. In all of this the paper represents itself as a virgin schoolmarm violated and betrayed by her most trusted pupil, an act so long in the tooth that even its subscribers can't read the *Union Leader* with a straight face.

Back to Buchanan. During the Q&A, only two people, May Gruber—who does not raise the issue of Pandora Mills but instead suggests that Jesse Helms's interference with the NEA amounts to government censorship—and a young woman from Merrimack, who describes Buchanan's position on AIDS as ignorant, challenge the candidate on any of his obvious whoppers. Given the general attitude of Pat's fans, this takes more guts and conviction than the windbag on stage ever possessed in his life. I'd like to think that these two intelligent, humane voices insert just enough dissonance to sully an orgy of ugly feelings, or at least plant a few suspicions that the Wizard of Oz cannot really give the Scarecrow a functioning brain.

On the way out of the theater, an obsessed, elderly, goofily dressed John Bircher strikes up a monologue aimed at the *Voice* photographer, who happens to be African American. The man carries a bundle of literature charting a vast, ongoing conspiracy by the Trilateral Commission and David Rockefeller. "I've had this crap up to here. This country's gonna go right down the goddamn tubes. Someday you're gonna have United Nations troops in here. George Wallace got ten million votes, he said we're fed up with this crap, what happened? Boom. Robert Kennedy knew who killed his brother, all of a sudden, bang, Robert Kennedy, right? Martin Luther King was so exposed he was no longer any use to these people, what happened? Bang!" Like flies to a steaming pile of ordure, the weird creatures of eternal night draw close to the flame that is Pat Buchanan. Meanwhile, some workers roll out the set, a temple-like construction of plastic milk crates, for the Palace Theatre's current production, *The Tempest*.

FADE TO BROWN

In a large auditorium with level seats, pale olive walls, dark neo-Georgian olive trim, festooned with many portraits in gilded frames of men who resemble Alistair Cooke, a number of dew-lapped, earnest preppies and environmentally conscious residents of Exeter and nearby towns have gathered at Phillips Exeter Academy to experience Jerry Brown.

Out in the hall, volunteers are stacking Jerry's videotape and piles of Jerry's literature. As I write this, I keep hearing Sandra

Bernhard's dialogue from *The King of Comedy* echoing through my head. Jerry.

Jerry Brown has enough sense of humor to joke about the space cadet rap he's getting in the press. Just enough. Perhaps infected by the sober and enlightened atmosphere of this great hall where countless maiden blowjobs began as humid, hungering glances across rows of brilliantined schoolboy hairdos, Jerry strikes a serious yet scrappily boyish note. He reminds us that he is the only candidate with a classical education, schooled in Greek and Latin. For three years he toiled and thought and really examined himself and who he really was in the silence of a Jesuit seminary. He traveled to Japan and spent some quality time in Japan and knows the Japanese, knows the culture and what makes it tick. After that, Jerry spent three months in Calcutta, working with Mother Teresa in her Home for the Dying, eager to see what human caring, human compassion, even in the absence of a mutual language, could do amid so much suffering and dying.

And that isn't all. If I were to write down everything Jerry Brown has done, or even just everything Jerry Brown says he's done, you would still be reading this next Tuesday. Jerry's introduction of renewable energy technologies in California alone would cover many pages, as would his hands-on approach with the state legislature in Sacramento, where he moved into a small apartment right across from the statehouse instead of taking residence in the ugly expensive mansion built for the Reagans. Did I tell you what Jerry did about the dead-end welfare system in California? How Jerry actually lessened crime? The magnificent windmills and other devices that have made PG&E, thanks to Jerry, the most cost-effective and profitable gas and electric utility in the US of A? No? Sandra, would you please sing "Come Rain or Come Shine" just one more time?

As I listen to Jerry, something keeps irritating me. At first I believe it is the memory of a large crow I once saw bisected by one of Jerry's power-generating windmills outside San Luis Obispo while driving from LA to San Francisco. Then I realize it is a small child in a pink padded windbreaker seated beside me who is playing with a Nintendo Game Boy as Jerry speaks.

Just behind me, several young men who had been discussing, avidly, the various clues on Beatles albums pointing to the death of Paul McCartney (for example, on the *Sgt. Pepper* lyric sheet, John Lennon's finger seems to rest against the line "at five o'clock as the day begins"—possibly the exact time of Paul's demise) have stopped talking about that and are listening to Jerry with what seems, when I look at them, like respectful skepticism. Good day sunshine.

Jerry wants to take the system back from the politicians and the corporations and put it in the hands of you the people or rather we the people, and that's why he isn't accepting more than one hundred dollars from each individual to run his campaign. We can cleanse this system of corruption and provide health care for every American and cure the rot of our inner cities with a few simple techniques. All right, I'm sorry, I don't remember what they are, but Jerry knows them, and if you elect Jerry, he'll tell you himself. Or at least you should take a copy of his videotape. But if you do, be prepared to pass it on to five other people. This is how a grassroots movement gets started.

Jerry is wearing a white turtleneck and a blue denim jacket with brown leather strips on the collar and baggy, black corduroy trousers. Jerry has a large bald spot and strangely mottled skin, red in the wrong places, and just between you and me, there is something a little delusional about Jerry, even though I know he really was the governor of California at one time.

SEACOAST

In fairness to the candidate, he only sounds this way because America has evolved so far from the notion of direct rule that even people who agree with Jerry understand he has no chance of being elected. One thinks of direct rule in connection with local rather than national politics. Brown does have a constituency in New Hampshire, as would any ecology-minded consumer advocate, because local communities have seen what can be accomplished by write-in drives, petitions, and town meetings. This is, paradoxically, partly thanks to William Loeb and the politicians he supported over the years.

Loeb, by the way, never resided in New Hampshire. For decades he occupied an eighty-acre, high-security compound in Pride's Crossing, Massachusetts, furtively darting back and forth across the border, it is said, in order to avoid subpoenas. In league with a succession of vacuous New Hampshire governors, Loeb sponsored uncountable schemes to wreck the environment in the interests of various contractors, developers, and high-tech corporations. Sununu's Seabrook nuclear reactor was only the most recent venture to mobilize conservation groups throughout the state.

Before Seabrook, there was Durham Point. In 1973, Governor Meldrim Thomson Jr. (now an occasional columnist for the *Union Leader*) announced his vision that New Hampshire needed an oil refinery. No one had perceived this need before, but because of his campaign pledge of no new taxes, Thomson had to find money somewhere for deteriorating state services. At the same time, employees of Aristotle Onassis's Olympic Oil Co., posing as real estate agents, began buying options on three thousand acres of shorefront in Portsmouth, Rye, and Durham, under various guises: the establishment of bird sanctuaries and hunting preserves, retirement homes, etc. The biggest chunk of optioned land was at Durham Point. Onassis also optioned parts of the Isles of Shoals, a little archipelago ten miles off the coast.

In November 1973, Thomson announced that Olympic Oil would install a $600 million refinery at Durham Point. Supertankers would offload at the Isles of Shoals, where the oil would be pumped to Portsmouth via underwater pipe, then shunted to Durham Point through another pipeline. Onassis himself would visit the state on December 19. Loeb's front-page editorial announced, "WELCOME to the Two Big O's—Oil and Onassis!" Appalled property owners in the quiet university town of Durham quickly joined forces with environmentalists to block Durham Point, as the *Union Leader* devoted reams of fawning newsprint to Onassis, whom it characterized as "Santa Claus." According to Loeb biographer Kevin Cash, the Durham Point project would have been "the largest single-unit oil refinery ever built." It also would have transformed the countryside around the University of New Hampshire into a moonscape.

The project met its toxic avenger in the form of Mrs. Thomas Dudley, the town of Durham's representative to the state's General Court. (Mrs. Dudley's given name was also Dudley, therefore Dudley Dudley. She was a descendant of Joseph Dudley, who was governor of Massachusetts and New Hampshire between 1723 and 1728.) A Mrs. Nancy Sandberg, also of Durham, organized Save Our Shores, which opposed Olympic Oil with legal services to optioned property owners, a speakers' bureau, bumper stickers, etc.

Mrs. Dudley cast the Durham Point issue in terms of home rule. This had immense popular appeal. Town meetings throughout the Seacoast area rezoned the target properties to exclude the refinery, while House Bill 34, intended to override the local ordinances, went down to defeat 109 to 233. Onassis returned to Skorpios and Maria Callas. Cash speculates that Loeb never fully recovered from the rejection of Durham Point by New Hampshire voters.

Now, it seems, some kind of attitude shift is taking its gradual course in the state—very gradual, if you compare it with the mall and condo boom of the Reagan years, when developers and retail chains, greased by every tax break John Sununu could contrive, swept through southern New Hampshire like shit through a cane brake, transforming a landscape of harsh, bucolic beauty into one of unparalleled hideousness. Steady migrations of "Massachusetts people" into the southland have brought with them, unexpectedly, a burgeoning circulation of the liberal *Boston Globe*. This, combined with a generous cable range, has eroded the Loeb information monopoly. Even if people generally don't like Blacks and gays and other menacing elements, now they hear about them all the time.

There is still no alternative statewide paper in which to rebut insane accusations and slanders that appear in the *Union Leader*, but the influx of news from CNN and other sources has miniaturized the paper's impact. Simply to stay marginally competitive with the Maine cable chain and the *Boston Globe*, the *Union Leader* and WMUR Manchester have to report the unpleasant minority news they used to suppress, even if the paper's editorials—mainly crayoned by geriatric Loeb protégé James L. Finnegan—continue to sound like bulletins from a psychiatric ward. The era when William Loeb's campaigns against local college presidents could hound them out of the state—for allowing gay organizations on campus, or sponsoring "communist" lectures, as happened with Loeb's untiring persecution of Thomas Bonner at UNH from 1971 to 1974—is over.

NOWHERE TO RUN, NOWHERE TO HIDE

I drive to Keene one bleary morning with Martha and the Vandellas blasting in the car, up Route 3 to Pinardville, down 101 to Milford, Milford to Peterborough. Just before Dublin the Tsongas signs start appearing on trees and fence posts and mailboxes, *I wake up feeling sorry I met you, hoping soon that I'll forget you, when I look in the mirror to comb my hair—*

Well, Tsongas has very thinning hair, but this is the least of his problems. In a tiny conference room at the *Keene Sentinel*, surrounded by a restrained crowd of at least ten people, the candidate is defending his record in Massachusetts, not that anyone is attacking it, and expounding a fairly conservative philosophy of government, conservative but compassionate, and I know he can't help his face but it's full of little moues and funny tics and because

I arrived late I am practically sitting in a large potted plant just outside the conference room hoping he will raise his voice above a steady drone. Paul Tsongas looks like somebody who could do a fairly credible Lamont Cranston imitation if he really let his hair down, such as it is, but this morning he's stuck on a tone of infinite reasonableness and gentle self-mockery.

"Look," he says after a half hour, "I'm a Greek from Massachusetts who's had cancer, so I've got to be either really serious about what I'm doing or else I'm crazy."

This is followed by an unfortunate moment of silence. Note to press corps: if you find yourself in Keene next week, Lindy's Diner has terrific oyster stew.

À LA RECHERCHE DU DEBRA WINGER

There was bound to come a nadir, a point below which the tedium of the campaign trail could not dip without degenerating into chaos. I am a student of chaos, absurdity, and life's little ironies. Moved to tears one morning by a CNN report on unemployed factory workers in West Virginia, I then bring my cousin Kathy some lunch my mother's prepared; Kathy has just opened a tax accounting service in town, having left her job at a law firm that lost its major corporate client. Kathy is one of the least neurotic, most industrious people I have ever known. I tell her all about these poor laid-off steelworkers.

"Well," she says, "remember when we were kids in the sixties? And all we wanted was to do something in life where we wouldn't have to work in a factory?"

Of course she's right. It's impossible to listen to these visiting politicians jaw on about restoring New Hampshire's industrial base without remembering the sheer meaningless misery most of our relatives endured, day in, day out, some for twenty or thirty years, gluing on shoe soles or soldering circuit boards, an unending pointless-ness for which no number of quarterly raises and benefits packages could ever compensate. The idea that forty to sixty hours a week of mono-tony was good enough for us, for our class of people, was sufficiently appalling to propel us both into college and out of town.

But we came from that factory world, a little more directly than most of the people we know, which is why Kathy and I, in our different styles, have nothing but contempt for New Hampshire yuppies. And why, I suppose, the Conservation Center in Concord, a perfectly benign, tree-rescuing operation in a solar-heated, light and airy facility of dressed knotty pine, activates my class hatred in a way that Phillips Exeter Academy doesn't. I know I'm as smart as any given graduate of Phillips Exeter, but I will never be rich enough to spend all day worrying about acid rain and printing brochures about it on recycled paper.

The gorgeous assistant press officer wants to know if I think they should move the podium for Senator Kerry into the solarium from the observation deck. It is 17 degrees on the observation deck and everyone coming into the solarium shudders when they get a look at it, why on earth do we have to stand outside to hear him? Well, because of the photo op. On the observation deck you've got your panoramic view of a gazillion pine trees and the Route 93 access bridge over the frozen Merrimack River and the dome of the statehouse like a little burnished bubble of junk jewelry, whereas inside you've just got all this knotty pine and several cases of brochures on the culture of Christmas trees and timber management areas and some wall diagrams of the facility and the membership desk. Plus this long knotty pine table where I'm writing this.

"If you get any wind it's going to blow right into the microphone and you won't hear a thing," I tell the gorgeous assistant press officer, who doesn't believe me.

"We've tested it," he says. "You've got good audibility everywhere except in that corner over there."

I am about to say that Senator Kerry is already low enough in the polls without making the press corps stand around in 17-degree weather when the press comes pouring into the solarium, and there's actual excitement in the air, strange considering the candidate, a definite buzz, something's up, something's happened, SOMETHING HAS FINALLY HAPPENED, what can it be? "The write-in Cuomo campaign has opened an office in Concord," *Voice* photographer Brian Palmer explains.

On the tail of this news, Kerry's arrival is indeed an anticlimax, his little speech on the observation deck a nonevent of numbing proportions. One of his aides tells me Kerry's numbers have climbed from six to twelve. Wavering numbers, but the money's coming in, he's planning to hang in until Super Tuesday. Personally, I would ditch the undertaker's overcoat, change the tie, do a nice even rinse on the hair, and try to get him to stop doing that thing with his mouth where he looks like he's sucking a Fisherman's Friend. I now see the wisdom of keeping the podium outside, since most of us would fall asleep if it were anywhere else. At least he doesn't mention The Leg.

"He's gotten more mileage out of that leg," my aunt Beatrice complained when Kerry's commercial came on a few nights earlier. "And he can walk better than I can."

RETURN TO PEYTON PLACE

En route to Berlin, I detour onto Route 140, a hardscrabble two-lane of disintegrating asphalt, for a look at Gilmanton Iron Works. As a child, my role models were Grace Metalious, Emma Peel, and Oscar Levant. Poor tragic Grace ripped the lid off Gilmanton Iron Works in her immortal *Peyton Place*, made a fortune on that and the subsequent *The Tight White Collar* and *Return to Peyton Place*, then drank herself into an early grave. It's a New Hampshire kind of fate.

What I've forgotten is that Gilmanton Iron Works doesn't have much lid to rip off, consisting as it does of a Corner Store and a Post Office. And no one in the Corner Store or the Post Office knows who Grace Metalious was. No one in the Corner Store or the Post Office has decided who to vote for in the primary, either.

"Are there still Iron Works, anyway?" I ask the woman at the Corner Store deli counter.

"There never were any Iron Works," she says. "Not buildings. They used to take iron ore out of Crystal Lake and ship it off."

THE SMELL

Berlin, late afternoon. Big, bruisy skies with long, gray clouds rolling through them. Shops on Main Street all offering clearance sales, 20 percent off, 50 percent off going, going, gone. The only places to get a cup of coffee are the Woolworth's lunch counter and the local pizza joint. It's 11 degrees.

This is an incredibly bleak town, not really a city anymore. Snow piled everywhere, ice crunching underfoot, the streets almost empty. The *Berlin Reporter*, which has just gone from weekly to daily, reports an increase in head lice at local schools. "AIDS Victim Speaks to Berlin High Students," reads one headline. "Study Finds Shortness of Breath Among Older Mill Workers."

In LaVerdiere's Super Drug Store, amid a pile of Waylon Jennings and Lawrence Welk tapes, I find an Ink Spots compendium I can play on the long drive home.

We always knew of the paper mills in what Pat Buchanan calls the North Country and we always called "up there": grim clusters of silos and smokestacks, the Cascade Plant at Cascade Flats, the Burgess Plant a quarter mile up the Androscoggin River, the chemicals spreading out through the water, poisoning the Androscoggin, Tinker Brook, Pea Brook, Dead River, Peabody River, the dead trout, the cancer-riddled perch, the stillborn smelts, the perpetual sulfur-and-boiled-cabbage stench wafted on the mountain winds, covering Gorham, blowing down to Randolph, on a clear day you could smell it all the way to Shelburne, a smell that stank like nothing else on earth, a smell like something crawled up inside you and died, filling everything, like water rising in a sinking ship.

In Harkin headquarters on Pleasant Street, a buxom volunteer in a harlequin sweater set tells a middle-aged man sitting against the wall: "You know he's gotten over fifty awards from different disabled groups? Including Veterans with Disabilities? Because he wrote the Americans with Disabilities Act, you know. Which we're all gonna need some day. With arthritis and so on."

The man regards her coolly. He's my age, he resents this. "Well, I hope not."

By and large, an early middle age, late-ish thirtysomething, hyperthyroidal gathering. Working people, lots of beards, lots of mustaches, a number of Alan Alda types, turquoise down jackets, no pretensions in this place, everything ready-to-wear, maybe a certain Cambridge influence, the snack table covered with potato chips, ginger ale, pretzels, Ritz crackers, a jar of Cheez Whiz. Ratty green carpet. Looks like a furniture showroom.

Waiting and waiting and waiting for Harkin. I stand against the wall behind the chairs reserved for seniors and the disabled, with a clear view of the speaking area. It occurs to me, not for the first time, that I could easily have assassinated any of the major candidates. But they seem to be doing a good job of it themselves. A camera crew glides through the place, interviewing people out of work and people who are "just hanging on by a shoestring." Times are tough. The James River Corporation hasn't hired anyone in two years. Harkin's almost here. Some aides are holding open the door. No, not yet, they're still parking the car. Suddenly . . . something in the air . . . quite unpleasant . . . one of these senior citizens has farted . . . I move away from the chairs . . . the smell follows me . . . it's even over here in the middle of the room . . . a thick, rich, bean supper fart . . . wait, though, it's everywhere . . . my god, it's the James River plant!

Yes, folks, just leave a door open on Pleasant Street, and these factories that everybody wants to ram back into high gear have practically stunk out Harkin headquarters. Once the candidate is inside, the door closes and the fart smell gradually dissipates, like a minor motif in a symphony of hot air. A distinguished-looking man, like your favorite high school civics teacher, carefully raked gray hair, a cracker-barrel face that belongs on a dollar bill, light blue shirt, burgundy V-necked sweater, olive-gray slacks, a navy blazer—remember Jean Arthur in *A Foreign Affair*, swinging from a ceiling pipe in a Berlin (Germany) speakeasy, singing "Ioway, Ioway"? Harkin has that same wholesome, rolled-up-shirtsleeves quality, and his rap has the plainspoken, blocky style of Harry S. Truman, on whom Harkin's modeled himself. Trailing just about everybody in the polls? Big deal.

"I love history. 'Course you know my favorite president was Truman. One night Truman was speaking to the young Democrats. And he was way down in the polls. Strom Thurmond had walked out with the Dixiecrats, Henry Wallace had walked out with the Progressives, *Life* magazine in that summer had run a picture of Dewey calling him President Dewey. One young Democrat yelled out, 'Who's gonna be the next president?' Truman looked at him, he said, 'Young man, next January, there's gonna be a Democrat in the White House, and you're lookin' at him.' And that's what I say to you. You're lookin' at him. 'Cause we're gonna win.

"I sense a hunger to turn away from the legacy of the Reagan-Bush administration. Those policies that have made the rich get richer, the poor get poorer, made the middle class pay the freight both ways. Those policies that have cost you your jobs, exporting them out of this country ... young people can't get a college education, don't know where they're gonna get the money ...

"If you're a junk bond dealer, a corporate trader, best of times. If you're a corporate CEO with a golden parachute, best of times. But if you're a working person, lost your job, no job training, don't know what to do? Worst of times. If you're a family, unemployed, you don't know how you're gonna pay your health care bills? An elderly person? Worst of times."

There is nothing to argue with in Harkin's broad-brush portrait of America today, though his vignettes about what is wrong are more than a little stale by this time. Free trade is a two-way street. Jobs. Tell Japan to open its doors. Level playing field. Reciprocity.

If I ever go to Japan, I won't be taking along the three top auto executives. They can't even figure out to put the steering wheel on the right-hand side. Bring the money home, invest it here. Rebuild our infrastructure.

Tell you the truth, this guy is a little too calculatedly down-home for my taste. OK, they've all got an answer for everything, but the tone . . . this picture of America as a land of happy workers, raring to go, to pitch in . . . the way everything is us versus them . . . and the way everybody's complaints feed directly into his argument . . . and frankly, he hasn't said one word about minority issues, racial divisions . . . of course, none of the others have, either, except in code. You go to White America, you talk the White America talk.

"WHAT ABOUT THE DRUGS?"

This question punctures the rhapsodic upswing that was supposed to conclude Harkin's speech, and the candidate is clearly irritated, but game:

"We've gotta beef up our Coast Guard. Anyway, who was it that put Manuel Noriega on the CIA payroll? George-Herbert-Hoover-Bush!" And he goes on. Rather alarmingly. If I understand him correctly, Harkin has no qualms about sending the Marines into South America. With its permission, of course.

"Mr. Harkin," a boozy-sounding woman in the back pipes up, "why should we send billions of dollars to Russia, when they have always been our enemy? And Poland, and Yugoslavia, and all those countries instead of keeping the money in this country?"

Before Harkin can open his mouth—well, it's already open, but before he can say anything—a large, craggy old man with a face like Lionel Stander's chimes in:

"Ten billion going to Israel to put these guys to work on the Golden Heights for Russian immigrants! What the hell is this? Everybody afraid of the Jews?"

"Now, sometimes you—" Harkin begins, but the man is implacable.

"I'm not a bigot, I'm not—but on the other hand, they're human beings, but we're human beings, looking for jobs too."

"That's why you need to make sure that they are investing back in this country, that's exactly what I've been telling you."

The woman from earlier is also implacable:

"What I feel, you go into a store, and myself, I buy US made. Made in the USA."

"You bet," Harkin panders.

"If it's made in USA we keep our own people working, right?"

"That's right," he says.

"But what you see in most of the stores, is Made in China, Made in Taiwan, all that. What's the point of these countries—and if those articles were not on the shelves, people would buy US made. It wouldn't be there. So you pay a dollar more for the product. But our people don't work for nothing, they don't live twelve in one apartment. We have a nice way of living. And we wanna keep it that way. And I don't want to support the Russians, believe me."

Harkin talks about a bill he's introducing, instructing US representatives to the IMF and the World Bank to vote against any loan to any country that spends more on its military than on health and education. This sounds nice, until you consider that the US itself wouldn't qualify for such a loan, though most other countries in the world would.

"They never pay it back. Did they ever pay it back?" the woman screeches.

"There's one country that has paid back every loan."

"Which one?"

"Israel."

"Well, the Jews, they have more money than everybody in the world!"

Harkin quickly takes a question from another part of the room. For me, anyway, he has just collapsed into nonexistence. I suppose one can, in these bankrupt times, in a state where the only major paper once ran an editorial entitled "Kissinger the Kike?" expect a little Jew-baiting on the campaign trail. But I cannot imagine Mario Cuomo or Jay Rockefeller letting such remarks just sit there in the room, just to grub a couple of votes. Not in a million years.

On November 7, 1960, John F. Kennedy stood in Victory Park in Manchester, directly across from the Manchester *Union Leader* offices, and said:

"I believe there is probably a more irresponsible newspaper than that one right over there somewhere in the United States, but I've been through forty states and I haven't found it yet."

The kind of ignorant sentiments sounded at Harkin's Berlin headquarters can be heard throughout the state of New Hampshire, and even if they originated generations before Loeb's acquisition of the *Union Leader*, the paper has fueled them for decades. As a result, bigotry has been institutionalized among the less educated, who believe their lives have been ruined by the Jews, the Blacks, the Japanese, the communists, or invaders from Massachusetts rather than by bad choices, bad leaders, and a refusal to learn from the larger world. The candidates certainly know this coming in, and at the risk of sounding idealistic, I think any presidential candidate stumping through this backward but maybe not entirely hopeless state has some moral duty to offer a corrective example, to show some high-mindedness, instead of just promising jobs and money and material aggrandizement.

During the years of artificial plenty, New Hampshire was happy to sell off the intangible wealth of livably scaled towns, forests, and wide-open spaces for a quick buck, three or four extra Kmarts within driving distance, and an idiotic abundance of worthless consumer goods. Now that people have to live in the debris, their fields and meadows long vanished under now-vacant malls and abandoned tract developments, they might reflect that this all happened once before, when the great Amoskeag Mills shut down earlier in this century, and that history has repeated itself as farce instead of tragedy. Of course people are "hurting"—you usually do hurt after shooting yourself in the foot. And instead of yacking about wake-up calls and level playing fields and "sending a message" to the rest of the planet that America intends to remain a vicious bully among nations, first in everything but human reason, any candidate worth voting for, however hard the times, ought to offer people an appeal to their better natures, as well as to the part that eats. Nobody did.

(1992)

THE BROTHERS

The Brothers:
The Road to an American Tragedy
Masha Gessen

On June 24, Dzhokhar Tsarnaev, the younger of two Chechen-American brothers responsible for the Boston Marathon bombing on April 15, 2013, was sentenced to death in a Boston federal court. (His older brother, Tamerlan, died following a street battle with police in Watertown, Massachusetts, several nights after the bombing.) The brothers had placed, and detonated by remote control, two explosive devices fashioned from pressure cookers stuffed with shrapnel; three people were killed in the blasts, and more than 260 others suffered serious, permanent injuries, including sixteen limb amputations.

Footage from multiple surveillance cameras overlooking the Boston Marathon dispelled any reasonable doubt that the Tsarnaev brothers had planted the bombs and set them off. At Tsarnaev's trial, notwithstanding his "not guilty" plea on thirty separate capital charges, his chief defense at-torney told the court "it was him." This effectively confined the defense case to the assertion that Dzhokhar had acted under the powerful influence of Tamerlan, and would not have carried out the bombing on his own, counting on character witnesses in the trial's penalty phase to dramatize this idea to the jury. One witness testified that Dzhokhar had been "like a puppy following his brother," a characterization eerily illustrated by surveillance videos of Dzhokhar trailing Tamerlan by several meters on the sidewalk lining the marathon route.

The defense team's sole objective was a life sentence for their client, an unlikely outcome from the outset, given that the court denied motions to change the trial venue from Boston itself to a town where jurors' friends or families were less likely to have been affected by the bombing. In a non–death penalty state like Massachusetts, a federal case in which execution is an option can still be heard so long as the jury is "death-qualified"— i.e., all the jurors have declared themselves willing to deliver a death verdict. Since 80 percent of Massachusetts residents specifically opposed execution in the Tsarnaev case, the jury was necessarily drawn from an unusually narrow pool and was therefore disproportionately likely to impose capital punishment. Dzhokhar Tsarnaev has since been moved to federal death row in Terre Haute, Indiana, since—although a non–death penalty state can deliver a death verdict—the executions themselves must be carried out in a state that has death penalty statutes. This risible scruple has a practical aspect: such states also have the requisite killing equipment on hand, and often seem to relish the chance to use it. (In recent Ohio, Arizona, and Oklahoma executions, a European export embargo on lethal injection drugs has prompted mix'n'match improvisations with untested pharmaceuticals, with results Josef Mengele would consider plagiarism.) Timothy McVeigh, whose trial venue was shifted from Oklahoma City to Denver, Colorado, got transferred post-trial to the same death row in Terre Haute.

Whether Tsarnaev will, as McVeigh did, forego the often decades-long appeals process to hasten his end is an open question. While hiding from police inside a boat in a backyard in Watertown, Massachusetts, Dzhokhar managed to write a rather long note on the boat's hull that began: "I'm jealous of my brother who ha [bullet hole] ceived the reward of jannutul Firdaus (inshallah) before me." ("Jannatul Firdous" is a name for "the highest paradise" in Arabic, as well as a line of specialty fragrances available online from Givaudan Roure, "the oldest perfumery house in the Arabian Gulf.") For all we know, Dzhokhar's jealousy may already have cooled. If so, ample grounds for appeal exist. There is the venue issue. Then, too, US district judge George O'Toole Jr. refused to give the standard jury instruction which says that a single holdout juror can avert a death sentence permanently—that is, without the penalty phase of the trial being repeated until a unanimous verdict is reached. The grotesqueness of executing a teenager is not considered grounds for appeal: the death-qualifying age, so to speak, is eighteen.

Unlike several recent books on the marathon bombing, Masha Gessen's *The Brothers* is uninflected by consoling homilies, Manichean narrative framing or civic propaganda. Gessen's is a superlative work of reporting that locates the Boston atrocity and the Tsarnaevs in the queasy context of the modern world, where atrocities happen every day, in places presumed to be "safe" as well as those beset by civil war. *The Brothers* provides essential Soviet and post-Soviet geopolitical background, charting the Tsarnaev family's peregrinations from Kyrgyzstan (where Stalin brutally transplanted the entire Chechen population in 1944) to Novosibirsk in south central Russia, where the brothers' parents, Anzor and Zubeidat, met (he was finishing his Soviet military service, she was seeking her eldest brother's permission to move to Moscow). They later moved to Kalmykia, the Soviet republic where Tamerlan was born; back to Kyrgyzstan, where two daughters, Bella and Ailina, were added to the family; then to Chiry-Yurt in Chechnya, Dzhokhar's birthplace.

From Chechnya they returned again to Kyrgyzstan to escape the 1994 Russian bombing of Grozny. In 2000, they moved to Makhachkala in Dagestan, where the Second Chechen War was spilling over the border. Wahhabi fundamentalism had spread through the Caucasus, its suspected adherents a target for Russian troops and local police. As Gessen writes:

> Makhachkala and much of the rest of Dagestan became a battleground.... This was the Dagestan to which Anzor and Zubeidat

brought their four children, including Tamerlan, who at fourteen was on the verge of becoming that most endangered and most dangerous of humans: a young Dagestani man. [They] had to move again, to save their children—again. They would go to America after all.

The Tsarnaevs weren't always fleeing incipient war zones. Sometimes they just rolled elsewhere in search of a better deal. More often than not, Zubeidat, the more willful and ambitious of the parents, decided where they would go. Bad timing, bad luck, and defective reality testing all feature prominently in the story Gessen tells; so do seemingly miniscule ethnic and religious distinctions that caused the Tsarnaevs to feel out of place wherever they lived. They were Chechens outside Chechnya, Muslims in only the nominal sense that their ethnic codes reflected a vaguely Islamic influence.

Things didn't work out in America. The Tsarnaevs arrived soon after 9/11, when Muslims began to replace communists as objects of fear in the media demonization industry. Chechens, who had once been welcomed as refugees from Russian aggression, became suspect after Russia and the US began collaborating on the "war on terror." (The US ignored Russian atrocities in Chechnya in exchange for air bases in Uzbekistan and Kyrgyzstan.) While it's unclear whether the Tsarnaevs experienced egregious anti-Muslim, anti-Chechen or other discrimination in the US (they didn't wear Islamic dress, and one daughter successfully copped a Latina identity for a while), their ethnicity and religion complicated the legal status of some family members, and they must have seen themselves as part of a despised, if nebulous, minority.

The travails of the Tsarnaev clan are almost too numerous and tangled to itemize. The new life in America started with the thorny process of asylum seeking, scrambling for housing and off-the-books work (asylum applicants are prohibited from employment or collecting benefits for a year), finding schools for the children, and trying to decipher local conditions. As the Tsarnaevs landed in Cambridge, Massachusetts, the location was a mixed blessing: a liberal enclave of top-notch universities and rapidly gentrifying neighborhoods, its contiguous working-class areas a Hogarthian reminder of the destiny awaiting failure. A well-educated, Russian-speaking, guardian angel landlady, Joanna Herlihy, entered their lives at a propitious moment. Herlihy, who "for most of her adult life had been trying to save the world," can be viewed retrospectively as a mixed blessing too. Untiringly helpful in practical matters, she sheltered her new tenants behind a baffle of contentious idealism, ratifying their feelings of persecution when wishes didn't come true. The stellar expectations of the Tsarnaevs eroded in increments. Within a few years, they collected grievances like baseball cards.

Gessen writes that kids in newly immigrating families "stop being kids, because the adults have lost their bearings . . . they go through a period of intense suffering and dislocation made all the more painful for being forced and unexpected. But at the other end of the pain, they locate their roles and settle into them, claiming their places in the new world." Most of the Tsarnaev children, however, did less and less well as time went on. The family pattern had been set by their parents: when troubles piled up after each fresh start, they just moved somewhere else. Gessen's narrative makes the Tsarnaevs palpable enough, but unworldliness mists the atmosphere around them; Anzor and Zubeidat sound too narcissistic, too skilled in extracting sympathy and favors from new acquaintances, to compromise much with American reality. No one in the family stuck to any ambitious plan long enough to realize it. Anzor, whose bogus claim to have been a prosecutor's assistant in Kyrgyzstan got him nowhere, took up his previous trade as a freelance car mechanic; Zubeidat, after thwarted efforts to translate documents for human rights groups, became a home care worker, later a beautician. With the exception of Dzhohkar, the undoubtedly bright children began to stumble in their new surroundings.

Zubeidat, who believed him "perfect" and "destined for greatness," no doubt instilled a great deal of self-belief in Tamerlan. But, as Gessen writes, "he had lived in seven cities and attended an even greater number of schools," entering tenth grade in Cambridge at seventeen. He struggled for good grades and struggled to learn English, but as the oldest child was also the most wrong-footed by repeated dislocation. Hopes for him shifted to a career in boxing or music. Catnip to women, he dressed like a gigolo and kept himself gym-solid shapely. He played the keyboard, and thought of becoming a music star, but never really pursued it. After dropping out of community college, he delivered pizzas and sold weed. He married, and fathered a child. He won some impressive boxing matches and an amateur Golden Gloves trophy but was afterward barred from title contests because he wasn't a US citizen; his application was held up after he was arrested for smacking his wife. At the time of the bombings, he was living on benefits and dealing drugs.

The daughters, Bella and Ailina, despite some early promise, scuttled their educations; they married Chechen men (a cultural ukase), had children, divorced, got busted for passing counterfeit banknotes and selling weed. Nothing reachy was expected of them in the first place and they soon seemed fated for a life of welfare and sporadic work in service industries. Their designated roles were to marry within the clan, have babies, continue the blood line, and embrace domestic servitude, as per the will of Allah. They were independent enough to get out of bad marriages and free enough to keep their own children (in the old country, children were the husband's property), but otherwise their American road turned into a dead end.

Dzhokhar, having spent his whole childhood in Cambridge, was the most assimilated of the family, and the last to stumble. A sweet, smart boy loved by all, he graduated with honors from high school (Cambridge Rindge and Latin, alma mater of Matt Damon and Ben Affleck), despite spending much of it stoned out of his mind.

He also was dealing, like Tamerlan. While he couldn't have afforded a prestige university, Dzhokhar's choice of UMass Dartmouth—in Gessen's generous description, a "non-competitive" college—reflects a dazed, amiable passivity. The Tsarnaevs were a "tight-knit family" in the most ruinous sense that the family alone provided each member's total sense of identity and direction. If one ran awry, eventually they all did.

All the descriptions of him that have emerged from conversations with people who knew him, including people who cared for him deeply, are spectacular in their flatness. Those who watched him from a distance describe him as a social superstar. To those who thought they got closer, he was charming. Indeed, charm appears to be his sole distinguishing personality trait. Teachers thought he was bright but uninterested in thinking for himself.

In his sophomore year at Dartmouth he began failing subjects, stepped up his marijuana sales, and narrowed his social circle to a small band of other immigrant Dartmouth students—Dias Kadyrbayev and Azmat Tazhayakov from Kazakhstan, and Robel Phillipos, an Ethiopian with US citizenship—and their occasional girlfriends. He tweeted, he Facebooked. He spent much of his time away from his dorm room, at a New Bedford apartment the Kazakhs rented.

The group spent three or four evenings a week on the sofa, getting stoned, watching movies and eating. The boys played video games; the girls talked about which of the boys might be the hottest lover, though it doesn't seem as though anyone but Dias was getting much action.

In 2009, Tamerlan and his mother "began studying the Koran." Tamerlan also began studying *The Protocols of the Elders of Zion*, ever popular in Russia and the bible of anti-Semites everywhere. One of Zubeidat's home care clients, a loose screw called Donald Larking, passed along conspiracist libertarian newspapers and magazines. The internet provided even more enticing forms of inflammatory propaganda—lectures by the al-Qaeda recruiter Anwar al-Awlaki and the like—and the opportunity to share festering resentments with thinkalikes all over the planet. Relatedly or not, Dzhokhar, a whiz at languages, opened an account on VK.com, "a Facebook clone site on which most Russians his age maintained their social media lives." By this time, evidently, everyone realized that America had been a wrong move.

Anzor, despite a few drunken fights and scrapes with neighbors, was an essentially passive, Soviet-made working stiff, svelte and athletic in his youth, gaunt and ailing by middle age, indifferent to Islamist manias and 9/11 conspiracy lore, resigned to fixing cars and getting by. His health deteriorated, and his marriage to Zubeidat, who had taken to wearing a burqa, fell apart. They divorced in 2011; in 2012, Anzor left the country for Dagestan. Meantime, after ten years, Joanna Herlihy got fed up with her rebarbative tenants and their increasingly cracked views. She asked them to leave, but gave them several months to do so.

Here, more or less, is where the train goes into the tunnel. More finely sifted details of all the above can be found in Gessen's extraordinary book. It's worth noting here that Zubeidat was arrested for shoplifting from the Cambridge branch of Lord & Taylor in 2012; she then took off for Dagestan, two weeks after Tamerlan returned from a seven-month visit. With both parents gone, Tamerlan was, by custom, now the head of the family in America, though Bella and Ailina, haphazardly in and out of Cambridge with their children, were living erratic lives of their own. Dzhokhar shambled back and forth in a cloud of smoke between Cambridge and New Bedford. "There was an understanding in the family now: Dagestan was the place to be." Dzhokhar spoke of moving there the following summer. Tamerlan was only waiting until he could get a US passport—a valuable commodity in a pinch.

At the time of the bombings, Tamerlan Tsarnaev was twenty-six, Dzhokhar nineteen. They had no known accomplices, though the bombs were far from simple to make, and no traces of their assembly were discovered anywhere. It's also unclear when the idea of bombing the marathon first occurred to either brother. In the months before the bombing, the brothers were rarely in the same place at the same time. It's easy to suppose they created a gang of two through phone calls and text messages, and fortified their gang's sense of mission with YouTube jihadist videos and al-Qaeda's online magazine, *Inspire*, which ran a DIY article entitled "Make a Bomb in the Kitchen of Your Mom." Had they held off for a year, the ISIS logo might have attracted the brothers to Syria, but the ISIS brand hadn't yet overtaken al-Qaeda's outside the Middle East and the Caucasus. It was widely reported that Tamerlan had been "radicalized" during his visit to Dagestan in 2012. Gessen thinks this is an exaggeration, having tracked his activities there very closely. He hung out with young Salafi Muslims belonging to the Union of the Just, "allied with Hizb ut-Tahrir, one of the largest Islamic organizations in the world. Hizb ut-Tahrir proclaims the goal of creating a caliphate that would unite the Muslim lands of the world . . . by peaceful means, through political and philosophical struggle only." Gessen notes that some analysts consider Hizb ut-Tahrir "a gateway organization that facilitates young Muslims' passage from peaceful civilians to jihadis," but all the same, Tamerlan did nothing much in Dagestan besides talk the Islamist talk and show off his fancy clothes.

Retrospective suspicion that Tamerlan had murdered three drug dealers in Waltham, Massachusetts, in 2011, by slitting their throats, insinuates the possibility that Tamerlan had killed people before visiting Dagestan, and was already disinhibited about inflicting lethal violence. However, we don't know, and we probably never will; the only purported witness/accomplice to the

Waltham murders, a gym-mate called Ibragim Todashev, was shot seven times and killed by an FBI agent in Orlando, Florida, a month after the bombing. According to the FBI, Todashev "became aggressive" while writing out a confession implicating Tamerlan, the uncompleted text of which was inconsistent with the Waltham crime scene.

This sort of obscurity is everywhere in the Tsarnaev saga. Why was a bevy of federal agents buzzing around the MIT area in Cambridge several hours before the Tsarnaevs shot an MIT security cop? Had the FBI, at the instigation of the Russian FSB, not just interviewed Tamerlan as a suspected extremist several times in 2011, but tried to recruit him as an informant? An informant who "went rogue"? If this were the case, could the FBI have hoped to take him out before he could spill, if the police caught him alive?

Gessen has taken flak from the *New York Times* for merely asking such questions, in a ponderous review by Janet Napolitano, director of the Department of Homeland Security at the time of the marathon bombing. A beloved figure of the surveillance services, Napolitano dismissed the book's descriptions of FBI malfeasance, abuses of the deportation laws, and draconian prosecutions on accessory charges as "conspiracy theory." This seems quite unfair to Gessen, who tries for several pages to imagine a plausible scenario in which the FBI agent who shot Todashev seven times could have been acting in "self-defense." That she is unable really to do so is hardly her fault. The FBI itself issued several different versions of what happened before settling on something remotely credible.

Well before the Tsarnaev brothers were identified as suspects, tabloid, TV, and print media launched a free-ranging witch hunt of Muslims, people who looked like Muslims, and unaccountable others, picked out of footage of the marathon crowd, or out of nowhere; at one strange moment of the frenzy, even the actress Zooey Deschanel was identified as a bombing suspect on a news broadcast, perhaps because of the slightly unusual spelling of her name. After the police shoot-out (in which Tamerlan's nearly dead body was recovered, Dzhokhar having run over it in a van), authorities asked residents of the Boston area to "shelter in place," putting an entire American city under lockdown.

After Dzhokhar's arrest, various provisions of the US Patriot Act permitted authorities to question the gravely wounded suspect, a US citizen, for hours before he was read his Miranda rights; in the days and months that followed, almost anyone in the United States with the faintest connection to the Tsarnaevs was either harassed, deported, or prosecuted for minor, even unconscious infractions that, if shoved under the umbrella of "terrorism," can be magnified by federal prosecutors into major felonies. Dias Kadyrbayev, Azmat Tazhayakov, and Robel Phillipos, who removed some of Dzhokhar's belongings from his dorm room in a stoned panic, are currently doing long stretches in federal prison; another friend who deleted the search history on his own computer has been in custody for two years awaiting trial. The charges brought against these people presumed deliberate obstruction of the bombing investigation, or of making "materially false, fictitious and fraudulent statements" to police and the FBI, when in any reasonable view, nothing they did, or told or didn't tell authorities, had any effect on the investigation whatsoever. They had no knowledge of the bombing before it happened and were in an even greater state of shocked confusion afterward than everyone else in Boston, simply because they happened to know the Tsarnaevs.

What passed between the brothers in the ten months after Zubeidat's departure to Dagestan is terra incognita. The chances are no specific event or Svengali-like radicalization inspired the Tsarnaev brothers to blow up the Boston Marathon. As a policeman in Yasmina Khadra's 2007 novel *The Attack* puts it, "I think even the most seasoned terrorists really have no idea what has happened to them. And it can happen to anyone. Something clicks somewhere in their subconscious, and they're off... Either it falls on your head like a roof tile or it attaches itself to your insides like a tapeworm. Afterwards, you no longer see the world in the same way." The media fantasy that Tamerlan was schizophrenic and "heard voices" is highly improbable. The consensus among terrorism experts is that terrorists are normal people. "He was a perfectly nice guy." "The last person I'd imagine doing something like this." After the fact, neighbors, friends, and coworkers invariably say the same things about terrorists that they say about serial killers. It's worth noting that there isn't a single provable instance of the legendary FBI profiling unit in Quantico, Virginia, actually instigating the capture of a serial killer: it tends to be when someone is stopped for driving with a broken tail-light that the dead body in the trunk is discovered. It's only afterward that we're told they "fit the FBI profile."

Why did they do it? How could they? In the world we live in now, the better questions are: Why not? Why wouldn't they? To quote Khadra's novel again, on suicide bombers: "The only way to get back what you've lost or to fix what you've screwed up—in other words, the only way to make something of your life—is to end it with a flourish: turn yourself into a giant firecracker in the middle of a school bus or launch yourself like a torpedo against an enemy tank." Everything the US has done to prevent terrorism has been the best advertising terrorism could possibly have. The "war on terror" has degenerated since its ugly inception in Afghanistan and Iraq into a two-pronged war against the US domestic population's civil rights and the infrastructures of Muslim nations; every cynical episode of this endless war has inched America closer to a police state, and turned people minding their own business in other countries into jihadists and suicide bombers. If the United States were at all interested in preventing terrorism, it would first have to acknowledge that the country belongs to the citizens its economic policies have impoverished, and get rid of emergency laws that violate their rights on the pretext of ensuring their safety. This would involve dismantling the surveillance state apparatus that inflates its criminally gigantic budgets with phony terrorism warnings and a veritable industry of theatrical FBI sting operations. And then the country would have to address the systemic social problems that have been allowed to metastasize ever since the presidency of Ronald Reagan. As everyday existence becomes more punitive for all but the monied few, more and more frustrated, volatile individuals will seek each other out online, aggravate whatever lethal fairy tale suits their pathology, and, ultimately, transfer their rage from the screen world to the real one.

(2015)

ROMANIAN NOTES

> Thanks for a country where nobody's allowed to mind his own business. Thanks for a nation of finks.
> —WILLIAM S. BURROUGHS, "A Thanksgiving Prayer"

•

In Bucharest, the psychological damage inflicted on a society subjected to surveillance terror is apparent everywhere when you scratch the surface, even twenty-four years after the fall of Ceaușescu—in the suspicion older Romanians show toward each other; in the furtiveness and compulsive cheating rampant among shopkeepers and service providers; in the resigned abjection of young people who can imagine no future options besides (a) colorless, lifelong conformity in a degrading job or (b) membership in a neo-Nazi gang; in the atmosphere of demoralized powerlessness that suffuses daily life in Bucharest as perceptibly as melancholia pervades Istanbul. No problem too small to be insoluble, no conflict unthreatening enough to resolve without trauma. And in the countryside, people say, it's worse.

•

In line at an airport immigration check, the couple ahead of me debated which of their passports to use. They each shuffled at least five, like cards in a poker hand, all issued by different countries. The two sounded postcoitally blowsy, absorbed in their own sleepy dithering. They asked if I'd been around Taksim Square the night before. They had been sprayed, it turned out, with the same wave of tear gas I had walked into three blocks further down the street. Like me, they'd spent all night rinsing their eyeballs, and now could easily fall asleep on their feet.

We just got married, the woman said, making a little snort, as if they shared a few doubts about whether this had been a great idea. She was fortyish, dubiously blond, pale, strong-chinned, gray-eyed, very pretty, of unguessable nationality, wearing a frazzled old Chanel suit and no makeup. Her partner was a hefty man, possibly Lebanese, with a stippled whitish fringe along the trim line of his thick, black hair. Youthfully loose-limbed, but paunchy and quite a bit older. One pale-aubergine shirttail fluttered at his zipper; the other was stuffed into his pants. He was trying to be amusing and, unlike most people in airports, succeeding. *Guess where we're going*, the woman quizzed with mock haplessness. *Cairo, jewel of the Nile*, her new spouse chimed in, rolling jaded eyes at the predictable ironies of travel. I had a half-conscious flash that these people weren't touring or jetsetting at all, but testing out a much-revised script for incipient flaws, a fiction close enough to reality to go unchallenged in public. The immigration person waved them forward. *And then, what the hell*, the woman laughed as she walked away, *Beirut. How's that for a dream honeymoon?*

•

It's possible that people intending to do bad things use the telephone and the internet to plan them, if they are also morons. However, morons are not noted for their planning skills. I suppose it would be nice if some bad things could be prevented before they happen without turning the world into a police state. The "eye in the sky" in casinos nips a lot of card counting and skimming and other scams in the bud. But if you place every human being or even everybody in a single country under invasive surveillance, a police state is what you get, even if the collected data is scattered around unsorted in a mainframe until a particular person becomes "a person of interest."

The overriding imperative of any bureaucracy funded by the state is its own self-perpetuation. If its purported reason to exist threatens to disappear, a bureaucracy will create whatever conditions it was supposed to eliminate. A drug enforcement agency will deal drugs. An anti-terrorism agency will breed its own terrorists, attracting weak-minded, potentially volatile people into bogus conspiracy cells. A central intelligence agency or so-called department of homeland security will manufacture threats to security, for example the recent "increased chatter alarm" that closed all the embassies in North Africa for a week.

If these glue traps for federal revenue are allowed to collect unlimited information about everybody, they can also make anybody into a terrorist, a drug mule, or whatever other menace a potential agency or department budget reduction calls for, cutting and pasting together a flimsy but widely believable, totally distorted version of any individual for public consumption, using bits of his or her data that have been parked in a massive hard drive in North Dakota or Utah or one of the other storage states. Last words of Lee Harvey Oswald: "I'm just a patsy."

•

In *Kiss the Hand You Cannot Bite*, a book about the rise and fall of Ceaușescu, Edward Behr quotes a former Securitate official: "Imagine a huge apparatus spreading rumors, fear, and terror, an atmosphere in which common people feel that if they try and do the most insignificant thing identified as an act of opposition . . . they will disappear. It was psychological terror that paralyzed the Romanian population, and the most outstanding piece of disinformation was the rumor, deliberately spread by Securitate itself, that one out of every four Romanians was a Securitate informer."

•

Local "unrest" distracted me from Egyptian news in Sofia, where comparatively festive marches "turned violent," as the wire services put it, only once, on the forty-first consecutive night of demos, when protesters trapped journalists and politicians in the Parliament building, then stoned a police bus sent to extract them. It felt much easier to identify with angry Bulgarians, angry Turks in Taksim Square, than with the factional mix of Islamists in Cairo. The Istanbul demos targeted once-popular prime minister Recep Erdoğan after he proposed razing Gezi Park and replacing it with an Ottoman Disney Mall. (Erdoğan's biography features the most piquant dependent clause I've come across recently, citing the fecund marriage of the former sesame bun seller and anti-Semitic playwright to Emine Gülbaran "despite his homosexual background." About which, there isn't another word.) The Bulgarians, unusually effective street agitators (aside from bringing down the whole government last February, demos recently produced a total ban on shale oil extraction), were enraged by the government's ongoing collusion with crime-syndicates-turned-corporations that control much of the country's industry and resources. These things made sense. I understood where they came from. It takes no imagination at all to perceive the US since 9/11, notably New York under Mayors Giuliani and Bloomberg, as a more elusively layered, distractingly overdecorated version of Bulgaria Today or Istanbul Now, if you throw in an electronic upgrade of the East German Stasi, the Romanian Securitate, the Soviet KGB, and the Albanian SHIK. Egypt, however...

•

To pilfer the tide of Ivana Lowell's brilliant recent memoir, why not say what happened? According to Alan Taylor's *The Civil War of 1812*, even before the American Revolution scores of colonists in every trade and profession fled the soon-to-be-United States for remote parts of Canada, disgusted by the corruption and unbridled avarice that already permeated life in American towns and cities. By 1871, reporting on the fantastic chicaneries of the Gilded Age robber barons and the rotten judiciary they manipulated to thwart one another, Charles F. Adams Jr. was able to write of an atypical judge, with no fear of intelligent contradiction: "At this particular juncture Mr. Justice Sutherland, a magistrate of such pure character and unsullied reputation that it is inexplicable how he ever came to be elevated to the bench on which he sits..." How different the US might be, today when the practical ruthlessness of the Gilded Age amounts to a pimple on Lloyd Blankfein's ass, if every school child were taught the actual history of the country, instead of being stuffed with platitudes glorifying the supreme greatness and goodness of the place where he or she happened to be born.

•

I registered Egypt as a creepy smudge when it appeared on Bulgarian TV, which I only turned on for news of Edward Snowden, marooned at the time in the Moscow airport. Now, in Bucharest, I catch myself doing the same: Egypt seems even more distant, a catastrophe with no solution and no exit. I don't know how to reconcile the contradictions embedded in it. I can't look at it. Among other things, it would force me to consider: Do I honestly "believe" in democracy?

I'm old enough to know America itself doesn't, since until very recently, any democratically elected head of state or popular leader anywhere whom the US couldn't control swiftly experienced a CIA-sponsored insurgency or coup d'état—Arbenz, Mossadegh, Allende, Aristide, Sukarno, Lumumba, Trujillo, Diem, Goulart in Brazil, Nkrumah in Ghana, to name just a few, and then there are all the failed coups, against Castro, Chavez—the list covers every continent except Australia, where I think the US mainly just rigs elections. Everybody in this world, except in America, understands exactly what the single mission statement of US policy is: "You do it our way or we'll push your face in."

•

No answer, no exit: asking people to choose between the Egyptian military and the Muslim Brotherhood is the same as asking if they prefer Auschwitz or Treblinka.

•

Beside the veranda of his carpet emporium, Ahmet's ringlets brushed John-from-Melbourne's ear while they sipped mint tea, slouched on fat embroidered pillows. In the mid-afternoon heat, they lolled like pashas on a vast Soumak carpet rolled out on the ground. Ahmet's piccolo, a cherubic but very pushy fifteen-year-old, had "teasingly" escorted me the length of the bazaar, from a fabric shop also owned by Ahmet, where I had been on the verge of getting laid by one of his employees. Ahmet had been there earlier, striking Mae West poses and exhausting his supply of sexual innuendoes. Ahmet was what used to be called a camp. Not my thing. Now I had to deal with him again, taking in a tableau of pudgy, effeminate carpet shill nuzzling lanky, louche-looking retiree from Down Under, which strongly suggested that Ahmet and John were *carnally familiar* old friends. I took John for an expat living in Istanbul since at least the Battle of Gallipoli, if not the Crimean War.

After a lot of misfounded conversation, I gleaned that he was nothing of the kind. Depressingly, he was two years younger than I was. He had arrived two days before on a loosely organized package tour and had met Ahmet for the first time that morning. He wasn't gay, or not much, just comfortable with body contact. This was the six-hour anniversary of Ahmet's campaign to sell him a carpet, subtracting an hour for lunch and another for Ahmet's mosque duty. Merchants in the Old Bazaar not only drip charm and oblige you to drink tea with them for hours but will happily fuck you in the ass to make a sale. The playfulness involved often looks and feels more personal than it is, though.

•

Democracy, Schmemocracy. It's irrelevant to the people who manage the country, a joke to the people who own it. A local example, of course, is New York's City Council, led by Christine Quinn, abolishing mayoral term limits after they were set by a voter referendum—the most unambiguous expression of the citizens' wishes in a democracy (unless the ballot question is constructed by Californian Jesuits). What I'm not certain about is whether I support, believe in, advocate, adhere to, "democracy," if the outcome is or might be something very evil.

•

Silence was the enemy of Ahmet's trade. He had a Wagnerian opera's worth of rug chat stored in an otherwise fallow brain. At times, weirdly, losing himself in the throes of a marketing aria, he appeared to mutate, like a human CGI effect, into a more urbane, philosophically detached, European personality, even a hereditary duke or viscount, from a country far west of Turkey. Or an actor, perhaps, researching the role of a faggy Levantine rug peddler, who sets off for lunch at the Four Seasons before remembering he's still in greasepaint and a cheap rehearsal costume. These improvised personality touches—ruminative, skeptical, fitfully dismissive, florid, conflicted, judicious, brazenly unctuous by turns—began to suggest that somebody else was trying to sell him the carpet. He made two paltry sales all day, both dismayingly irrelevant to his current business plan. His current business plan was to somehow unload a centuries-old Isfahan consignment item, valued at two hundred thousand euros. Everyone entering the shop wanted a look at it, since Ahmet invoked it as if it were the Holy Grail. Absurdly, I thought, he went as far as to tell people he expected the thing to triple in value on its next appraisal and prayed some devilish shrewd customer wouldn't wrest it from his inventory before that. However, Ahmet could divine with amazing accuracy the net worth and disposable income of any living human being and saw that none of the day's marks had remotely enough assets to buy it. He was just fucking with himself. It seemed mildly endearing.

•

The Obama administration scrambles to glue a happy face on its out-of-control spy agencies, while the director of the NSA lies to Congress, not only about the fact of rampant domestic spying, but about the number of terrorist plots the NSA has thwarted by means of *any* of its surveillance programs. At first it's fifty, then it's ten, then it's down to five, finally it's "I don't have the exact figures in front of me." Exactly none, apparently. Even Joe McCarthy was less obviously full of shit. By the time James M. Clapper, if that really is his name, finished testilying under oath, news of the illegal liaison between NSA and the DEA had already leaked from the cache of yet-unpublished Snowden documents. It's brilliant to release the sordid truth one item at a time, right after The Clapper or some other federal sinkhole has been forced to admit the last one and indignantly denied that the logically inevitable next one could even be possible.

*

When Ahmet disappeared to cook tea, John mentioned that Cairo was the next stop on his itinerary. The question of whether to cancel hovered in the muzzy air. *Of course you should go*, I said, yawning. *They're not rioting in Luxor or Alexandria, are they?* I had no idea if "they" were or not, but it was just rioting, as far as anyone knew. Maybe it would stop, the way the bazaar stopped when the prayer call, crackling with dense static, bleated like a scary foghorn from the Fatih Cadde mosque across the road. *Not yet*, John said.

Unless all hell breaks loose before Tuesday, I'm going. I only get away from Melbourne once a year, anyway it's already paid for.

I meant not to sound *too* encouraging, but life really is cheatingly brief. And people who never travel tend to imagine, when trouble erupts in a distant country, that its entire landmass has seized into convulsions. I reminded John that he knew better, though I had scrubbed Egypt from my own vague plans that morning. John wasn't American, I rationalized, he would be less unwelcome than I in a combat zone, or else less attractive as a hostage, if it came to that. *Either things will calm down before you get there,* I said, *or you'll have a great story to tell your grandchildren.*

Anyway, John said, *I check the embassy travel advisory every day.*

Sometimes, I said, *even when there's a war, if the Hilton stays open, it means you can travel around and still avoid the whole thing if you're careful.*

It really didn't occur to me until 3 a.m., when I was feeding cats in the streets near my hotel, to ask myself what is always somehow an untimely question: *Why the fuck did I say that?*

•

Obama—not to be outdone in devising the "least untruthful" excuse for a money-gobbling vortex of warrantless searches and supine FISA court judges who sign off on anything put in front of them—assures us that he had planned some purgative review of the NSA even before Edward Snowden was a drop of cum in his father's balls, *so there!* How sad that the still-inspiring symbolism of Obama's election has turned out to be the only unqualifiedly positive thing about his presidency—even Obamacare is so deeply compromised by concessions to the insurance industry that its main value is likewise located in the realm of the symbolic. I'm rarely moved by the rhetorical style of Ivy League valedictorian addresses, so when people say "the president made a great speech," it's just an unnecessary reminder that actions speak louder than words. And in the matter of Edward Snowden's immeasurably laudable and invaluable public service, and regarding the NSA, CIA, FBI, DEA, et al., the next shoe to drop will doubtlessly be federal collection of all citizens' medical records—and, since all the acronyms are having a gang bang, why not let the IRS in on the fun, along with the family doctor?

(2013)

BEING AND NOTHINGNESS AMERICAN STYLE

These are the generations of America.

> And Lee Harvey Oswald shot John F. Kennedy. And Jacqueline Kennedy shot Mark S. Goodman and Mark S. Goodman shot Beverley Davis. And Beverley Davis shot James Willwerth. And James Willwerth shot John J. Austin. And John J. Austin shot Nancy Jalet. And Nancy Jalet shot Leah Shanks. And Leah Shanks shot Christopher Porterfield . . .
>
> —J. G. BALLARD, *The Atrocity Exhibition*

On November 7 of this year, the usually infallible Bernard Weinraub ("Special to *The New York Times*," and to each and every one of us) assured his readers that Oliver Stone's forthcoming *JFK* "will be the most widely discussed movie of the Christmas season." Not *The Addams Family*! "The fact that the movie, budgeted at $35 million to $40 million, features Mr. Costner, one of the top stars in Hollywood, and is supported by one of the more prestigious studios, Warner Brothers, adds considerable weight to the impact of the film's thesis, which presents the killing as a conspiracy but does not pinpoint the conspirators."

Notwithstanding Oliver Stone's recent description of prestigious Warner Bros. as an organization of "cocksucker vampires," it does seem that the lavish bankrolling of a studio film supporting the four-shots-from-the-grassy-knoll theory has started a lot of talk. The *Times*, for example, titled Weinraub's article "Substance and Style Criticized in *J.F.K.*," when neither the style nor the substance of

Stone's film had yet been viewed by anybody. The *Washington Post* and *Time*, twin pillars of credibility, have been pooh-poohing Stone's assassination theory with uncharacteristic fervor for months, apparently on the basis of a stolen first-draft script of the film.

Stone's partisans in the a priori controversy swirling around his movie include Carl Oglesby, founder of the Assassination Information Bureau, Herbert L. Schiller, professor emeritus of communications at UC San Diego, and Zachary Sklar, coauthor of Stone's screenplay. These people sense dark forces at work to discredit Stone, and to keep the searing truth about the Kennedy assassination from reaching the American public. The same dark forces, perhaps, that converged that fatal day in Dealey Plaza. In the scenario favored by this particular mindset, a public awakened to the possible collusion of the Mafia, the CIA, and even J. Edgar Hoover in the murder of an American president is a public that will march on down to the government and put a stop to this sort of thing. "One purpose of our movie," Stone asseverates in a letter to the *Washington Post*, "is to see that in at least one instance history does not repeat itself."

Given the résumé of the current White House occupant, there would seem to be little danger of history repeating itself in quite the same configuration any time soon, but Stone's faith in the public's thirst for truth is nevertheless admirable. Granted, the conclusion reached by the House Select Committee on Assassinations in 1979 that there had, in fact, been a conspiracy to kill Kennedy caused barely a flutter in the pop heart and mind. The House Committee, however, is no Oliver Stone. A Gallup poll commissioned by Stone revealed that 70 percent of people questioned had "a positive interest in seeing an Oliver Stone film on the assassination," a clear leap in numbers over those who had a positive interest in seeing one about Jim Morrison.

Troubling to *Time* and *Washington Post* reporter George Lardner Jr., Stone's script closely follows the 1988 book *On the Trail of the Assassins* by Jim Garrison. In 1967, then New Orleans district attorney Garrison indicted Clay Shaw, "director of the International Trade Mart and fixture of New Orleans high society" (Garrison's description), for conspiracy to murder Kennedy. Lardner flatly states that "Garrison's investigation was a fraud." Clay Shaw was found not guilty after less than an hour of jury deliberation. (Lardner was very much on the scene in those murky days and months that followed the assassination. He was, piquantly enough, the last to see one of the key conspiracy suspects, David Ferrie, alive.)

To digress for a bit: by this time, close to thirty years after the fact, at least half the American people believe the Kennedy assassination was a conspiracy. Many believe that Oswald was a patsy set up by the conspirators, that the conspiracy was covered up or ignored by the Warren Commission, and that the assassination was a virtual coup d'état. Plenty of evidence supports these notions. Oswald's supposed weapon was a mail-order Mannlicher-Carcano rifle with a defective scope. To kill Kennedy he would've had to fire it three times in six seconds with preternatural accuracy. Oswald was a poor shot. The spent cartridges were found in a neat arrangement near the sixth-floor shooter's window, whereas, vide Garrison, "when a rifle is fired the cartridge is flung violently away." Bystanders on and near the famed grassy knoll saw puffs of smoke and heard rifle fire coming from behind them. A fresh bullet nick on the freeway escarpment indicated a direct trajectory between the area of the picket fence at the top of the grassy knoll and the death car.

Somewhere between impact and autopsy, Kennedy's brain disappeared. Or the brain wasn't sectioned for trajectory data at autopsy and could not be subsequently located. The coffin bearing the corpse out of Parkland Hospital was a different coffin than the one it arrived in in Washington. Doctors at Parkland Hospital saw a man whose entire rear skull had been blown off; autopsy photos from Washington show a single, tiny bullet hole in the top rear of a virtually intact head. If Kennedy had been shot from the rear, i.e., from the sixth-floor window of the Texas School Book Depository, he would have slumped forward with his face obliterated. Instead he was knocked backward and sideways. Certain incongruities, such as Governor Connally's back and wrist wounds, were accounted for by the so-called magic bullet theory: a single bullet exiting Kennedy's body struck Connally and passed through his body and was found, later, undeformed, despite impact with numerous bones and organs. This is ballistically impossible. The Warren commissioner responsible for the magic bullet theory was Arlen Specter, the rat-faced Republican inquisitor of the Hill-Thomas hearings. I rest my case.

At this juncture, the underwater narrative of conspiracy becomes one of suppositions and shadows. One scenario has Jack Ruby traveling to New Orleans in mid-1963, ostensibly to hire strippers for his Dallas clubs, secretly meeting with mob bosses Carlos Marcello and Santos Trafficante. Through Chicago mob boss Sam Giancana, three hit men from the Sicilian Mafia in Marseilles are hired to whack Kennedy in Dallas. Meanwhile, dupe Oswald is set up by anti-Castro nut and former high-ranking FBI official Guy Banister, whose Anti-Communist League headquarters were located at 531 Lafayette Street in New Orleans. The same building, with a different entrance at 544 Camp Street, housed Oswald's Fair Play for Cuba headquarters!

Enter David Ferrie, described by Lardner as "a vain, nervous flight school instructor," and by others as a virtually hairless chicken queen whose eyebrows and toupee were held in place with Elmer's Glue-All. After the assassination, "authorities" were tipped that Ferrie "knew Lee Harvey Oswald and might have hypnotized him, that he might have gone to Dallas as a 'getaway pilot' for a presidential assassin," etc. Lardner claims that Ferrie, one of many collateral actors to die mysteriously, was "employed as a private investigator for attorneys of reputed Mafia kingpin Carlos

Marcello ... [and] had been sitting outside a federal courtroom in New Orleans waiting for the verdict in a case against Marcello (not guilty) until several hours after Kennedy was killed." Moreover, "he went to Texas for a weekend trip ... but went to Houston and Galveston, not Dallas." That "(not guilty)" speaks volumes. Marcello, Trafficante, Ruby, Ferrie, Shaw, and Banister float through many scenarios besides Garrison's, sometimes in connection with "maverick elements" of the CIA, veterans of the Bay of Pigs, the army, and an array of malcontents.

To wade through a fraction of the existing conspiracy literature is to feel oneself inexorably sinking into quicksand. We may never know what really happened, any more than we will ever know the true identity of Jack the Ripper. Vital parts of the jigsaw puzzle, like Kennedy's brain, have vanished forever; you can keep shifting the other parts around as long as you please, but there will always be gaping holes in the big picture.

For this very reason, the Kennedy assassination lends itself to fictional treatment, see William Richert's classic movie *Winter Kills*, based on the Richard Condon novel, and Don DeLillo's brilliant novel *Libra*. The submerged, partly unknowable quality of the assassination narrative has always struck a welcome chord in lovers of suspense. In actual fact, most people don't really care who shot Kennedy; as the one element everyone agrees on, Kennedy is the least interesting figure in the story. The atmospherics give the thing its malignant tone: the feeling that something sinister was taking its course under the American veneer of prosperity and two-car garages, something that ultimately brought disillusionment and cynicism into a world that had seemed shadowless and full of possibilities. After all, look what happened afterward: expansion of the Vietnam War, race riots, more assassinations, hippies, LSD, Kent State, Woodstock, Altamont, the Black Panthers, and then all that unpleasant stuff in the '70s followed by ten years of Reagan-Bush Incorporated.

The coup d'état angle, the suggestion of powerful, implacable enemies of democracy masquerading as businessmen, flight-school instructors, pedestrian gangsters, and nightclub proprietors, has plenty of allure. Throw in the embittered Cuban exile community and the lunatic fringe of the VFW and it's hard to imagine who wouldn't like the story. As with Jack the Ripper, there isn't enough hard evidence to make any particular version of the story stick; one's free to believe whichever variant provides the satisfying twists and turns of good fiction.

In the immediate wake of the assassination, of course, the deranged-loser-acting-alone scenario also held great charm. Oswald: a tiny, insignificant figure who failed despite the myriad opportunities offered by a flourishing America. Kennedy: the pinnacle of other-directed success and the most important person in the world. There seemed at first to be a tragic and very legible lesson in this disparity, an illustration of absolute good and absolute evil, and Oswald's murder, following twenty-three hours of mysteriously unrecorded interrogation by the Dallas police, drew down the silence of Iago on the meaning of the bloody deed.

Since that faraway era of violated innocence, the conspiracy industry has furnished sufficient motive to make Kennedy's murder seem practically belated. Judging only by Stone's pronouncements about JFK, and his demonstrated compulsion to recast the entire 1960s in the image of his own dippy, Iron John notions of truth, justice, and the American way, Stone intends to show exactly why JFK was bumped off. This information is so explosive, so menacing to the established order, that the minions of darkness have already mobilized against him. In case Oliver Stone gets assassinated and all the prints of *JFK* are destroyed before the truth can reach the American people, I feel obligated to reveal a secret that has flummoxed historians and all concerned Americans ever since the tragic afternoon in 1963 when those three, four, five or six shots rang out in Dealey Plaza: Kennedy wanted to pull troops out of Vietnam, end the Cold War, and normalize relations with Cuba. Pass it on.

Those of you who have not already taken to the streets upon hearing this news may wish to ponder the evolution of motive in relation to the JFK hit. In the deranged-loser-acting-alone schema, Communist Oswald, who had once defected to the Soviet Union, was trained in Moscow to kill the president, in which case he wasn't really acting alone; but if he was acting alone, it probably had something to do with his love of Castro and Cuba, our Communist foes, because he did have that Fair Play for Cuba thing going in New Orleans and even got into a scuffle while handing out leaflets. (In the conspiracy scenario, this scuffle becomes a piece of theater intended to make Oswald's presence in New Orleans stick in certain memories.) He'd also tried to assassinate General Edwin A. Walker, a John Bircher, plainly demonstrating his left-wing sympathies.

The idea of a commie-inspired hit by a lone nut, though ideologically soothing at the time, was also rather frightening. Visions of nuclear war were never far from the public mind in those days, especially after the Cuban Missile Crisis, and what if the government found Castro or Moscow at the bottom of the assassination, what then? Soon enough, however, our government was able to brush away those suspicions and paint Oswald as a disgruntled crackpot. Given the obvious ineptitude of the Warren Commission, it seems fair to say that the commission's purpose was not to discover anything really scary, but to "prove" Oswald acted alone.

As the Kennedy killing receded in time, and America generally proceeded to fall apart, the conspiracy models gained plausibility. There was the Mob angle: as attorney general, Bobby Kennedy had been out to break up organized crime, and JFK had done nothing to stop him. Furthermore, the Mafia pined for its lost casino empire in Havana, which it had hoped to win back when assorted bits of Miami-based flotsam of the Scarface variety washed up in the Bay of Pigs, but Kennedy failed to provide air support and the coup failed. Jimmy Hoffa wanted Kennedy dead. Carlos Marcello wanted Kennedy dead. The Five Families who control all the tiles of that gorgeous mosaic, New York City, wanted Kennedy dead in a big way. To read some of the literature on this subject (i.e., *Contract on America: The Mafia Murder of President John F. Kennedy*) is to become convinced that a hefty percentage of the populations of New Orleans, Miami, and Dallas, as well as a daunting number of federal employees, wanted Kennedy so dead that a list of possible assassins could easily fill all twenty-six volumes of the Warren Commission Report.

For a long while, these sounded like sufficient reasons for JFK's murder by the Mob and/or the Cuban exile community. More recently, the apparent wish of the Kennedy brothers to force J. Edgar Hoover's retirement has added another motive, one that ropes in the FBI, Lyndon Johnson, and Hoover spouse-equivalent Clyde Tolson. Even more recently, the theme of Kennedy-with-drawing-from-Vietnam, a notion rather flimsily supported by a peace-oriented speech Kennedy gave in June 1963, has been cranked up by assassination theorists who claim that the end of the Vietnam involvement would have jeopardized the CIA-Mafia heroin network in Southeast Asia.

What emerges in these latest revisions, strangely enough, is a fantasy rewrite of the Kennedy administration's agenda. Oliver Stone's public statements about JFK reflect a strong wish to reenchant Camelot and its clanking Cold Warrior ghosts with their long-faded myths of nobility and good intentions. In the Stone paradigm, historical cause-and-effect is direct and obvious; if the policies of the Kennedy administration, coldly examined, seem continuous with what happened before and after, i.e., imperialistic, conservative, given to military adventurism, then Kennedy's death must be accounted for by an impending reversal of those policies. Thus, neatly, a single cause, Kennedy's assassination, accounts for all the icky things that followed.

Stone may be very mistaken about this: read Taylor Branch's *Parting the Waters* for a dispiriting picture of a Kennedy whose relationship to the civil rights movement was both cynical and expedient. Read Stanley Karnow's *Vietnam* for scholarly evidence that the Vietnam buildup was proceeding at the time of Kennedy's death, unimpeded by anything except an eye for public opinion. Skim the many volumes of case abstracts issued by the Subversive Activities Control Board covering the era of Bobby Kennedy's attorney generalship, replete with federal suits against the Civil Rights Congress, the Labor Youth League, the Communist Party, et al.

It's hard to conclude that Kennedy was philosophically much different from Nixon. But he was different in a way that Hollywood is uniquely able to convey: he had the charisma of a movie star. Though the right wing still doesn't get it, the fact that JFK was boning hundreds of women in the White House merely adds to his protean legend as chief executive. We have been ruled by gray, dropsical, humorless men with mob ties and the so-called intelligence community ever since, excepting always our strange interlude with the humble peanut farmer from Georgia. (Carter is the only living ex-president who devotes his time to public service rather than the collection of payoffs.) Stone is quite correct when he claims that America changed after JFK's killing. The style of government has become ever more imperial, secretive, and punitive; the presidency is now a vortex of negative glamour. The substance of government has always been kept out of public view, in secret memoranda and drunken jigs around the campfire at Bohemian Grove.

Stone may also be right when he says that some elements of the media have been working overtime to discredit his movie. Lardner, intelligence and CIA reporter for the *Washington Post*, has perpetrated several jeremiads against Stone, Garrison, and the conspiracy model, taking the droll position that all questions were impressively settled by the Warren Commission. Lardner threatened a libel suit over Stone's description of him as a "CIA agent journalist." "The only subject I have covered for years is sin and corruption," writes Lardner. Though no spook, Lardner does seem imprudent when he brags about being the last person to see David Ferrie alive, at four in the morning, as if that automatically refuted the idea that Ferrie was bumped off. Ferrie "died of natural causes," Lardner writes. And left two suicide notes. Which seems to rule out homicide. Sort of.

It may also be true that Stone's treatment of the Vietnam War, Wall Street, and the Doors has made many people wary of his broad-brush technique, and his melodramatic penchant for personifying Good and Evil in absolute terms. And in a more general sense, some just naturally resent having a history they can remember tailored into a two- or three-hour entertainment that may, things being what they are, come to represent "historical memory" for still others whose memories begin after the events being pictured. This resentment takes on a certain edge when the entertainment in question costs $20 million to $40 million to produce, and anywhere between $5 million and $20 million to advertise; its claims and representations can't be meaningfully contested by a review or a letter to the editor. Young people do not read books, and so whichever interpretation of the long-ago recent past reaches the screen first tends to be definitive. Stone himself is sensitive to this rule of market research; allegedly he muscled a competing JFK-kill flick, based on DeLillo's *Libra*, into turnaround through his clout at CAA.

The representation of "living history" can never satisfy the people who lived through it, either at the center or on the periphery. Every human memory is an incessant editor uniquely adapted to the primordial wishes of its owner. Visual evidence and visual fiction can both play havoc with what we think we have stored in our neocortex. Many years after the Kennedy assassination, a poll revealed that an overwhelming number of Americans—at least as many as believe the Dallas events were part of a conspiracy—believed they had seen the assassination live on television, though the Zapruder film was in a vault at Time-Life until five years later.

Like so much of modern life unanticipated by the Constitution, the saturation booking of two thousand theaters for a single director's version of Gandhi or Jesus Christ or the shooting of JFK is something we just have to live with, along with the easy purchase of Uzis and AK-47s. It's part of the touching megalomania of film directors to imagine that people should only quibble with this state of things after the finished product is on display for $7.50 a pop. At least some of the negative feelings aimed at films and filmmakers taking on large, still-resonating chunks of recent history have to do with the industrial scale of the product itself, which renders ex post facto analysis and criticisms practically moot. On the other hand, the people most upset about Stone's *JFK* have an unseemly investment in the lone-gun explanation of every American assassination—as someone once wrote of the fall of the Austro-Hungarian Empire, "it just sort of happened."

If it does nothing else, Stone's film will at least teach a fresh generation of video renters that nothing bad just sort of happens in America.

(1991)

WEINER'S DONG, AND OTHER PRODUCTS OF THE PERFECTED CIVILIZATION

Several miles outside central Sofia, in an industrial park in the Izgrev District, the Museum of Socialist Art occupies a blocky modern low-rise that could pass for a progressive high school in any American suburb, garnished on one side by a garden where much of the local sculptural residue of bygone Communist regimes—the Stalinist reign of Georgi Dimitrov from 1946 to 1949; the less stifling, more prosperous era of Todor Zhivkov, first party secretary from 1954 to 1989—has migrated from more imperious altitudes in the hub of the Bulgarian capital.

Marooned in this far-off scruff of greenery, the old order's monuments to its ideals and protagonists retain the patina of immutable, hortatory literal-mindedness characteristic of the Soviet period's official art and literature. Now, though, they appear less frighteningly exalting of a pushy idea than like fragments of a nightmare drained of nocturnal menace, planted in glassy sunlight like an assortment of lawn elves mixed in with massive fantasy figures who, so we're told, once upon a time were real and walked the earth.

Like the indoor exhibit of socialist realist posters celebrating factory openings and heroically met agricultural quotas, the sculpture garden features depictions of many nameless humans incarnating ideological rectitude and civic virtue—*The Award Winning Builder, Head of a Worker, Machine Operator, Women from the Farm, Participants in the Uprising*, etc.—grouped near, or around, charismatic, historically legible individuals. The relatively liberal Zhivkov is somewhat mingily represented, as is the first Communist prime minister, Vassil Kolarov, whereas the hard-liner Dimitrov is amply depicted in granite, bronze, and marble likenesses, of various sizes. There are busts and statues of Hristo Karpachev, Poet of the Revolution; Dr. Mara Maleeva-Zhivkova, Zhivkov's wife ("she loved the people"); and Tsvaytko Radoynov, a colonel in the NKVD who worked in the Bulgarian Communist underground during the Second World War, was captured and executed by firing squad, and posthumously promoted to general.

No Bulgarian, however, appears anywhere as often—in the museum or garden—as Stalin. Busts and full figures of the Red Tsar far outnumber the many of Lenin, who, despite an unusually ugly, gigantic rendering in stone (many of these statues, and almost all the posters, are actually gorgeous, contrary to reputation) looming over a whole quadrant of garden in a stance resembling that of a lunging grizzly bear, unavoidably evokes John the Baptist vis-à-vis his ubiquitous successor.

It occurs to me that I have never seen a sculpture of Adolf Hitler dating from the Third Reich. The only plastic representations I can think of at all, off-hand, are the Hitler dolls and marionettes in Syberberg's film *Hitler: A Film from Germany* and Maurizio Cattelan's *Praying Hitler*, which were made decades after the Primate of Linz ate the gun in his bunker. Portraits of Hitler were everywhere in the Reich, of course, from classroom walls to postage stamps. Once, he was even pictured as a Teutonic knight in armor, mounted on a horse. Perhaps it was forbidden to make a three-dimensional effigy of Hitler, as it must be to fashion one less than thirty feet tall of Kim Jong-Il in North Korea. On top of everything else, Hitler was neurotically superstitious, and probably feared the voodoo power of the replica. Effigies can be pricked with pins, cursed, sexually assaulted, ripped to pieces, incinerated, or decapitated in the privacy of a citizen's home, where until recently the fact that there is no privacy in a citizen's home eluded collective awareness, which in turn inhibited privacy invaders from acting too directly or drastically on the objects of their surveillance for fear of giving the game away. In Stalin's case, an endless profusion of sculpted Stalins planted from Moscow to Vladivostock served the cosmetic function of smoothing out his smallpox craters and filling out his withered arm.

Aside from an old woman inside the museum who resembles a wary crow pecking the ground cover in a graveyard, her embittered, devout expression leading me to suppose that she is, in every sense, *an old Communist*, everybody I meet here (the man in the sentry box at the front of the drive, the woman collecting the entrance fee, the lady who runs the video exhibits and the souvenir concession) signals, in one way or other, that they perceive this museum's horde "ironically." The Communist period, for them, survives here as an increasingly weightless novelty of recollection, yet one worth preserving, as it is, after all, history.

It's the intelligent thing, to have museums like this. I'm convinced almost any revolution, uprising, or military victory that begins by toppling the absurd statues and glorifying kitsch commemorating the once-adored is likely to end with the worship of someone or something even worse, or to devolve into chaos and savagery—as in Cambodia with the Khmer Rouge, Iraq after Saddam Hussein, Afghanistan after the Taliban demolished the Bamiyan Buddhas, and China when the emperor burned all existing books and built the Great Wall, the most overreaching monument to human stupidity ever erected. Tomorrow's monsters always insist on changing everything that reminds people of the day before. The French have it right; there is still a Stalingrad Métro station in Paris, and myriad other place names belonging to people who landed on the wrong side of history, and to events that embarrassed the state, like the plaque in front of Brasserie Lipp where Mehdi Ben Barka was kidnapped.

•

I leave Sofia on Deathtrip National Airlines and land an hour later in Bucharest, where I draw cash from an airport ATM and, distracted by someone I decide is a dangerous maniac talking to invisible people in a belligerent voice, forget my card in the machine and get into a taxi.

Within seconds, I glean that the driver is a dubious piece of work, asking "casual" questions he'd ask gullible, anxious, miserably horny tourists with lots of money: Am I here on vacation? Business? What am I going to do in Bucharest? He reveals that the city is full of easily available, clean, and respectable whores. I'm not going to shut this asshole up by telling him I like men, first of all because it's none of his business, and second because he'd just offer me his brother or, god forbid, himself. He's about thirty-five, clearly eats too much, and has a greasy film all over his skin that seems also to coat his grubby clothing. He delivers me to the wrong hotel, despite having entered the address in his GPS and consulting some crony on his cell phone, and insists it's the right hotel that just has a different name over the entrance. This after inquiring whether I would be interested in an erotic massage and being told that I don't need a pimp. He becomes enraged at my use of the word "pimp," though that is unmistakably what he is. "It's legal in Romania," he grumbles. "Not a pimp." OK, a ponce, a procurer, a pander, a whore-monger, a man who lives off the earnings of women: take your pick. I know he's deliberately driven to the wrong address, but fail to deduce that he does so to avoid the right hotel's security camera, as he plans to rip me off for a startling amount of Romanian New Leus, seeing that I have them confused with Bulgarian Levs and am so impatient to get away from him that I fail to consult the currency converter on my phone. He has the aura of a human oil slick. I pay him quickly and roll my luggage into the lobby of what I know is not my hotel. Luckily, the staff is nice; they fetch another cab.

When the second driver pulls up to the correct hotel, miles away, and shows me the fare on his meter, I realize the oil slick took me for a truly audacious ride, and, while paying the new fare, discover an empty flap in my wallet where the bank card is normally tucked. A disaster scenario briefly unfolds in my head. I only know three people in Bucharest well enough to have their current phone numbers, and seriously doubt that any of them has the price of however many hotel nights I will need to fix this sudden pennilessness. But I've trained myself over the years to process panic-inducing situations like this as welcome material for a novel, in case I ever write another one, so walk into the peculiarly situated but very nice Hotel Vila Arte, and quite calmly explain to the woman at the desk that I have, at the moment, only cash, and only enough cash to cover a single night. After a flash of visible skepticism, she tells me not to worry and to relax in a little parlor off the lobby while they make up my room. It would be very funny indeed to end up a clochard in the gutters of Bucharest after the life I've had, but I'm not going to think about that. I didn't bring American Express, which I'm told will crawl over broken glass at the summit of K2 to replace a lost or stolen card, or any other credit cards on this trip: it becomes too tempting to buy things I couldn't afford when I was younger and certainly don't need now, when the end always seems unavoidably in plain sight.

I've had some dealings with my regular bank over the phone from Havana and know that its "toll-free from outside the US and Canada" line is not a working number, and never has been. I call instead the number you're charged for, am put on hold for twelve minutes, then learn that the bank will send a replacement card by regular air mail but not express overnight delivery. This will take five or six days. Not good enough. By the clock it's too early to call the branch office, where I'm pretty sure I can talk someone I know into sending a new card by next day UPS. I find that I have a Chase debit card in my wallet, for my other checking account, which has,

I think, twenty-five dollars in it. I could call someone in New York and have them deposit money in the Chase account. But I don't have checks for that account, or the number written anywhere, so call the allegedly toll-free number on that card, hoping to easily get the account number. I am told by a man on the other end of the line whom I picture as tall, nondescript, twenty-seven years of age, with medium-length, straw-colored hair, wearing a muted check blazer, a pale blue shirt, and teal corduroy trousers, that I will need to answer a few security questions.

I realize that I picture every male voice I hear when I call places like a bank as issuing from exactly the same blandly affable person, wearing exactly the same imaginary clothing. And that I somehow assume this person was a fan of the Jerry Seinfeld show and follows baseball without fanaticism, rents instead of owns, drives a Prius, dates a woman finishing a Master's in marketing for the twenty-first century at an inferior college, and has occasional problems sustaining an erection with her, or comes prematurely. Once a month or so, he hooks up with a pre-op transgender prostitute in the skanky part of whatever city he lives in. I realize too that I have not used my Chase account in over a year and have undoubtedly forgotten how I answered any security questions, and say so.

"Oh, no, these aren't answers you've given us," he tells me. "They're questions based on publicly accessible information about you that we have at the bank."

"Oh."

"All right, first question. I'm going to read you five addresses, and want you to tell me if you've ever been associated with any of these addresses. 15 Buckingham Road. 94 Chestnut Avenue. 109 St. Mark's Place. 43 Thalia Massie Drive. Finally, 12 Winterville Road. Have you ever been associated with any of these?"

"Not that I know of. Why exactly is this a security question? St. Mark's Place is close to where I live in New York, but—well, wait. I just remembered. I lived in a little apartment on St. Mark's Place for three months in 1978."

"That's correct!"

"What do you mean, 'that's correct'—why the fuck do you know where I lived for three months, thirty-five years ago? I didn't even have an account at Chase Bank in 1978. I didn't have any bank account in 1978. It wasn't even called the Chase Bank in 1978; it was the Chemical Bank, Chase Bank was Chase Manhattan. They merged. Which, come to think of it, I only opened an account at Chemical Bank in 1980, when I was living somewhere else."

"Well, that's the information I have here."

"But why do you have it? Where did the bank get the information, who did they get it from? Is David Rockefeller listening to this call, by any chance?"

"Forgive me, sir, but that's a little like asking why the sky is blue, at my end of this. I have no idea why the bank has this information . . . public records of some kind or other—"

"No, but wait, I'm not anybody—I don't have a trillion dollars on deposit at Chase Bank, I'm not a drug kingpin, or a spy, I'm just some little person with a checking account at your bank. Why do you have all this kind of detailed, private information about me? You know something, I've been writing a memoir for three years, and really, you should write it for me, you know more about me than I do."

The man in the checked blazer giggled. This reminded me that people who work on Maggie's Farm, so to speak, do not own Maggie's Farm, and find its inner workings just as mysterious and probably as obnoxious as I do.

"Are you ready for the next question?"

To crop this to a forgivable length, the next question cited five corporations, all with acronymic names, and asked if I had ever had dealings with any of them. It seemed safe to say that I hadn't, since I'd never heard of them, and never worked for a corporation, for that matter, though I supposed that somehow, anyone who ever works at all actually works for some corporation, somewhere, that owns or controls the non-corporations they may have worked for at one time or another—and further supposed that I was having dealings that very minute with some surveillance company owned by, say, WXY Corp, or SBRQ Corporation, or one of the others Mr. Pleasant Ordinary was reeling off the names of.

I've forgotten what the final question was about, only that it was equally invasive, structured around a harvest of data mining, and the kind of query that should be illegal, and isn't, like the obnoxious "recommendations" from Amazon.com based on our previous purchases; the very special selection of movies urged on us by Netflix after we've used the site precisely once to watch one episode of *Breaking Bad*; and the digital profiling that occurs automatically whenever we order a pizza, buy a roll of film, check in at the airport, or do anything else that obliges us to identify ourselves. This story does not have a happy ending, simply because it doesn't have any ending, but just continues, as if we each had a personal Stasi officer assigned to monitor our existence. However, the episode itself ended painlessly enough, with someone in New York putting cash in the Chase account, no doubt becoming himself an object of the surveillance connected to me, quite aside but not apart from the already existing surveillance connected to him.

•

> He ain't no sheik, that's no great physique, and Lord knows he ain't got the smarts... —*Chicago*, the musical

We've all heard about it, read about it, and some have even seen it. I refer, of course, to former congressman Anthony Weiner's penis, an object of limited curiosity for those of us amply acquainted with male genitalia, and of even less interest to those familiar with Anthony Weiner's overall physical envelope and personality, yet for a considerable time an organ of rapt, though possibly feigned, fascination to a woman named Sydney Leathers—which seems not only improbable, but an almost unforgiveable lapse in taste on the part of

Ms. Leathers, who will soon essay a sin queen in a whalebone corset for one of the higher-end adult entertainment ventures. Judging from the white-cotton-veiled intimation of Weiner's virile member featured several months ago in the *New York Post*, the artifact in question is what Norman Mailer, describing his own equipment, once characterized as "an average Jewish prick." For the record, I am wholly in favor of anyone wishing to promote his or her genitals of whatever dimensions on Facebook or Instagram to feel free to do so, and don't find mildly quirky sexual impulses like Weiner's, or really any sexual quirks that don't involve involuntary pain, or murder, or cruelty to animals, at all abnormal or reprehensible. But given what Weiner has claimed to be his career ambitions, putting his cock online after getting caught doing it once already indicates not only lamentably poor judgment but sufficient idiocy to exclude him from the kind of public employment that involves decisions about other people's money, the placement and timing of urban construction projects and street repairs, zoning enforcement, noise abatement, police deployment, and a host of other responsibilities far too boring for most of us to even contemplate, but necessary in a grossly overpopulated world full of incompatible life forms. Unfortunately, the realm that would otherwise seem the most appropriate venue for Weiner's self-realization, namely Vivid Entertainment, is one where his physical endowments would not be greatly in demand, and his inevitable next mea culpa will probably not create copious opportunities as a television talking head, since anything he has to say is bound to be interrupted by questions about his penis. In Croatia, I caught a half-hour TV interview with Dominique Strauss-Kahn in which an earnest discussion of world economic policy lurched suddenly into a barrage of questions about pimping. This sort of thing is vastly entertaining the first time, and box office poison forever after.

Weiner seems doomed to a season on *Celebrity Apprentice*, followed by his complete disappearance from public life, and some bucolic aftermath as an accountant in a small town in western New York. Or, perhaps, he could carve a new future growing hydroponic vegetables for sale at farmers' markets, if he can resist raising cucumbers and zucchini squash. Weiner may be an asshole instead of a creep, but sometimes even an asshole flaunts his inability to control himself once too often.

(2013)

PASOLINI, *MAMMA ROMA*, AND *LA RICOTTA*

Indefatigably productive, ingenious, exasperating, narcissistically didactic, slyly self-promoting, abject, generous, exploitative, devoted to the wretched of the earth with honest fervor and deluded romanticism: Pier Paolo Pasolini can easily exhaust the adjective-prone, as man and artist, his person and his work riddled with contradictions.

He is unique to postwar Italian culture and politics, unique in his degree of loathing for its '50s and '60s economic miracle and its impact on the country's cities, the countryside, and its dialect subcultures, unique in his nervous mingling of intense, alienated Catholicism with Gramscian Communism; in *La Ricotta*, the words of his own poetry, spoken by the film director played by Orson Welles (which had, alas, to be dubbed in Italian by Gregorio Bassani), "I am a force out of the Past. Only in tradition do I find my love . . ." embody the contradictions that made Pasolini the most controversial and certainly the most persecuted Italian artist of his day. For this worshipper of vanishing times and values was the victim of the most entrenched prejudices surviving from the past. Embracing the stereotype of the noble peasant, he was hounded throughout his career by the homophobia and pious ignorance of peasants, and finally got murdered by one.

His entire output as an artist—poems, plays, films, novels, essays, and journalism—adds up to more than the sum of its parts, and it's especially the films that seem hit-or-miss on the vertiginous level of Pasolini's own ambition. Pasolini's cinematic legacy is a jumble of brilliant moments and fizzles, a sprawl in which almost everything is interesting yet much of it reflects the hazards of both lyrical and experimental film.

Mamma Roma, Pasolini's second feature, and in its antic way, the thirty-five minute *La Ricotta*, which immediately followed it, are among Pasolini's most audaciously shaped and satisfying movies. *Mamma Roma* is the story of a prostitute who rises from the subproletariat to the lower middle class, reclaims her son, Ettore, after an absence of many years, and moves him to Rome with her, where she tries to transcend her past while concealing it from him. This project of self-gentrification and of "urbanizing" an illiterate provincial youth is doomed, however, not least by the reappearance of Mamma Roma's old lover and pimp, Carmine—quite literally "a force from the Past"—who twice compels her to moonlight from her hard-won position as a market stall proprietor and return to the streets she walked for thirty years.

From a formal viewpoint *Mamma Roma* is both an extension of the postwar neorealism of Rossellini and De Sica and its repudiation, a film of mostly short, even stuttery scenes broken by longer, surreal passages where Anna Magnani, in the title role, strides along the kind of ill-lit outdoor brothel found in every city, which American pimps and prostitutes refer to as "the track," soliloquizing about fate as various interlocutors momentarily fall into step with her and then fade into the night.

Mamma Roma's attempt to give her son a better life has, thanks to Magnani's grandiloquent acting, the flavor of tragic opera. As one character tells her, "You'd hang on the cross for him, wouldn't you?" But Ettore, whom we first see sitting alone on a bench of a revolving carousel, has no real interest in "bettering himself," despite some initial enthusiasm for a waiter job his mother and two accomplices have blackmailed a restaurant owner into giving him. He prefers the company of other aimless boys and their adventures in petty crime. His resentment of his mother for his long abandonment (it is never clear who raised him) quickly eclipses the novelty of her outsized personality and her copious affection for him; he feels suffocated by her determination to improve his lot, and completely at sea in his new urban environment.

Mamma Roma's own desire to rise has a strangely oscillating quality. The world she aspires to, a belt of dreary housing flats and petit bourgeois businesses on the Roman outskirts, is an up-market version of the ugliness she endured as a prostitute. Her efforts at "respectability" consist of going to Mass, hawking fruit and vegetables from a street wagon, and avoiding her previous profession. She visits a priest for advice, but when he tells her, "You can't make something of nothing," she readily draws on the wiles of the very underworld she has struggled to escape to get what she wants for Ettore.

And this is the crux of *Mamma Roma*. It isn't that Mamma is morally flawed—though Pasolini viewed her attempt to find a place in a rapidly changing society as an expression of moral decay, because of this new society's consumerism and spiritual vacancy—she is socially doomed, and the forces that have made her life a bitter struggle for longer moments of joy than the few she gets to experience (teaching Ettore to tango, clinging to him as the motorcycle she's bought him roars along the roadway) are the same that literally doom her son.

The overt Oedipal aspect of this film is a familiar element in Pasolini's work. Strange to say, we never learn whether Carmine is actually Ettore's father (something assumed by many critics), since Carmine never claims to be, and Mamma Roma, in one of her hallucinatory night-world promenades, says that "her husband" was Ettore's father; but she also says this husband, presumably a young man, was arrested and taken away right after their wedding, leaving her "a virgin at the altar." Moreover, at an earlier point she describes her forced marriage as a teenager to a man over sixty, who has outlived both her parents. (Where is he? She never tells us.) Carmine accuses her of seducing him when he was a simple country boy, and says that she was already forty at the time. One would almost conclude that Ettore has no father and that Mamma Roma is, like the city she's named for, "eternal," the archetype of the mother whose fatherless child is also her lover, if only in her own imagination. (Pasolini, whose sexual tastes ran to street boys like Ettore, loathed his father, who died in 1958, and worshipped his mother, whom he then lived with until the end of his life. He cast her as the Virgin Mary in *The Gospel According to Saint Matthew* [1964].)

Mamma Roma was attacked by both the Right and the Left, for opposite reasons, momentarily censured after its premiere at the 1962 Venice Film Festival when a local cop charged it with obscenity, and it caused a minor riot when a group of neo-fascist students invaded its Roman premiere. In a more subtle sense, even its star and director attacked it, or each other, over the issue of Magnani's performance, which both (mistakenly) found less than wonderful, also for opposite reasons. The stormy reception of the film failed to reap the usual commercial success, and was hardly the first of Pasolini's troubles (his novels and other writings had incited prosecutions and protests before he ever picked up a camera, and his first film, *Accattone*, had raised a formidable hue and cry). The "scandal" of Pasolini's work made him a large public figure, and a large public target.

But none of Pasolini's earlier provocations were quite as incendiary as *La Ricotta*, the director's contribution to the compilation film *Rogopag* (Rossellini, Godard, Pasolini, and Ugo Gregoretti). A profoundly religious film, *La Ricotta* is an explosion of disgust at consumer society and its vulgarity, a scabrous reproach to the Catholic Church for its abandonment of the poorest members of that society, a film about a film about the Crucifixion that shows Christianity's central symbolic event being staged within a circus of depravity. Its Christ is a starving film extra who gives his own box lunch to his hungry family, loses a meal he's stolen to a visiting movie star's lap dog, and, after managing to stuff himself with ricotta cheese, dies from indigestion on the cross.

As Enzo Siciliano puts it in his biography of Pasolini, "this movie set is nothing but the temple overrun by the moneychangers." *La Ricotta* uses all the technical and moral ironies of filmmaking, the disjunction between "reality" and artifice, to paint a world of implacable cruelty ruled by money and cynically contrived spectacle.

Soon after its release in 1963, *La Ricotta* was seized "for insulting the religion of the state." Pasolini was put on trial, found guilty, and sentenced to prison for four months, a conviction voided by an appeals court the following year.

While Pasolini was far too prominent and prolific a figure in Italian culture to be silenced by lawsuits and scandals, the pattern of harassment and denunciation that bedeviled his career from the beginning intensified after the successive polemical and legal brawling over *Mamma Roma* and *La Ricotta*. International fame made him a potent gadfly in Italian politics and arts. His films and writings were considered a real threat to the substantial remnants of fascism in modern Italy. His murder in 1975, shortly after completing his most scandalous and blatantly antifascist film, *Salò*, remains fogged by rumors of conspiracy, though many have said Pasolini found a martyrdom he was looking for, in the shabby streets of the abandoned poor he celebrated and mourned.

(2004)

THE SADEAN CINEMA

Up or down, for or against—Pasolini's *Salò* makes it clear at the outset that no such judgment can attach itself to the spectacle the filmmaker distills from Sade's *The 120 Days of Sodom*. The film gives the book a different locale, in the last republic of Mussolini, an unnamed villa replacing the Chateau of Silling as the site of orgies, tortures, mayhem.

The essays by Simone de Beauvoir, Pierre Klossowski, Maurice Blanchot, Philippe Sollers, and Roland Barthes cited in the film's "bibliography"—an unprecedented title card, underscoring the thesis quality of Pasolini's film—are justly famous, difficult, even irritating in their complexity; we may or may not be familiar with them, but Pasolini assumes a far greater familiarity than most filmgoers would venture, an intense involvement that assumes an interest in the questions they raise.

Yet such an involvement would require a special temperament, much like Pasolini's own. We recall that the filmmaker's first poems were written in Friulian dialect, that he was preoccupied with linguistic questions throughout his many years of productivity in many media (newspaper columns, journals, novels, film, poetry), that *Salò* was preceded by numerous efforts to depict what Barthes calls the rhapsodic epic.

And there, to be honest, this viewer confronts his own nervous sense of the texts, the body of work they address or speculate about, almost the wish that Pasolini had simply smeared his canvas with his own "manias," as many assumed that he had when, several months after this film was completed, he was murdered, quite grotesquely, on the beach in Ostia.

It's a peculiar demand for a film to make, even in the form of "suggested reading," and *Salò* demands a lot from any audience without a bibliography. It drags us through an ordeal that many find unendurable, in certain ways a harsher ordeal than that of reading Sade himself.

If the exegetes of Sade agree on one thing, it's the "ordeal" quality of Sade's writings. Whether we agree or not with Sollers that "we have not yet decided to read Sade," and, moreover, that it's because "the reading we should be able to give Sade does not exist within this society and this culture," that Sade "represents a radical denunciation of the kind of reading we still perform and project indiscriminately"—this is perhaps not the point that most occupies our attention.

What *Salò* shows, and what it never shows, aren't exactly the same thing as what's present in the Sadean dramaturgy, and what's absent from it. In Sade's writings, the sexual acts Pasolini's film shows in a peculiarly unexplicit way are "shown" by the writing— the text describes for us the collision of organs and orifices that *Salò*, except for the tortures unto death at the end, depicts by way of "suggestion," though if we were to say what happens in a scene, the language might be closely similar.

Like Sade, for whom the act of writing is no ordinary act but a defiance of circumstance, the literal text is already a substitution. Like Sade, *Salò* is a conjuring act, but a different one, the record of an artificial spectacle, staged with chocolate excrement and artificial sexual organs, a "special effects" cinema in which nothing is what it appears to be.

In the spirit that Sade, quoted by Beauvoir, has "imagined everything conceivable in this sort of thing," but has "certainly not done, and certainly never will" do everything he's imagined, Pasolini presents us with an *idea* of the thing he pictures, a re-presentation, a faux-everything game performed in mirrors and obscuring long shot (the libertine pile-up on Sergio's "wedding night") or horrific, "impossible" close-up (the chocolate mess on everyone's face at the Banquet of Excrement), with studio bullet holes (the riddled corpse of the single defiant militiaman), or, at the finale, reverse-telescoped, yet obviously fake, scalpings, burnings, and hangings in the villa's inner courtyard—the enactment of horror takes the place of real horror.

Our understanding that this spectacle has been faked is presumably the only reason we can watch it; if it purported to be "true," or so we might assume, the film would have deserved the prosecutions and bannings it encountered when it was released into the world, in very limited circumstances, and Pasolini might have deserved the charges of obscenity, pornography, and what have you that arose from it.

Instead, and this is one function of the bibliography, we're asked to look at the conceptual scheme behind the acts we're obliged to witness. From the outset, when the four libertines agree on the strict rules to be followed by everyone at the Chateau of Silling—in *Salò*, the nameless villa, but like the Chateau, a place where the victims have been subtracted from the world, removed from the context of their lives, where nobody knows they still exist and therefore they are, as far as anyone is concerned, already dead—we're in the realm of the metaspectacle, as Barthes virtually diagrams it in *Sade/Fourier/Loyola*, a clockwork mechanism in which each element has some recognizable function, a perpetual motion machine.

As Pierre Klossowski illustrates in *Sade, My Neighbor*, the Sadean text is an act of inverted religiosity. The atheism espoused by the libertines is in some sense flawed by their own extreme rationality, since Sade's protagonists are caught in the paradox of defying something they declare doesn't exist.

Pasolini's own ambivalent relation to Christianity necessarily comes to mind. It's impossible to watch *Salò* without the troubled awareness that the same director who made it filmed *The Gospel*

According to St. Matthew, and this awareness makes us doubly attentive to the film's transgressive movements, from mania to murder. Instead of following the morality that demands that we treat our neighbor as we want to be treated, Sade, as noted by Beauvoir, Klossowski, and Blanchot, resists this Christian form of moralism and replaces it with Nature, or an idea of Nature in which human nature, specifically, says, "As this is what gives me pleasure, it's what I have to do"—Nature replaces God, and "man" becomes, like any animal, ruled by instinct.

Blanchot formulates it this way: "Given that all beings are equal in the eyes of Nature, this fact allows me the right not to sacrifice myself to preserve others, whose ruin is indispensable to my happiness."

Yet this has the effect of "equalizing" desire among human beings, awarding every impulse the same value. As Blanchot notes, Sade approaches this idea from a split perspective. The idea in itself would make the libertines empty objects, and their victims the recipients of an undifferentiated rage. (As in Sade, in *Salò* the harshest punishment is reserved for those who cry out to God for deliverance; their names are entered in the book of death; their sobbing and lamentation do nothing but excite the fury of their captors, make them excited, spur them on to greater excess. But to be moved to this rage by the mention of something absent validates the reality of the absent thing, in a sense ratifies the idea of a deity.)

So Sade must have it two ways. He first demonstrates that power is everything, that life is ruled by force. The libertines embody a social framework that imprisons everyone in its mechanism: capital, religion, jurisprudence. They operate in an economy of waste matter recycled through their own bodies as well as those of their accomplices and victims.

Again, Sollers tells us "the reading we should be able to give Sade does not exist within this society and this culture," and that the reading Sade requires can't exist until we abandon thought as the cause of language, because Sade's project "is concerned ... with language without cause, with the writing of the signifier as pure effect."

The films Pasolini made immediately before *Salò* prepare us to "read" this film as a sequence of episodes without cause, scenes as fragments of an unfilmable, seemingly endless duration. *The Decameron*, *The Arabian Nights*, and *The Canterbury Tales* are all picaresque novels in which stories are nestled within stories, like Russian dolls. As Barthes characterizes the rhapsodic novel, these epic narratives don't "advance," but achieve a circularity by wearing out the reader's attention.

The 120 Days of Sodom is similarly interminable, a narrative container that itself never develops or moves forward, that bores us (in the sense of a dentist's drill)—exhausting, endlessly repetitive, monotonous.

Salò, perhaps because its moralism is betrayed by its own bibliography—we're shown these things in order to "learn" from them, to become enlightened; Pasolini cannot avoid moralism—does "move forward," in the direction of death, from the opening scenes of young people being harvested from a ruined countryside to serves as victims and enforcers of the libertines' pleasures.

It's not all that surprising that a film about the seduction and pleasure of fascism, which *Salò* partly is, should produce a fascinated disgust, which *Salò* does. I think this is where Pasolini and Sade, to an extent, part company, although the viewer of *Salò* and the reader of Sade are similarly made to enjoy the recounting of horrific things. When we watch *Salò* or read Sade, we're forced into complicity, like the paramilitary youths, themselves prisoners, who enforce obedience, and we become both victims and victimizers.

(2000)

MURDERING THE DEAD

She came to Los Angeles during World War II from nowhere special, a pretty girl with big hair and bad teeth who liked to go to bars and nightclubs. She believed in love and romance and lived on hot dogs and Coca-Cola, lavished hours on her makeup in dollar-a-night furnished rooms. A drifter, something of a cipher, she was a person people remembered vaguely but could never quite pull into focus. A good-time gal who didn't really seem to have a good time, demanded a little too much sympathy and hardly ever returned a favor. She sometimes spoke of a husband killed in the war, a baby who died, but these were figments of a waking dream that carried her through sleepless nights. If someone hadn't cut her in half, the world would know precious little about Elizabeth Short.

She had been nicknamed the Black Dahlia, a name so movie-perfect for the era of noir that her murder became symbolic of everything weird and inexplicable festering under the city's gleaming surfaces. Steve Hodel's best-seller, *Black Dahlia Avenger*, is the latest in a long procession of novels and nonfiction books to treat the Dahlia case as Los Angeles's emblematic homicide, a killing affixed to the city the way Jack the Ripper is to Victorian London and the Strangler is to Boston. The Dahlia killing engraved itself into urban mythology; it seemed to say something stark and ugly about the emptiness of glamour and the wages of sin. Short's dead body became a movie star, a cautionary tale and a magnet for a large assortment of patholo-gies, many of them literary.

The symbolic message of Short's corpse as the killer arranged it at Thirty-Ninth Street and Norton Avenue in Leimert Park in early 1947 could not in itself be less mysterious or more readily aligned with notions of Hollywood as a sausage factory for the young and beautiful. Like the Manson killings, the Hillside Strangler slayings and the Night Stalker spree, the Black Dahlia murder was carried out with its effect on the public very much in mind. The perps in all these cases had something to tell the world, posing the bodies, writing things in blood, sending a garbled telegram about the incur-able in human nature.

The classic account is John Gilmore's *Severed*, which achieves the almost impossible feat of turning the very blankness of Elizabeth Short's brief life into a thing of riveting oddity. According to Gilmore, Short had a rare vagi-nal deformity that made the image of a sexually easy creature of the night nothing more than an image; if we accept this premise, the Dahlia story be-comes the dark tale of a hapless mimic whose grasp of adult relations extended only to what they looked like in the movies. There's no reason not to credit Gilmore's fastidious account, in which one drifter kills another, then dies in a flea-pit hotel fire: this cruddy, depressing solution to the mystery is utterly consistent with the pathos of the world the Black Dahlia traveled through on her way to the big nowhere.

For a certain mentality, however, prosaic justice demands that an unusually vicious, legendary murder turn out to have been committed by a truly unlikely, preferably famous individual or, failing that, someone connected to famous people. Hodel, a former homicide detective for the Los Angeles Police Department, manages to implicate several famous personalities in Short's murder. *Black Dahlia Avenger* has the added *frisson* of its author's bizarre discovery, after two entire years of research, that Short's killer was—gasp!—his own father.

Hodel is not the only person in recent years to discover exactly this skele-ton in the family closet. In 1995, a book called *Daddy Was the Black Dahlia Killer* revealed that its co-author, Janice Knowlton, a former lounge singer, had discovered through recovered memory that her father murdered Short after Short left an aborted fetus in her father's garage. Horrifically, Knowlton was forced to witness much of the torture and mutilation inflicted on Short and to help him dispose of the remains.

Knowlton's is the kind of book it doesn't do to argue with: its author seems to have channeled a rich vein of snuff pornography while gazing at healing crystals in some quack's office. Hodel, having been a homicide cop, would seem a more rigorously fact-driven investigator. And yet Hodel's father, like Knowlton's, was named George. What Hodel considers proof is strangely tangled with nebulous memories. Could Steve Hodel be an "alternative personality" of Janice Knowlton?

Let's call this personality Steve and see what he has to say. After an obligatory shock-horror opening that whisks us back to Leimert Park on that dreadful morning in 1947, Steve recounts his own bittersweet and strained relations with his father, Dr. George Hodel, up until his death in 1999. There would be no funeral, as per his will, but Steve flies to San Francisco to console Dad's widow, June. She gives him a small photo album that belonged to his father, unwittingly opening Pandora's Box.

Among the pictures Dad—at one time a professional photographer, among many other things, and an intimate of Man Ray—has kept through-out the years are two of a woman with her eyes closed. Something tries to bubble up from memory. The face is familiar yet unknown. At last it hits him: it's the face of Elizabeth Short.

There are also pictures of Hodel Jr.'s first wife, Kayo, whom we now learn had been, unknown to Steve, one of Dad's mistresses before Steve married her. We later find out that she cheated on Steve and lied about her age (that is to say, lied about her age extremely). Steve now realizes that the love between Kayo and his father was a deep and tumultuous one, rather than a silly fling, and concludes that Kayo married him to wreak revenge on Dad.

To get to Short, Steve seems to have taken a cherished bromide of American prosecutors a bit too much to heart—that is, that circumstantial evidence is often more valuable than eyewitness testimony.

He tells us first about his father's extremely rangy life. Dr. Hodel had been, at various times, a concert pianist, a crime reporter, a radio an-nouncer, an artist, finally a surgeon and psychiatrist. In 1947, he and the family were living in the posh Lloyd Wright's Sowden house at Franklin and Normandie avenues, in Steve's account a brooding Gothic pile full of secret rooms straight out of *Vathek*. Dr. Hodel operated a venereal disease clinic downtown, presumably another accursed lair of dark secrets. Among his friends were Henry Miller and John Huston.

The picture Steve paints of his father unavoidably calls to mind those sinister doctors in novels by Raymond Chandler and Jim Thompson, usually found at a starlet's bedside at three in the morning brandishing a syringe. There were, at the spooky Lloyd Wright house, orgies. There was, among Dr. Hodel and his famous friends, an interest in the Marquis de Sade. One of Steve Hodel's older brothers recalls seeing Dr. Hodel write something on a woman's breast in lipstick at a typical get-together. Shortly after the Dahlia slaying, another unsolved homicide became known as "the Lipstick Murder."

At various moments in the book, after depositing such tidbits, Steve announces that he has "proven" something, perhaps meaning something in the realm of the occult. Dr. Hodel, we are told, admired Man Ray, who did a famous portrait of the Marquis de Sade and was a surrealist. The surrealist group once made photo-booth portraits of themselves with their eyes closed to emphasize the belief that dreams and reality are the same.

In the pictures of Short that Steve found in his father's album, her eyes are also closed. Moreover, the way the dismembered

Dahlia was posed bears a close resemblance, *qua* Steve, to the figure in Man Ray's photograph "Minotaur." The Marquis de Sade left instructions that he did not want any funeral obsequies or memorial, virtually the same stipulation found in Dr. Hodel's last will and testament.

There is more, much more. Dr. Hodel was—or so Steve claims—the "prime suspect" in the Dahlia police file, though which file, discovered in what year, in whose department, and by whom are questions so muddied by Steve's account that any methodical reader would be skeptical. Steve's reve-lations occur to him by way of "thoughtprints": products of free associa-tion. An accomplice of Dr. Hodel's named Frank Sexton is remembered by a witness; photographs and "thoughtprints" summon him as a "swarthy" man. Steve is later made aware of the presence of a swarthy man in some fifteen murders, including that of James Ellroy's mother.

The Dahlia body site is only a few miles from the Sowden house. So are a million other things in Los Angeles, but this kind of pataphysical eureka defines this entire book's methodology. The mere physical proximity of one thing to another suggests a rela-tionship—Dr. Hodel lived in Los Angeles, so did Elizabeth Short; an interest in the Marquis de Sade (an interest shared by Simone de Beauvoir, Pierre Klossowski, Maurice Blanchot, and many other literary figures) becomes solid proof that Man Ray, Huston, and Dr. Hodel were "sadists" and that Dr. Hodel, at least, along with swarthy Frank, had no inhibitions about perpetrating the tortures and mutilations of Sade's novels in real life; a man claiming to be the Dahlia killer who called a reporter spoke in a refined, sibilant voice, Dr. Hodel had once been a radio announcer and also had such a voice; and so on.

Perhaps aware that his portrait of a libertine, murderous coven in his childhood home is only marginally more plausible than Janice Knowlton's acrobatic feats of memory, Steve eventu-ally rolls his sister, Tamar, onto the proscenium. Tamar, once a freewheeling buddy of Michelle Phillips, is now an older and wiser mom of two daughters, named Fauna 1 and Fauna 2.

As a teen, Tamar told police who picked her up as a runaway that her father had molested her. This resulted in an indictment, a trial, a scandal. After being acquitted, Dr. Hodel fled the country, staying away for most of the following forty years, leaving Steve in the clutches of his mother, a drunk. Man Ray went back to Paris around the same time.

Like Steve, Tamar is willing to say anything about anybody as long as they are dead. John Huston, Tamar asseverates, tried to rape her when she was eleven: he was, she says, exactly like his character in *Chinatown*. According to Steve, Dr. Hodel had such powerful goods on the high and mighty because of his VD clinic that Tamar's accusations would never have resulted in formal charges, except for a bureaucratic screwup. Man Ray, he implies, somewhat contradictorily, might also have been snared by the webs of justice had he, also, not been "powerful," but he fled the country just in case. The notion of Man Ray as a person with awesome power over the Los Angeles police and district attorney's office is itself rather ponderous.

What we have here is a wacky parody of a police procedural, with a rich and fascinating subtext of delusion. There is also something plangent and, in an underdog way, tragic about somebody so wounded by a lousy childhood that his father becomes a veritable Minotaur in his adult imagination, a scourge to all women, faceted and diabolical as Fu Manchu. Remember that Oedipus, too, was a kind of detective.

All the same, it isn't nice to drag a lot of famous dead people into your family muck, unless you have witnesses a little more reliable than someone who differentiates her children by numbering them.

It is, finally, and not at all sympathetically, appalling that a homicide detective would sell out his professional integrity to produce this piece of meretricious, revolting twaddle, which amounts to evidence manufacturing, litigation-proof slander, and chicanery on a fabulous scale, and does ab-solutely nothing to answer the question: Who killed Elizabeth Short?

(2008)

HAZARDS OF A SNOWBALL FIGHT

Adapted from the famed samizdat novel of the French Resistance, Jean-Pierre Melville's first feature, *Le Silence de la mer*, despite critical and commercial success, gained its director little glory: overshadowed by the book and its author's celebrity, Melville got credit for supplying a beloved narrative with serviceable illustrations.

Novel and film are both chamber dramas in which speechlessness and claustrophobia act as metaphors for the refusal to accommodate the enemy in any uncoerced situation. Since all but a handful of shots show the characters in a single room, the film's most remarkable achievement is its theatricalization of the character who speaks, while retaining the mood of naturalism. Each evening's ritual, repetitive structure, its shifting nodes of tension held in unvarying abeyance, has curious affinities with Sartre's play *Huis clos*, in which three characters trapped for eternity in the same room all speak, and by doing so make an even more extravagant case than Melville's for the conclusion that "hell is other people."

The power of withholding, the psychic deformities produced by one person's silence and the other's hysterically reactive talkativeness, have their supreme expression in Ingmar Bergman's *Persona*—a horror movie in the deepest sense, the almost unbearably revelatory spawn of Strindberg's two-hander, *The Stronger*.

The deceptively serendipitous proximity of people adrift in a shared private dream world made Jean Cocteau's wildly popular 1930 novel, existentialist avant la lettre, *Les Enfants terribles*, a slyly plausible successor to Melville's debut feature. Compared to the

Dreyeresque camera setups of his first film, *Les Enfants* moves with the restless pace of a Marx Brothers movie, but siblings Paul and Elisabeth, who share a bedroom in a Paris flat, deflecting anomie with a repertoire of incestuously entangling games, nonetheless inhabit a bell jar as airless as the drawing room in *Le Silence de la mer*. The siblings cling to a neurotic interdependence they should, judging from their apparent ages, have long outgrown. But it's tricky to decide how far beyond puberty they really are. The film opens with a schoolyard snowball fight at the Lycée Condorcet—where both Cocteau and Melville, at different times, went to school—in which darting camera movements and intricate cross-cutting catch the rough and tumble of very young boys. Paul, who looks a little mature for a schoolboy, is hit with a rock-spiked snowball thrown by Dargelos, his lycée crush.

Dargelos, called to account and finally expelled, is played by the somewhat diminutive actress Renée Cosima—which extends the impression that the film is about schoolchildren, since Cosima, despite a game panache and swagger, more closely resembles a preadolescent, feminine boy than the muscular embodiment of virility and arrogance Cocteau describes in his novel. (Dargelos crops up in several Cocteau works; in the writer's own film, *The Blood of a Poet*, Dargelos kills a boy with the same type of snowball.)

A brutish hunk Cocteau adored at school bore this surname, and was arguably the psychic prototype, if not the unvarying physical model, for the lovers Cocteau launched, or tried to launch, in artistic careers: Raymond Radiguet, Jean Desbordes, Marcel Khill, Jean Marais, and Edouard Dermit. Dermit, in a further stroke of casting "against" the novel's delineation of types, plays Paul in *Les Enfants*. (Unlike Cocteau's real-life projections of Dargelos, of course, neither Dermit nor any of the others would've dared brutalize him, unless that was pre-established on an evening's bedroom menu.)

After these opening scenes, once Paul has been helped home by his chum Gerard, he endures, or enjoys, the demanding torpor of an invalid, teased and nursed by Elisabeth, who's a few years his senior and has to look after the house and their ailing mom.

Somewhat reversing the terms of the novel, the delicate, unambiguously rejected lover is changed into a well-constructed, sexually interesting, indolent, and self-satisfied young bundle of petulance and unpredictable mood changes, albeit afflicted with chest problems, while the godlike rebel/rough trade Dargelos, even if we mistake the actress for a male, is slightly built, too light on his feet, an impish brat only slightly more formidable than a feather boa. In any case, he vanishes from the film after marching out its main gate in an unbowed gesture of "good riddance."

Another off-kilter detail is Paul's incapacity: he manifests no dramatically alarming evidence of illness. But lying prone in bed, he heightens suggestions of sexual availability. His habitual lassitude, his habitation of an oneiric playpen of a room unbelievably cluttered—it all suggests that Paul's "recovery" may never conclude, because he was already this way before Dargelos's attack. His immobility compounds his passivity, making him more malleable to his sister's capricious inspirations and the physical play that, certain commentators to the contrary, signals incest in unambiguous terms.

The incest issue holds little interest for me. I have always assumed incest and sexual experimentation to be common phenomena among siblings of every class, and find nothing remarkable about it. It may look more sordid in a trailer park than in a Venetian palace, but I think that's mostly because the trailer park itself is more sordid than a Venetian palace. I could also credit reported denials by Cocteau and others that sexual acts transpire between Paul and Elisabeth. Why debate it, since the force of the taboo is nowhere in evidence—as it is, say, in a film like Stephen Poliakoff's 1991 *Close My Eyes*, in which Clive Owen and Saskia

Reeves, playing grown-up siblings, convey a sense of the social and psychic gravity of their transgression.

The Melville-Cocteau collaboration seems neither to have been a grudge match nor a picnic. Whether the director and the writer liked each other (they did) has nothing to do with the movie. Cocteau admired *Le Silence de la mer* and approached Melville about filming his novel. This may have had something to do with Melville's having been in the Resistance, while Cocteau played the social butterfly throughout the Occupation, hobnobbing with the German officer elite, but it might have had more to do with Cocteau's desire to turn his latest flame, Dermit, into a movie star.

On Melville's part, it would seem odd to follow one thanklessly adapted famous novel with the adaptation of another famous novel, but he genuinely liked the story, and film money was desperately scarce at the time. As he probably anticipated, critics endlessly parsed the finished film to decide what belonged to Cocteau and what came from Melville.

Melville later said he had been "flattered" to be chosen by Cocteau, adding that he "quickly got sucked into it." Cocteau wanted far more control than Melville would give him. When the author tried to change his own script, Melville told him that if Cocteau planned to write a new *Les Enfants*, Melville wasn't interested in filming it. Melville gave way on two points he regretted: the casting of Dermit as Paul, and the "updating" of the action from 1929 to 1950. When Cocteau "inadvertently" called "cut" in the middle of a scene, Melville had him thrown off the set.

In *Melville on Melville*, the director acerbically speculates that Cocteau hoped Melville would die during the shooting so Cocteau could simply take over the film.

The novel *Les Enfants terribles*, written during opium withdrawal, instantly electrified a generation of French youth. Young people Paul's age—whatever that was, exactly—found in its ungovernable, impulsive characters reflections of their own inner worlds, and their deep-rooted alienation from the spirit of the age, an alienation most viscerally expressed a few years later in Sartre's novel *La Nausée* (1938).

Cocteau's was a sensational book, not merely "daring," but one that tapped the antagonism between French institutions—school, family, police, military—and the generation not quite adult, but already more clear-headed about what they wanted, and especially what they didn't want, than their parents had ever been. In book and film, we're presented with the superannuated, spiritually mildewed figures of the school prefect, the family doctor, the family lawyer, the spectral French professional class unchanged since the time of Balzac, that did things a certain way because things had always been done that way. *Les Enfants* deals with these figures in a manner suggesting that what all such people actually do is keep the wheels of social boredom in stabilizing slow motion and the joy of living in a state of rot.

The core characters—Paul, Elisabeth, Gerard, and the clothing model Agathe whom Elisabeth invites to live with them, after Elisabeth takes a job in a fashion house—become a tribe of indoor campers, all clustered in the magic bedroom, a commune with all the thinly repressed power struggles and inegalitarian subtexts of hippy communes of the 1960s.

Paul's and Elisabeth's magnetic field of pranks, games, and playful sadisms takes precedence over everything, including the possibility that one or the other sibling might form an attachment to someone else. A band of nomads who never go anywhere, build tents from blankets and collect dysfunctional, arresting objects for their "treasure," a chest of drawers reminiscent of the Surrealists' discoveries in flea markets.

Gerard and Agathe often look like extras hired to witness the siblings' performances, though Gerard secretly loves Elisabeth and Agathe falls in love with Paul. Agathe's strong resemblance to Dargelos eventually prompts Paul to fall in love with her, too.

Elisabeth, whose imperiousness alternates with schmaltzy tenderness for her brother, sisterly coziness with Agathe, and patronizing kindness to Gerard, essentially runs everybody's life. Of course this story is patently unreal, Melville's surprisingly sure-handed appropriation of the dream realm Cocteau's work specialized in. To keep its unreality within limits, Melville vetoed most of Cocteau's "suggestions," and brought an edgier kind of unreality into play. He vetoed Cocteau's desire to use a jazz motif, choosing the baroque instead, Bach and Vivaldi, which is woven into the film to optimal effect, heightening the disorienting interior spaces and the characters' movements inside them.

This choreography of sound and image owes its quality of unfolding surprises to cinematographer Henri Decaë's idiosyncratic framing, switches from high to low angles, the unusually mobile camerawork that anticipates the handheld camera of the New Wave. Aside from directing films of his own, Decaë shot two of Melville's three "Resistance" films, *Le Silence de la mer* and *Léon Morin, prêtre*, as well as the director's *Bob le flambeur*, *L'Aîné des Ferchaux*, *Le Samouraï*, and *Le Cercle rouge*. Decaë gave Losey's *Eva* its brutally gelid blacks and stolid whites, Clément's *Plein soleil* its unforgettable, interior pans so dark that not only did the colors of a wall take a long stare to register on the eye, the movement of the camera itself takes a while to distinguish from stasis. Ducaë kept surpassing himself, in work with Chabrol, Franju, Duvivier, Malle, George Stevens, Michael Ritchie, Peter Glenville, and a score of other top-grade directors.

If the film begins innocently, with prickly, mildly sadistic exchanges between Paul and Elisabeth, the film's evocation of childhood morphs strangely into young adulthood without any apparent passage of time, the characters just suddenly seem a lot older than they were and convey all the innocence of battery acid. From the outset, Elisabeth betrays a precocious bitterness at the prospective duties of adulthood, at her responsibilities at home, at the likelihood that nothing except her physical beauty will ever make her a truly exceptional person, something she can only be for Paul and their credulous friends.

In this sense, Gerard and Agathe do appear naive, though neither is really oblivious to the dead-endedness of the charmed circle, nor unaware that the game they've walked into is rigged against them both. But they have an intrinsic goodness about them that blinds them to Elisabeth's perversity, or at least to its bottomless quality.

Elisabeth's nimble skill at manipulation and her superior insight into other people's emotional weaknesses come increasingly to define her, first with her mother's death, and then, after a ridiculous marriage to a rich American who's killed in a car crash the day after their wedding, with her inheritance of a fortune and a vast townhouse.

The tribe migrates to this peculiarly designed new home, where the old games resume, the clutter and intimacy of the old bedroom reproduced in a virtual corner of a salon the size of a football field. Paul, in a moment of exasperation, takes his bedding and drags it off to another part of the house. Elisabeth has already discovered that Paul walks in his sleep, and long before this surmised that the magazine pictures tacked above his bed in the old place all feature young men resembling Dargelos. She intuits the danger Agathe's resemblance to Dargelos really threatens. Paul's homoerotic fixation on his schoolmate no longer distresses Elisabeth. Paul's confession that he loves Agathe, on the other hand, deranges her.

Nicole Stéphane, as Elisabeth, not to be vulgar about it, really owns this film. As skilled and enjoyable to watch as the other actors are—including Dermit, whose part demands several kinds of inertia, but includes several scenes in which Paul becomes vividly animated in one fashion or another, and which Dermit performs more than adequately—Stéphane mesmerizes the viewer into tense and basically unwanted sympathy with her increasingly unsympathetic character. As Elisabeth, vileness becomes her. Elisabeth's vivacity is the cosmetic glow of the death instinct. Her feral, assured technique of destroying everyone around her makes the others seem enslaved by sentimentality and confusion.

Elisabeth has the predator's gift of dissembling motive and intent. Like María Casares's astonishingly foolproof, elaborate revenge on her former lover in Bresson's *Les Dames du Bois de Boulogne*—a film for which Cocteau wrote the dialogue—Stéphane's Elisabeth methodically takes inventory of the strings she has to pull on each of her victims and displays an almost wistfully meditative pleasure at the moment she's about to give one of them a tug. Sabotaging Paul's rather stupidly complicated effort to convey his love to Agathe, Elisabeth soon has Agathe gushing her thanks to this guardian cannibal for steering her into an idiotic marriage to Gerard.

In Alexander Kluge's riotously funny, cerebral film *The Power of Emotion*, a couple guilty of near-murder nurse their brain-injured victim by reading aloud to him for hours, attempting to "undo the crime" by returning reality to the moment before it happened. Kluge has often suggested that such a procedure is philosophically possible, but existentially futile. In the end, this guilt-ridden duo reach their living dead end in a shitty hotel in Barcelona. Kluge's voiceover tells us of the woman: "Now she has exactly what she wants." Trapped in a squalid, narrow room, forced to forever endure each other's company, with nothing at all good or bad ahead of them: heaven for the dead, liberation from choices.

One element of Kluge's mastery is evidenced by the fact that the commentary framing its subject is enough: the viewer has no need, no inclination to ask why this is "exactly what she wants." We know. We don't want to know, but we do.

Spun out differently in Melville's movie, the wish and its fulfillment leave us no mental wiggle room in which to misunderstand, and, worse still, no way of looking at this film's end without looking into a mirror. These extreme characters, these defiantly nonsensical pleasures, these delectable theatrics and transparently fake joys of remaining a child, in a world where childhood magnifies the cruelties that follow it and nurtures sadism with the fertilizer of intimacy, may seem even more alien at the end than they did at the outset.

Or, they may tell us something about how little the things that are broken inside us ever really get left behind.

(2007)

MISSIVE IMPOSSIBLE

The Letters of Samuel Beckett, 1941–1956, volume two of a projected four-part compendium, is an endless Chinese banquet at which all but the most determined gourmands are likely to feel stuffed somewhere between the crispy pig ears and the thousand-year eggs: some may thrill to the hairpin turns and daredevil high jinks involved in the translation of *Molloy* from French into English, but many with more than a glancing interest in Beckett may find by page 200 or so that his correspondence and its staggeringly detailed footnotes have, to torture a phrase from Jane Austen, delighted them quite enough for one evening, and will put this tubby, ill-proportioned book aside until that fortuitous and chimerical month in the country they've set aside to read Proust in his entirety.

From an archival standpoint, the scholarly apparatus attached to these letters is impeccable, though it was Beckett's ukase that only letters with bearing on his work be selected for publication. As a result, a lot of what the editors have included here—responses to fussy editorial queries, business negotiations, and fine points of translation—would be utterly opaque without exegesis. Footnotes are so profuse that the rare, perfunctory missives without them look almost forlorn.

The worst to be said of the massive research appended is that it fractures any sense of an unfolding personal narrative of the kind one gathers from reading the letters of Chekhov, say, or Rosa Luxemburg; what does "go forward" is Beckett's steady refinement of an aesthetic, his insistence on a severe, pristine, ascetic literary practice that extends to the presentation of his plays—this volume mainly deals with *Godot*, and to a lesser extent with *Endgame*, the indicated staging of which was informed by Beckett's exhaustive knowledge of representational painting. With *Happy Days*, Beckett proceeded to distill theatrical spectacle into increasingly static, painting-like tableaux. "I do not believe in collaboration between the arts," he writes, startlingly, to the art critic Georges Duthuit. "I want a theater reduced to its own means, speech and acting, without painting, without music, without embellishments."

As we learn from letters to various theater directors, Beckett was by no means as strict about enforcing his own vision as has often been claimed. ("You ask me for my ideas about *En attendant Godot*, extracts from which you are doing me the honour of putting on . . . I know no more about this play than anyone who manages to read it attentively.") His personal fondness for Roger Blin, among others, allowed for a good deal of leeway with respect to staging and mise-en-scène, though when Beckett directed his own plays, and sometimes when merely advising a production, he often reduced actors to jelly with his notes. One gets the feeling that if he hadn't been terribly shy, he would have preferred to act all the parts himself, since he had quite elaborate ideas about every detail. After the period covered by this volume, Beckett found his ideal interpreters in Jack MacGowran, Billie Whitelaw, and David Warrilow; here, the early productions of *Godot* were highly troublesome, as it seemed every big-name actor from Ralph Richardson to Marlon Brando wanted to bring his special magic to Beckett's austere masterpiece, but never did so, either because of manifest incomprehension or scheduling problems.

Little brilliantines of excremental wisdom, blithe self-contempt, and unassuageable futility make up for a great deal of numbing palaver over payments and book deals; Beckett often refers to his own writing as shit, or snot, or a turd swirling in a toilet bowl. ("My God how I hate my own work," he wrote in 1956.) He is allergic to any kind of publicity and refuses to give interviews, sit on panels, or indulge in the careerism of writers' conferences and literary festivals. One can't help admiring this extreme self-effacement, considering the fatuous self-promotion so typical of the literary world today. If the business correspondence of this volume is occasionally redundant and tiring, the collected emails of the current OK list promise to be so much worse!

Beckett's enthusiasms are often a surprise. He declares *The Catcher in the Rye* the best thing he's read in years, and remarks on the "extraordinary pathos" of Barbara Stanwyck in *Chaînes du destin* (released in the US as *No Man of Her Own*). The austere image of Beckett conjured by his work, which could make him seem to exist entirely on his own frosty planet, has eroded over the years. It was once difficult to imagine him swimming, or playing tennis, and it is still rather startling to learn that he also played *golf*. The more important revelation in the letters is the great range and perspicacity of Beckett's interests, in music, painting, dance; in this connection, his activity as a translator of other people's writing (Sade, Ponge, Bataille, Genet) reflects an engagement with the cultural matrix around him one would never suspect after reading *Watt* or *Malone Dies*.

There is, less surprisingly, the kind of hypochondriacal complaining that most writers, trapped at a desk with their swirling innards a favored distraction, are wont to interrupt themselves with. We hear much about Beckett's implacable, recurring cysts, dental mishaps, episodes of writer's block, spells of depression, and other maladies. This sort of casual information places him squarely inside the familiar, etiolated universe of his fiction and theater; it's interesting to see how closely Beckett's work mirrors a chronic state of physical distress. Interesting too that Beckett's discomfort living in his own skin never leads him in real life into the kind of misanthropy his characters often lug around with them from bog to bog.

Beckett's enthusiasm for the paintings of Bram van Velde, articulated at ponderous length on what feels like every third page, occasions many intriguing reflections on the plastic arts in general. In van Velde, Beckett seems to have discovered a kind of dead-ended, self-contained practice he imagines to be the visual equivalent of his prose; in this connection, the reader might apply Beckett's views on this artist to more substantial exemplars like Dubuffet or Giacometti. In any case, Beckett's avid support for an appreciably less fascinating friend reflects an appealing generosity and kindness that everyone who knew him has remarked on.

Aside from hard-to-imagine love letters, the most conspicuous lacuna here is the absence of any correspondence from the period between 1941 and 1945, when Beckett and his companion, Suzanne Dechevaux-Dumesnil, evaded the occupying Germans, finding refuge with friends and acquaintances in various French cities and towns before settling in a small house in Roussillon in the Vaucluse—a village advantageously out of the way that served as a storage depot and meeting point for the maquis. Since Beckett was a noncombatant partisan in the French Resistance, this longueur was arguably the most interesting period of his life, and it's a pity no publishable letters survive from it.

(2012)

PEAK ATTITUDE:
THE NOVELS OF RENATA ADLER

Renata Adler's newly reissued novels, *Speedboat* (1976) and *Pitch Dark* (1983), consist of anecdotes, vignettes, jokes, aphorisms, epigrammatic asides, and longer passages of prose—eclectic inventories of consciousness. Their immediate effect is that of a flea market in Samarqand or Ouagadougou, where the items on display (vintage clothes, military decorations, photo albums, broken appliances) are fractionally different enough, in style and provenance, from their cousins at the local swap meet to look like artifacts of an alternate universe. Adler's eye and ear for the peculiar are unmatched in American letters.

Adler herself is regarded as peculiar in literary circles; her reluctance to publish anything is almost as legendary as Fran Lebowitz's writing block. At a more prolific time, Adler wrote often, mainly for the *New Yorker*, reporting with great perspicacity on civil rights marches in the South, the '60s student movement, Biafra. For slightly over a year in the late '60s, she was the daily film reviewer for the *New York Times*, a job no one else has filled quite as memorably since. ("Even if your idea of a good time," began her first review, "is to watch a lot of middle-aged Germans, some of them very fat, all reddening, grimacing, perspiring, and falling over Elke Sommer, I think you ought to skip *The Wicked Dreams of Paula Schultz*.") Since then, Adler's work has appeared with diminishing frequency, though almost always with seismic reverberation.

Her 1980 review, in the *New York Review of Books*, of *When the Lights Go Down*, a collection of film reviews by Pauline Kael, is still being written about, albeit for the wrong reason—i.e., that it was "mean." In the Kael review, as in, among other things, her pieces on Watergate, the Starr Report, Monica Lewinsky's biography, and the "institutional carpet bombing" she received from the *New York Times* in reaction to four lines about Watergate judge John Sirica in *Gone*, her book about the *New Yorker*, Adler has diagnosed systemic maladies that the media hue and cry over transient symptoms—the Jayson Blair affair, for example—have effectively masked from public view. In Kael's case, a debased use of language spreading into every area of public discourse. With respect to the *Times*, the abuse of institutional power to stifle dissent. In such matters, Adler has taken the high road, according to her lights, and suffered the opprobrium of doing so, at a time when the high road is scarcely visible to many people, in large part because of the problems Adler has written about.

Adler's fiction has received less contentious reception than her essays, although an excerpt of *Pitch Dark*, deemed by a narrow band of cognoscenti to be "about" real people, prompted the gossip columnist Liz Smith to issue her only known work of literary criticism. The two novels range over many subjects treated in her nonfiction, but the difference, I think, is this: the equivocal, insecure, self-doubting cogitations of Adler's first-person narrators are instantly disarming in ways that Adler, speaking with relentless logic as herself, in polemical mode, is not. No one else has a dog in a fight against yourself, and despite countless minor casualties in Adler's two novels, the main event in both of them is "I" versus "I."

The writer-narrator of *Speedboat*, Jen Fain, travels a lot, for work and fun. Sometimes she reports for a newspaper, or teaches at a city college. Her friends are lawyers, doctors, other writers, judges, politicians, socialites. She encounters many other sorts of people too. At least as often as she speaks of "I," she relates stories about "we"—meaning her generation, the one that went to college during the second Eisenhower administration. How their childhoods were, what school was like, what they expected to happen next, and how they are faring so far: "Dispersed as we all are, though, what we seem to have entirely in common is a time, a quality of meaning no harm, and a sense that among highly urban and ambitious people we are trying to lead some semblance of decent lives." These stories convey a class solidarity that has less to do with money than with education and an interest in politics and culture, a fair degree of social polish (often observed in the breach), and ethical scruples that preclude certain forms of success and facilitate others—in the legal field, medicine, publishing, scholarship, science. Also a fair degree of patriotism, faith in incremental progress, and the durability of democratic institutions. Of this cohort's influence on the state of things, *Speedboat* keeps a running score. "We may win this year. We may lose it all. It is not going as well as we thought."

Various riffs present themselves as witty examples of Hobson's choice, or coercive inanity, or misapplied wisdom. Often, Adler records nuances outside the perceptual range of any other recent American novelist:

> We were talking about *No, No, Nanette*. I said I thought there was such a thing as an Angry Bravo—that those audiences who stand, and cheer, and roar, and seem altogether beside themselves at what they would instantly agree is at best an unimportant thing, are not really cheering *No, No, Nanette*. They are booing *Hair*. Or whatever else it is on stage that they hate and that seems to triumph. So they stand and roar. Every bravo is not so much a Yes to the frail occasion they have come to make a stand at, as a No, goddam it to everything else, a bravo of rage. And with that, they become, for what it's worth, a constituency that is political.

Jen Fain ruminates on everyday ephemera: allegedly bulletproof taxi partitions, for example, or the enigma of the "self-addressed envelope," or bizarre form letters. In company, she is drawn as if by hypnosis to the flaw, and, implicitly, the void. Attuned to the wrong word, the malapropism, the gauche remark, the fatuous rejoinder, she finds something wildly skewed, insensible, ominous, untenable, intolerable, or at least a little off in nearly every situation. Hilarious in description, this something is essentially monstrous. Whether it is a symptom of a world gone mad, or evidence of herself cracking up, is another question she ponders in her spare time. Her tendency to paranoia and the giggles is extreme.

> I don't think much of writers in whom nothing is at risk. It is possible, though, to be too literal-minded about this question. In a magazine, under the heading "$1,000 for First-Person Articles," for example: "An article for this series must be a true, hitherto unpublished narrative of an unusual personal experience. It may be dramatic, inspirational, or humorous, but it must have, in the opinion of the editors, a quality of narrative interest comparable to 'How I Lost My Eye' (June '72) and 'Attacked by a Killer Shark' (April '72). Contributions must be typewritten, preferably *double-spaced*..." I particularly like where the stress, the italics, goes.

Speedboat reveals at every turn bewildering forks in the route ahead, confusions between literal and figurative, a widespread misapprehension of scale and scope, a general loss of equilibrium; in the episodes of daily life, nothing presents itself in the form of a single entendre. Seduction and threat are indistinguishable; reciprocal incomprehension begins to look like the salient feature of social existence. A friend's idea of a little surprise before dinner turns out to be five hours of *Parsifal*. The incipient horror of it all is diffused throughout by framing each occurrence as a funny thing that happened on the way to somewhere else—exactly where, though, is never indicated.

Jen shuffles life's imponderables in a vain search for cause and effect, an elusive organizing principle that is surely somewhere, some secret raison d'être, just really any kind of explanation. Reality's failure to make sense promotes feelings of panic that oblige her to draw her own conclusions, invariably in the form of nervous jokes.

The second rat, of course, may have been the first rat farther uptown, in which case I am either being followed or the rat keeps the same rounds and hours I do. I think sanity, however, is the most profound moral option of our time. Two rats, then.

She writes directly to the reader, in sections of a single line, a paragraph, a page. The epigraph quotes Evelyn Waugh; many of this novel's bit players would be at home in *A Handful of Dust*, or *Scoop*. *Speedboat* is very funny, in an archly reserved way. It is so diverted by eccentric data that Jen is scarcely more present as a character than the odd people she runs across, or the men she is involved with at different periods, who are practically spectral. She is there on the page; she tells us things about herself, about the world. Still, we wonder who she is, and so does she.

The staccato brevity of Adler's *contes* keeps them at the constant temperature of a well-turned after-dinner recitative at a table in Elaine's, with what that implies of a coterie sensibility, gamesmanship, and emotional cool. The conspicuous limitation of this novel is that it looks like something written for the *New Yorker*, by the *New Yorker*. But Adler accomplishes something reachier simply by adhering to the *New Yorker*'s notions of decorous writing with a kind of defeating fanaticism. From a certain abstracted angle, *Speedboat* evokes an antic American version of a Robbe-Grillet novel—not quite *Le Voyeur* as a musical, but still—its narrator a mental camera, incidents pared to the bone, sinews hidden in negative space.

The "missing page," what we sense behind what's shown, is a deferred awareness of death coming—not now, not yet, but sooner or later, none of this is going to last forever; not a shadow narrative, exactly, but a steady inference between the lines, in the white space where everything evaporates. I do not mean to suggest a prevailing spirit of morbidity, but rather a tropistic avoidance of it that becomes ominous. In the end, this assemblage of anecdotal evidence that appears to build a case, and regales us so implacably with sinister ironies, arrives at no conclusions, but opts for an agnostic optimism that could easily travel south.

Pitch Dark is murky—not in a turgid sense, but clouded, rather, by troubled reflections, ambivalence, regrets. The weather of *Pitch Dark* is colder. Secondary figures are fraught with shadowed histories. Incidents and asides illustrate a hapless, estranging condition of things: a bitter libel case, a dying raccoon, solitary escape to charmless islands, *The Blue Angel*, "how I both was and failed to be a citizen of my time." A central episode in Ireland resembles a parody of gothic horror. Kate Ennis is an older version of Jen Fein, acquainted with disappointment and less innervated by amusing minutiae. She too writes. And travels, though more to flee her life than for any sort of fun. She often addresses one particular reader, a man she has left, or is leaving, or who is leaving, or has left, her. Her stories are longish and less sanguine in contrast with the ones in *Speedboat*.

Comparing Gertrude Stein and Thomas Wolfe, she writes, "She went on and on, too, of course, but only in a state of tension: drawn to the sentimental rhythm and the sentimental substance, but mocking and concealing it, reining it back." This could suitably describe the precarious balance Kate Ennis maintains between observant detachment and a nervous breakdown. The central matter obscured by Kate's tales—of Penelope sleeping with all the suitors, of hate mail received since high school from Rosalie Kamarski, the story of the dragon of the passport office, the one about the Chinese hypnotist, and so on—the long love affair ending, ended, or maybe not, seeps into narrative cracks, sounds a medley of stuttering refrains. ("Look here, you know. I loved you." "You are, you know, you were the nearest thing to a real story to happen in my life.") The *faits divers* in *Pitch Dark* frequently end on these plangent, mournful notes of heartbreak. One wishes they were less plangent, and less frequent, since they don't always work, though scenes depicting Kate and her lover, Jake—at night, for instance, after leaving a party, with Jake's wife also in the car—are brilliant.

> Late that night, on the road back, he said, "Honey, right there in that heavy snowstorm, I saw two deer." There was a silence. I thought, he calls her honey. I could not imagine what his wife thought, or why she said nothing, or why the silence seemed so long and deep. His words were clearly not addressed to me. He had already told me about the deer. He has never called me anything but Kate. Then it dawned on me. He had told his wife, too, and forgotten that he'd told her. She must have thought he was telling me for the first time, and that, whatever honey has come to mean between them, he now calls me that. I could be wrong, of course. She may not even have been listening, or maybe she never answers at that hour. There we both were, though, together in our silence.

For Kate, everything has started to make too much sense, and to point all in one direction. The comparatively blithe era of *Speedboat* has segued into twilight time, decline and fall.

> But from the highest public matters to the smallest private acts, the mugger, the embezzler, the burglar, the perjurer, tax chiseler, killer, gang enforcer, the plumber, party chairman, salesman, curator, car or TV repairman, officials of the union, officials of the corporation, the archbishop, the numbers runner, the delinquent, the police; from the alley to the statehouse, behind the darkened window or the desk; this is the age of crime. And recently, I think the truth is this, over a period of days and nights some weeks ago, I became part of it.

Adler's novels employ time like a keyboard, playable in either direction, and proceed unfettered by plot, qualities they share with

Robert Walser's stories and feuilletons, Burroughs's cut-ups, and Elizabeth Hardwick's *Sleepless Nights*. They follow associative patterns we're not given a key to, conceivably akin to the synonymies expounded in *Speedboat*:

> "So for these purposes, digitalis, adamantine, apple orchard, gonorrhea, labyrinthine, motherfucker, flights of fancy, Duffy's Tavern, Halley's Comet, birthday present, xenophobic are all synonyms," the great professor said. "Synonyms in terms of meter, that is."
>
> "I see."
>
> "And words that rhyme," he said, "are synonyms, in terms of rhyme, with all the words they rhyme with. Cat, gnat, flat. Fang, sang, sprang, you see."
>
> "Yes."
>
> "So that in the study of poetics, we have. Rhyme synonyms. And meter synonyms. I leave aside pure synonyms of meaning. There are not really very many. And there are other factors, of course."
>
> "Of course."

Jen Fain and Kate Ennis are children of the kind of liberal Jewish family where the Dow Jones Averages are toasted on the father's birthday. Products of genteel country life and first-rate universities, they entered adulthood expecting the world to be a certain way. Not necessarily their shucked oyster, but at times, at least, a place that would yield something to reason and recognize worthy behavior. Coming of age in the 1950s, setting out for the city in the '60s, they encountered instead a culture of irony spreading everywhere like kudzu, choking off the oxygen supply, and epidemic dissonance dissolving every solid value. From *Pitch Dark*:

> We watched *The Newlywed Game*. The moderator had just asked the contestant, a young wife from Virginia, What is your husband's least favorite rodent? "His least favorite rodent," she replied,

drawling serenely and without hesitation. "Oh, I think that would have to be the saxophone."

And from *Speedboat*:

They were saying "Make peace, not war," and so, the Commander of the Ohio State National Guard testified in the course of the Kent State trials, he threw a rock at them.

A perception of important things becoming lost to history figures in the literature of every era. In *Sentimental Education*, Flaubert describes a moral and emotional aphasia produced by the Revolution of 1848; the First World War, in Stefan Zweig's *Beware of Pity*, erases an entire code of sentiments particular to the Austro-Hungarian Empire. Adler is a cartographer of surface disturbances *d'avant-guerre*, like Musil in *The Man Without Qualities*, observing the slow fade of values and ideals associated with liberal Republicanism. One tension in Adler's novels arises from their narrators' desire to stay engaged with the world as it worsens, and the evident futility of trying to do so with the tools at hand—training in logic, reflectiveness, criticality, kindness, good manners, and basic morals being clearly inadequate to a criminal era that begins with the Kennedy assassination and the Kitty Genovese story, and runs rampantly on to this day.

That the narrators of Adler's novels are versions of Renata Adler by Renata Adler is hardly a question, and barely remarkable, except that Adler's other writing and what is publicly known about her make these seem even less fictitious than most novels.

It should be added that even if she had named these women Renata Adler, the novels, and Renata Adler, would still be works of fiction; diverse works such as Hardwick's *Sleepless Nights*, Aldo Busi's *Sodomies in Eleven Point*, and Curzio Malaparte's *The Skin*, among many others in which the narrator or protagonist shares the name of the author, are salutary reminders of why we have fiction. The imagination needs a safe harbor, insured against any documentary form of reality; our lives consist of many things besides facts. In fiction I may incarnate, even in my own name, someone who is not me, a person I might be if I were not constrained by the exigencies of my existence, who has other qualities, different habits of thought, a different sexuality, less money, more money, someone else's problems, a fondness for other things. Or, the fictional "I" can coincide with myself at every point, but live in a different country, behave differently toward other people, only know people I invent for him, etc.

No current literary label appealingly describes the kind of narratives *Speedboat* and *Pitch Dark* are. I doubt that any is needed. Their formal design, of self-contained pieces separated by a line space and periodic chapter breaks, is hardly sui generis, having been used in many different kinds of writing for over a hundred years, in collections of aphorisms, feuilletons, philosophical treatises, compendia like Humphrey Jennings's *Pandaemonium* and Walter Benjamin's *Arcades Project*, as well as seed catalogues, political pamphlets, and cookbooks, and works of fiction as diverse as Rilke's *The Notebooks of Malte Laurids Brigge* and Burroughs's *Naked Lunch*.

The kind of thought debris you find on the internet describes novels in this form as "experimental," which is predictive of a certain off-putting difficulty and self-indulgent esoterica. Often, too, it is declared by a gatekeeping sort of criticism that anything that deviates far from a nineteenth-century template is "not a novel." It seems late in the day for such parsing. But in fact, classifications that formerly reflected a delight in all literary forms and the intellectual pleasure of differentiating them—Mary McCarthy's essays "Novel, Tale, Romance" and "The Fact in Fiction" come to mind—now serve as filtering screens for the literary market, which is currently dominated by aesthetic conservatism of a depressingly conformist ilk: middle-class marriage saved, or ruined, or attacked by vampires.

Adler's novels concede the necessity of making fiction quicker, more terse, descriptively less elaborate than the traditional thing called a novel, not so much in deference to shrunken attention spans, but as the most plausible way of rendering the distracted, fragmentary quality of contemporary consciousness. Their reportorially even tone is quite distinct from the distorting lyricism found in most novels of sensibility; omitting much of what we expect in first-person narratives, Adler gets at the overfull yet depleted condition we find ourselves in now, peripatetic and restless, ever more deprived of the time and mental space to reflect on what we are really doing, or who we really are. They describe what it's like to be living now, during this span of time, in our particular country and our particular world. This is what the best novels have always done, and with any luck will continue to do.

(2013)

PARADE'S END: JEAN ECHENOZ'S *1914*

I n several recent novels the succinct, startling prose of Jean Echenoz has achieved the condition of a highly durable, transparent membrane, something like the trompe l'oeil mesh often used now to mask scaffolding on building facades under repair. Imposing a Beckettian principle that drastically less is immensely more, Echenoz summons a fulsome picture of his characters and their worlds with a scattering of surgically exact, granular details both irreproachably veracious and wildly defamiliarizing, such as the swarm of mosquitoes that attacks the protagonist of *I'm Gone* (1999) as his dogsled approaches the Arctic Circle: Yes, there is a mosquito problem in the frozen North. But who'd have thunk it?

Since his fairly-short-of-midlength masterpiece, *Piano* (2003), Echenoz has minted three novels that qualify, in a hilariously original sense, as biographies—of the composer Ravel, the inventor Tesla, and the champion runner Zátopek, three famous, real eccentrics whose rendered interiority is every bit as quirky, as enslaved by secret foibles, superstitions, antagonisms, and incongruous tastes, as any of the author's made-up creatures. These "nonfiction novels" are thrillingly compressed, without feeling truncated or egregiously contrived; their subjects "come alive" in a manner suggesting that extraordinary talents are like Christmas presents, not quite what one would have wanted for oneself, as lowering in their way as the rest of life's implacable pathology, however exalting they may be from time to time. That an amazingly gifted person is also just another asshole is conveyed without a smudge of condescension. In fact, what these eminent individuals manage to accomplish in spite of the existential haplessness Echenoz suffuses them with makes them more worth respecting than their conventional biographies do. Life is mainly inconvenient, rebarbative, and, after all, really, really short—the brevity of *Ravel*, *Lightning*, and *Running* underscores the latter point with terrific poignance that belies Echenoz's reputed "detachment."

His novels are not without sentiment, however frosty they may seem to an American reading public accustomed to gorging on sentimentality. In *1914*, the emotions of Echenoz's characters are not especially foregrounded, and the strongest expression of feeling is made by the phantom limb of an amputee, invisible to all. As a response to the brutal ugliness of the world's indifferent violence, however, the book is perfect: compared with the gooey, narcissistic literary responses to 9/11, Echenoz's nod to the powerlessness of ordinary people caught in the first great modern cataclysm is a veritable monument to human dignity.

In broad outline, *1914* etches the fates of five friends called up in the mobilization after Germany's declaration of war on France and Russia—young men from the hills of Vendée in the Loire region outside Nîmes. It opens on a blowy August Saturday afternoon when Anthime, the accountant of the footwear company Borne-Sèze, is spending his half day bicycling up a local hill from which several villages can be seen spread out across the countryside. This scene is an homage to Victor Hugo's last novel, *Ninety-Three*, wherein the Royalist Marquis de Lantenac "examined all the belfries on the horizon. . . . The cages of all these belfries were alternately black and white. . . . It meant that all the bells were swinging. In order to appear and disappear in this way they must be violently rung . . . and yet he could hear nothing. . . . This was owing to the distance and the wind from the sea. . . . All these mad bells calling on every side, and at the same time this silence; nothing could be more sinister."

In the town, where Anthime encounters Charles, the factory's deputy manager, "a smiling crowd milled around waving bottles and flags, gesticulating, dashing about, leaving barely enough space for the horse-drawn vehicles already arriving laden with passengers. Everyone appeared well pleased with the mobilization in a hubbub of feverish debates, hearty laughter, hymns, fanfares, and patriotic exclamations punctuated by the neighing of horses."

Charles is an intimidating figure in Anthime's life, a few years older, imperious, snobbish, his sense of his own importance seconded by the proprietors of Borne-Sèze; the company doctor, Monteil; and Blanche, the daughter of the company owners (whom Charles has recently impregnated). So much so that after he's assigned, along with Anthime and their friends Bossis, Padioleau, and Arcenel, to the Eleventh Squadron of the Tenth Company of the Ninety-Third Infantry Regiment, Monteil pulls strings to get him safely transferred out of harm's way, to the newly formed Air Service. It has not yet occurred to the French military that airplanes might be used for combat as well as reconnaissance. "The men had heard about them, looked at photos in the newspaper, but no one had yet actually seen any of them, these seemingly fragile airplanes."

While Charles abruptly disappears from the Ninety-Third (and ironically becomes its first casualty), Anthime and the others are left to experience the ground war, from its almost giddy inception as a political canard that everyone expects to finish up in two weeks, to somewhat after the Battle of the Somme—by which time they've experienced the innovations of chemical attack, high-yield explosives, and trench warfare, and the spectacle of their fellow soldiers (including the military band sent into battle with them, presumably to provide theme music) blown to smithereens in unimaginably grotesque ways.

There are muted echoes of Barbusse, Céline, Jünger, and Remarque, and of Stanley Kubrick's *Paths of Glory* (namely the scenes featuring the indomitable Timothy Carey), fantastically amplified by Echenoz's deadpan inventories of the design and contents of knapsacks, varying weather conditions, the declining quality of food rations, nuances of war profiteering not only by local peasants between the Loire and the Belgian border but also by Borne-Sèze and other provisioning companies, and various fatal injuries occurring among Anthime's regiment, e.g.,

> a fourth and more carefully aimed 105-millimeter percussion-fuse shell . . . produced better results in the trench: after blowing the captain's orderly into six pieces, it spun off a mess of shrapnel that decapitated a liaison officer, pinned Bossis through his solar plexus to a tunnel prop, hacked up various soldiers from various angles, and bisected the body of an infantry scout lengthwise. . . . Anthime was for an instant able to see all the scout's organs—sliced in two from his brain to his pelvis, as in an anatomical drawing.

Regardless of other echoes, Echenoz's true compadres here are Jean-Patrick Manchette and Raymond Queneau, as he has happily acknowledged elsewhere. This year is the centenary of our first experiment in worldwide carnage, the effects of which our lamentable species is still coming to grips with, albeit on a learning curve slightly slower than that of plankton. For those about to be bombarded by a year of patriotic drivel, lachrymose valediction, and militaristic brainlessness, Echenoz's little novel should provide a refreshing mental douche.

(2014)

DON'T BUY US WITH SORRY AFTER BURNING DOWN THE BARN

I will first reveal, without embarrassment, that I fell asleep five times during a morning press screening of Errol Morris's *The Fog of War*—which received its US premiere at the New York Film Festival last September and is currently playing in theaters around the country—and I left the auditorium with precious few impressions besides that of the spectacularly bad dental work that Robert S. McNamara, the former secretary of defense, ex-posed each time he was featured in close-up. Having now viewed the documentary three additional times, while fully awake, what ultimately seems most impressive about Morris's skewed framing, Philip Glass's brooding, ominous score, the cutaway montages of stock military footage from World War II and Vietnam, and the random clips of media moments from the era of McNamara's cabinet tenure under Kennedy and Johnson is how well they are deployed to contrive an illusion of deepening insight and imminent revelation while dispensing entirely with the factual glue necessary to place McNamara's role in either administration into any legible context.

Much of Morris's oeuvre to date (from 1976's *Gates of Heaven*, his documentary on pet cemeteries, to his 2000 TV series *First Person*, whose episodes bore titles like "Mr. Personality" and "The Smartest Man in the World") has consisted of a geek's-eye view of subjects only slightly geekier than the director himself—a view that is almost invariably glacial and contemptuous of both his subjects and his audience. Yet now and then, Morris's technique of staring "objectively" at the human oddities he collects achieves a transcendently hideous rendering of the lame and the halt in human nature, very much in the spirit of Francis Bacon's portraits of shrieking popes and lumps of human meat writhing about in barren interiors: while Morris's visual sense is rather quotidian and hardly as exalted as Bacon's iconic genius, he has a definite flair for turning humans into talking sea cucumbers obsessed with philosophical or historical matters clearly beyond their intelligence. That they also seem beyond the director's intelligence accounts for the quirky hilarity that rescues much of Morris's work from being taken seriously.

In McNamara, Morris has at last found a subject whose callow, self-serving evasions and stridently complacent banalities have a deep affinity with Morris's insufferable delusion that his work digs deep below the surface of things, enlightening the public in ever-more innovative ways.

Here the trope of audience improvement, spelled out in the film's subtitle, consists of "Eleven Lessons from the Life of Robert S. McNamara," which range from clichés as old as von Clausewitz ("Empathize with your enemy"), to specious dicta ("Rationality will not save us"), to secular mysticism ("There's something beyond one's self"), to corporate-training-manual exhortations ("Maximize efficiency"), to McNamara's personal notion about how warfare should be conducted ("Proportionality should be a guideline in war"), to pseudo-profundities ("Belief and seeing are both often wrong"), to blatant cynicisms epidemic among governments everywhere ("In order to do good, you may have to engage in evil"), and, penultimately, to a "lesson" routinely spouted by film stars, retired politicians, seasonally traded athletes, grocery checkout clerks, and uncountable other Americans who've acquired it through cultural osmosis: "Never say never." Last, and least, is the bromide "You can't change human nature."

This final "lesson" is demonstrably the case where McNamara himself is concerned. At the time of filming, he appears convinced that something that seemed the right thing to do in, say,

1962, though history has proven it to have been the wrong thing, was nevertheless the right thing because it seemed the right thing when he did it: "You don't have hindsight at the time," he astutely observes. And precious little foresight either, judging by the vast historical literature on the Cuban Missile Crisis and the Vietnam War. There is nothing resembling an apology, a mea culpa, anywhere in this film: McNamara admits that his role in the firebombing of Tokyo would probably have been considered a war crime if America had lost World War II, yet seems oblivious to the fact that he committed many war crimes over the course of a war we did lose, even at one point admitting that he can't remember if he was the person who authorized the use of Agent Orange. When asked who was responsible for the Vietnam War, McNamara unhesitatingly says "the president" but softens this pronounce-ment by kissing Johnson's ass with his very next breath, lingeringly enough that even LBJ would have been mortified by it.

The film blithely skips over the routine doctoring of military budget fig-ures and outright lying about casualties that was McNamara's specialty—connivances that made him LBJ's favorite inherited cabinet member—as the Johnson administration plunged deeper into a war that neither Johnson nor Kennedy before him believed could be won from its very inception, and glosses over the intense antagonism between McNamara and the Joint Chiefs of Staff (in this, at least, McNamara seems to have had the right idea, albeit in the wrong brain). In one of the few unobsequious moments in Morris's fogbound movie, we at least get to see McNamara jauntily as-serting, at a press conference, that the war is going very well indeed, at a moment when even the business community had soured on the whole sor-did enterprise, the Quaker peace activist Norman Morrison had incinerated himself directly below the window of McNamara's office at the Pentagon, and fifty thousand antiwar demonstrators had descended on Washington. (McNamara praises himself for refusing to allow the military guard around the Pentagon to load live rounds in their rifles; we then see footage of demon-strators getting clobbered with rifle butts—which proves that Morris can still work himself up to a sense of irony, if not actual humor.)

Unhelpfully, the filmmaker allows McNamara to repeatedly, with fervor, remind us that the world came "that close" to nuclear war during the Cuban Missile Crisis—often emphasizing the pure luck that saved us from worldwide annihilation by pinching his thumb and forefinger nearly to-gether. This is hardly illuminating. For one thing, anyone over forty-five has known this since 1962—and, unlike McNamara, few of us had a nuke-proof bunker at our disposal in which to weather the imminent holocaust.

True, McNamara argued successfully for a blockade and negotiations while JCS mental cases, notably General Curtis LeMay, were truculently lobbying Kennedy to launch a massive air and naval strike against Cuba, which already had over two hundred active warheads and the missiles to deliver them. By his account, McNamara applied the "lessons" of Cuba—whatever they may have been—to the war in Vietnam, a culture about which our government knew absolutely nothing. It's perhaps more surprising than it should be to hear, late in the film, that, at a conference in Hanoi years after the war's conclusion, McNamara learned for the first time that Vietnam, far from having been a puppet state of Moscow or Peking, had been fighting a war of national liberation, that the Vietnamese regarded the American incursion as a new attempt at colonization after the French had been driven out, and that Vietnam had been engaged in almost perpetual warfare against China for over a thousand years. McNamara's learning curve appar-ently works at the same speed as a Martian probe.

Morris's idea of a penetrating question is demonstrated in the film's epilogue: "Do you ever feel responsible for Vietnam?" he asks. McNamara refuses to answer one way or the other, though throughout *The Fog of War* it's abundantly clear that McNamara remains, on the cusp of senescence, in-capable of feeling much culpability about anything. At best, he feels rueful that history has already decisively pegged him as a monstrous bureaucratic wastebasket. A closing title mentions that after being fired as defense secre-tary in 1968, McNamara served as the president of the World Bank for twelve years, until 1981. Curious to learn if his own human nature had changed even a tad since his years of orchestrating the slaughter of millions in Vietnam, I phoned the brilliant investigative journalist Roger Trilling and asked him if he had anything to share about McNamara's tenure at the bank.

"Well, I do know . . . one thing," Trilling, a prodigious geyser of clandes-tine information, allowed. "When McNamara was handed his sinecure in 1968, he decided to choose a model nation as a testing ground for interna-tional development. He chose Thailand, since he was . . . obviously familiar with the region.

"'The primary problem in creating development for the whole country was the economic discrepancy between the impoverished north and the economically healthier south. . . . So McNamara proposed the develop-ment of a leisure industry that could benefit both areas of the country. This involved bringing girls from the north to the cities in the south to work in the sex industry, as a developmental tool." But of course as secre-tary of defense McNamara had already contributed greatly to the promo-tion of sexual tourism in Thailand, having negotiated the 1967 "R&R" treaty that would fill Bangkok's brothels with furloughed American GIs.

Under McNamara's stewardship, the World Bank monitored the entre-preneurial savvy of aging B-girls over a number of years, identifying which were capable of developing businesses that would help bring Thailand into the global economy. These country courtesans, on the verge of retirement, were qualified for microlending, enabling them to open messenger services, bridal shops, laundromats, and various other small enterprises. As these women turned out to be more adroit and quicker at turning a dollar than the males being groomed for private enterprise by the World Bank, this eventually resulted in a complete reversal of Thailand's traditional gender economics, with women suddenly dominating the economy. Perversely enough, the system worked, at least to the satisfaction of West-erners like Robert McNamara, who knows that in order to do good, you may have to engage in evil. But the evils involved in sponsoring a Third World sex industry in the interests of globalization are depressingly routine compared with the evil Robert McNamara perpetrated throughout his gov-ernment career. Concerning which, Errol Morris's *The Fog of War* never scratches the surface.

(2008)

THE P AND I

The Haldeman Diaries:
Inside the Nixon White House
by H. R. Haldeman

The publication of *The Haldeman Diaries* immediately after Nixon's funeral is the kind of prosaic justice our cooling thirty-seventh president most enjoyed: a coincidence that looks like a vendetta. Unrecognizable in the somber eulogies to the architect of detente, the canny elder statesman, and the man of peace, our Nixon—the mad Christmas bomber, scourge of Alger Hiss and Helen Gahagan Douglas, a loser in victory as well as defeat—has been restored to us in all his daft and whimsical glory: unlovable, paranoid, congenitally dishonest, and, like Richard III, entirely aware of his own wretched nature. "P was fascinated this morning to get a report on the Kennedy Center opening of the [Bernstein] Mass last night . . . he paused a minute, this was over the phone, and then said, 'I just want to ask you one favor. If I'm assassinated, I want you to have them play "Dante's Inferno" and have Lawrence Welk produce it,' which was really pretty funny."

And so it is. H. R. Haldeman's genius at playing straight man to Nixon's japes has been underappreciated in early reviews. Haldeman owes a little to James Boswell, a bit to Cosima Wagner, and quite a lot to Joseph Goebbels. Swirling in decaying orbit around a black hole, he too mixes the sublime with the tawdry, the monumental with the petty, the public gesture with the private tic. As diarist, however, Haldeman's perfected absence from his own narrative most resembles Andy Warhol's. Warhol said that he stopped having emotions when he bought his first television; for Haldeman this apparently happened when he became Nixon's chief of staff, if not earlier. There is hardly a trace of personality in Haldeman's day-by-day account—except, at the very end, a touch of asperity and disappointment. There is only the P, the P's lofty musings and valiant deeds, and the P's wacky collection of allies and adversaries.

This slightly posthumous work (Haldeman cooled shortly before P) is a comic masterpiece to place alongside Keynes's *The Economic Consequences of the Peace*. Yet the media, unable to wrench itself out of the somber/elegiac thing, has so far treated it with a leaden austerity. The *Wall Street Journal* notes "shocking anti-Semitic and anti-black bigotry" along with "fascinating glimpses of Mr. Nixon as a leader," as if they were different, reserving most of its contempt for Henry Kissinger—a.k.a. K—"an incredibly petty and insecure man." Jonathan Schell, in *Newsday*, sees Nixon's career, per Haldeman, as "a titanic struggle between concealment and revelation," though Haldeman renders it as an effortless manic-depressive segue. In the *Daily News*, William F. Buckley Jr. sniffs that the "supposed" "racial and ethnic prejudices" of Nixon were not "lethal," and were therefore not "the kind of racism we properly worry about." Ted Koppel, in a two-part *Nightline* program, plucked some of the juicier bits, e.g., "[Billy] Graham has the strong feeling that the Bible says that there are satanic Jews, and that—that's where our problem arises," but trod very lightly upon K, the book's second largest character and Koppel's favorite talking head. Michiko Kakutani, in the *Daily Times*, does note "moments of out-and-out farce," but concludes that the diaries "can only depress and perturb the reader." Oh, please.

Such tidings reflect a nervous discomfort with the obvious fidelity of Haldeman's portrait. Kakutani, for one, seems to believe that most Americans actually swallowed the funereal makeover of Nixon as "a visionary foreign-policy maker," etc., and recites his major crimes as if disclosing them for the first time. It is rather jejune to find anything shocking, or for that matter arguable, about Nixon's ethnic phobias, his inexhaustible resentment, his compulsive lying, or the fact that he was, in the only sense of the word, a crook. Haldeman's ideal reader takes all that for granted and basks in the author's hilarious, total identification with P.

Nixon's zesty drollery and hijinks are there from the beginning. Within a month of inauguration, he and K are cooking up the secret bombing of Cambodia, giving it the festive code name "Operation Menu." The sudden intoxications of power put P into scary overdrive. "Fascinated by Tkach report of people who need no sleep at all. Hates to waste the time.... Thinks you have to be 'up,' not relaxed, to function best." Even the White House staff's gift Irish setter, King Timahoe, feels edgy around P. "Had Tim in the office, both of them pretty nervous." K, like P, "swings from very tense to very funny."

Haldeman strikes the note of farce with recurring comic minor characters. "Poor Agnew slipped on the icy runway during troop review and smashed his nose. Then went on TV to introduce P with huge cut on nose bleeding profusely." "Almost unbelievable conversation at dinner as J. Edgar went on and on about his friends . . . and his enemies . . . A real character out of days of yore.... P seems fascinated by him and ordered me to have lunch with him twice a month to keep up a close contact." A theme of omnipresent enemies is also sounded with Warholian deadpan. "Interesting to watch Eunice Shriver last night and tonight, she obviously hates seeing Nixon as President. She talked to herself and winced all through the toasts, both nights, and must have been thinking back to JFK." "Big flap about proposed Ambassador to Canada, Turned out to be a guy P had met in '67 in Argentina. He was Ambassador there, and Nixon stayed at the residence, he left anti-Nixon literature and Herblock cartoons on bedstand. So now P has blocked this appointment, or any, for this guy."

The gang around P—an ever-shifting cavalcade of poltroons, buffoons, and sleazy opportunists, with a boorish core of constant retainers like Ehrlichman, Mitchell, Buchanan, Moynihan, Haig, and Connally, along with the largely irrelevant cabinet, the almost invisible Pat Nixon, and the spectral Bebe Rebozo—is soon swept up in the charade of rulership. Like the court of the Medici everyone harbors little secrets, everyone "leaks" this and that to the press, and all important decisions take place in an atmosphere of psychotic secrecy. "P issued strict orders that Ziegler and White House staff are to say nothing about Vietnam until further orders. Has to keep complete control and not let an inadvertent comment play into their hands." "Later called over, all upset because K making an issue out of State reluctance to bomb Laos. Rogers wanted a meeting, to argue P's decision. P told me to tell K to go ahead and bomb, don't make announcement or notify State just do it and skip the argument."

Even in an actual crisis, Haldeman's tongue-in-cheek rescues his pen from excessive melodrama. As South Vietnamese troops entered Cambodia, P "reviewed DDE's Lebanon decision and JFK's Cuban missile crisis. Decided this was tougher than either of those . . ." Minutes later, "Called again to discuss problem of locating his new pool table. Decided it won't fit in solarium, so wants a room in EOB."

After a few unsatisfying meetings with civil rights leaders and antiwar groups, P and his team decide to ignore the demonstrations and other unpleasantness occurring outside the White House. "Need to reexamine our appointments and start to play to our group, without shame or concern or apology. Should feel our way, appear to be listening to critics, but we have now learned we have gained nothing by turning to the other side." From Haldeman's marginalia, however, the reader gradually surmises that just below the immediate circle of P subluminous worker ants with names like Liddy, Hunt, Krogh, and Ulasciewicz are scurrying around the troubled countryside, planting spooks at leftist get-togethers, burglarizing offices, forging letters on other people's stationery, and delivering large amounts of cash in brown paper bags.

Meanwhile, the inner circle serenely goes about its imperial business. "The Apollo shot was this morning; the P slept through it, but we put out an announcement that he had watched it with great interest." The P is preoccupied with keeping the kooks, hippies, and yids at bay, holding the line on school desegregation, nominating ghastly judges for the Supreme Court, and planning nasty shocks for an ever-growing list of enemies. Despite his ingenuity in these domestic areas, the P feels unappreciated. "K, at Congress, didn't make the point regarding the character of the man, how he toughed it through . . . Why not say that without the P's courage we couldn't have had this? The basic line here is the character, the lonely man in the White House, with little support from government, . . . overwhelming opposition from media and opinion leaders, including religious, education, and business, but strong support from labor. P alone held on and pulled it out."

We will never know exactly how long the Vietnam War was protracted by K's on-again, off-again Paris Peace Talks, which in Haldeman's account seem mainly hobbled by K and P's capricious habit of following up each session with massive bombing raids. "The mad bomber" was Nixon's own term; he thought if the Communists believed he was really insane, they would be desperate to negotiate. K apparently agreed when it suited his mood, squabbled when it didn't. Haldeman's K is a Molièrean figure of fun, an incessantly grumbling, pompous, infantile worrywart who demands constant stroking from the P, threatens to resign every other day, and spends much of his time upstaging Secretary of State William Rogers, who he's convinced is "out to get him." What K and P share, aside from a child's love of secrecy, is the delusion that they function best in crises, which they frequently manufacture to rouse themselves from the torpor of omnipotence. They detect Soviet influence in various affairs the Soviets have little interest in—the India-Pakistan conflict, for example—issue blustery ultimatums, and work themselves into a prenuclear lather; when the bewildered Soviets acquiesce, K and P congratulate themselves on having forced the enemy to "back down."

They're equally gifted at spawning tensions within their own circle. "So I asked Henry to come in and join us. E then jumped on him pretty hard, on not only that, but also the intelligence thing, and the international drug problem . . . At this point Henry blew and said as long as he's here, nobody's going to go around him . . . E got a little more rough on him, and that resulted in Henry saying E couldn't talk to him that way, and getting up and stalking out of the meeting." Squalid internecine rivalries and craven favor mongering permeate every small and large issue, conference, meeting, state visit, and memorandum. From Haldeman's micromanaging perspective, the epochal Nixon visit to China and the Moscow signing of SALT I are slapstick, almost accidental triumphs of business over venality and pettiness. And after Moscow it's all downhill.

Haldeman first notes the Watergate break-in on Sunday, June 18, 1972. "It turns out there was a direct connection (with CRP), and Ehrlichman was very concerned about the whole thing. I talked to Magruder this morning, at Ehrlichman's suggestion, because he was afraid the statement that Mitchell was about to release was not a good one from our viewpoint." At first the little tapping of Plumbers is muted by the roar of P's landslide election victory. For a time, the gang is confident that the problem can be "contained," even turned to advantage. "He wants to get our people to put out that foreign or Communist money came in in support of the demonstrations in the campaign, tie all the '72 demonstrations to McGovern and thus the Democrats. . . . Broaden the investigation to include the peace movement and its leaders, McGovern and Teddy Kennedy." In fact, freshly mandated P feels nearly invincible. "He wants Ziegler to put a total embargo on *Times* and *Newsweek*, there's to be no background to Sidey regarding election night or anything else at any time. He wants total discipline on the press, they're to be used as enemies, not played for help."

As late as February 1973, the P still had other things on his mind. "He said, 'Don't discuss this with anyone else, but we've got to cover the question of how to handle the Nobel Peace Prize. It's a bad situation to be nominated and not get it.' Maybe there should be a letter to Miller, who is nominating him, saying the P feels he should not be honored for doing his duty . . . He wants a report on the Nobel Prize—who's on the committee, what's the process, can the P withdraw his name, and so on." By April, however, even the P's unflagging prankishness has waned. "The P had me in at 8:00 this morning. Said that if this thing goes the way it might, and I have to leave, he wants me to take all the office material from his—ah—machinery there and hold it for the library."

With impeccable comic timing, Watergate begins to unravel the P at the very moment that K secures a negotiated settlement in Vietnam, snatching defeat from the jaws of defeat. Just when K and P should be preening in the funhouse mirror of world history, unsavory drones surface from the netherworld for urgent nocturnal covens, scrambling to get their stories straight. Each story is quickly shredded by someone else's story. No one can recall exactly when and where who told who to do what to whom. "Talked to Dean on the phone this morning. . . . He's back to his cancer theory, that we've got to cut the thing out. Cut out the cancer now and deal with it." ". . . Jeb said that he and Mitchell were afraid Colson was going to take over the intelligence apparatus, so they went ahead, and Dean feels it was probably with Mitchell's OK." "Caulfield gave this letter to Dean, Dean told Mitchell about it, Mitchell told Dean to have Caulfield see McCord and take his pulse." ". . . some evidence that Colson had put Hunt into the Plumbers operation to spy on Krogh, and so on."

As all the P's men are hauled before the grand jury, P recalls—too late!—the trap he set for Alger Hiss, involving the question of perjury. P realizes with horror that he's walked into the same trap!

Here, Haldeman's narrative brilliantly captures the lunar panic of the final days, when one by one, sometimes two by two, the White House gang is thrown to the wolves by P. Frankly unable to recall his own lies, prevarications, secret meetings and the like, Haldeman starts to report other people's accounts of "Haldeman," as if he and the author were two different people.

Happily for us, Haldeman, along with Ehrlichman, is pretty much the last to go, unless you count the interim staff, special prosecutors, defense attorneys, and of course K, who surrounded the P when he was, at long last, forced to climb aboard his final presidential helicopter. Only a day before Haldeman's departure, P "shook hands with me, which is the first time he's ever done that." After announcing H's and E's resignations on TV, the P "asked me if I thought I could do some checking around on reaction to the speech as I had done in the past, and I said no, I didn't think I could. He realized that was the case." But the P just wouldn't be Nixon if he didn't ask.

And there Haldeman's delightful account closes, with the Vampire of Yorba Linda still clutching the frayed reins of power as he gallops toward . . . a full presidential pardon, his pension, and the mulch of historical relativism, shameless and saucy as the lounge comedian and used car dealer we, the people, always knew him to be.

(1994)

TOWN OF THE LIVING DEAD

Thirty minutes south of Springfield on I-65, engine sparks spitting under the chassis ignite the innards of an RV, which stops dead on the asphalt, disgorging a family of flustered, obese vacationers moments before the propane tanks explode. It's 90 degrees to begin with, and we're stuck, twelve cars to the rear, waiting for the who knows which fire department and the Missouri highway patrol, as a fat plume of velvet smoke rolls out of the gutted camper. The second explosion sounds like the foot of an angry god stomping on a large sheet of bubble wrap. You can hear a half ton of imitation wood grain furniture and Formica countertops and modular bedding crackle into toxic ash as people waddle from their cars for snapshots. Among the chorus of rednecks gawking at the blaze, there is palpable disappointment, thinly veiled as relief, as the news spreads that everyone got out of the RV okay, including the grandmother.

To put it simply, the fun begins even before you get to Branson, Missouri. Billboards thicken in the fields a few miles before Highway 76. Silver Dollar City. Shepherd of the Hills. Tony Orlando's Yellow Ribbon Music Theater. At the junction of 64 and 76, a cluster of two-story buildings—insurance offices, Baptist and Lutheran churches, clothing shops, and soda fountains—comprise the rural burg that existed before Branson became, in its own words, "America's fastest growing resort." This is downtown Branson—population 4,000—all fresh paint and gentrified storefronts and, emphatically, nothing special. It's roughly four square blocks sloping to a narrow arm of Lake Taneycomo, where a waterborne shopping mall in the shape of a riverboat broods near the entrance of a public park.

It would be pointless to look for an authentic, native Branson where the manna of tourist dollars doesn't require at least honorary tolerance of all but the most questionable foreigner. Folks might not cotton to the way you look or dress here, but as long as you're buying something you can count on a smile pasted over the homicidal wish behind the cash register. Now and then an overworked waitress or shopkeeper opines that Branson is "burning itself out," or complains that the "stars" perennially "settling" in Branson, like Bobby Vinton, come in for the quick cash and leave a year later. But Branson isn't Nashville—its indigenous attractions, like the Baldknobbers Hillbilly Jamboree, are the kind of rustic kitsch best exemplified by gift shop miniatures. There is nothing very precious being lost by expansion, except the landscape itself, which no one has much interest in preserving anyway.

Branson is one of those rural sites where temples to local folklore sprang up to attract tourists, who were first drawn to the area by the fishing and boating facilities on Lake Taneycomo. The lake, like the town, is artificial, created in 1913 by the damming of the flood-prone White River. Manmade lakes, with their dynamic impact on aquatic flora and fauna, are a specialty of the region.

There was, in the '30s, a movie house called the Hillbilly Theater, and a Hollywood Hills Hotel owned by a special effects director named Ned Mann. Local histories claim that movie stars stayed there but fail to mention any by name. In 1949, the manager of the Hillbilly Theater erected a gigantic Adoration Scene on a bluff overlooking downtown Branson. You know, the Adoration. Infant Jesus, Mary, cattle, the Wise Men, frankincense and myrrh. In 1953, the Chamber of Commerce started, during the Christmas season, an Adoration Parade to light the Adoration Scene.

About the same time, a family named Trimble opened a theme park devoted to the inspirational folklore found in *The Shepherd of the Hills*, a 1907 novel by Harold Bell Wright, which recounts the exploits of the Baldknobbers, an Ozark vigilante gang, and various mystically charged events following a bad drought. *The Shepherd of the Hills* was fashioned into an annual pageant, a sort of white trash Passion Play, performed in an amphitheater at the Shepherd of the Hills farm, which also offers a Homestead Tour, a wagon ride with Clydesdale horses, a blacksmith shop, Championship Frog Races, and a bluntly phallic Inspiration Tower, featuring "a truly awe-inspiring panoramic view of the Ozarks," restrooms, and snack bar.

Another theme park, Silver Dollar City, opened around the same time, and another lake, Table Rock, was added to the landscape by another dam. I-65 became clogged with vacationers. A four-lane bypass created an interchange with Highway 76. They opened a Wal-Mart on 76. The rest is history.

From the air—specifically, from a C-500 Hughes helicopter, which you can hire for six minutes for $22.50—Branson becomes a legible metastasis spreading across the woodsy, mountainous Missouri landscape, replicating the same cellular structures over and over: motels, music theaters, "rides," "attractions," souvenir shops, restaurants, specialty stores. This architectural melanoma starts as you hover west from downtown. The lack of any rational planning gives Branson the look of a fever dream, a horror vacui planted on either side of five miles of graded highway. The theaters, some with seating for 4,000, appear as massive swellings beside the weird spires and kooky shapes of amusement arcades, water slides, theme motels, and mammoth parking lots. On branch roads behind Highway 76, huge gouts of forest have been cleared for ever larger hotels and theaters, erected with the speed peculiar to contractors with friends named Gambino and Luchese. At certain hours, traffic is jammed on 76 heading west; at others, the east lane is blocked. Never both at the same time, but always one or the other.

NEARER MY GOD THAN YOU

The woman on stage is singing about Jesus. It is a gruesome tune, emphasis on Crown of Thorns, spear in side, physical torture, sung with a fervor bordering on necrophilia ("Feel his heart beat . . ."). She is wearing a mauve dress and clutching a cordless microphone the size of an old-fashioned cocktail shaker. Behind her, liturgical-looking shapes light up the wall above a large assortment of musicians. Deeply moved, the singer belts her way through the Crucifixion and His Blood soaking into the ground and Him being laid away in a tomb, and then, after a histrionic pause, the singer's mouth expands in a smile of blazingly white enamel, because, guess what, when they rolled away the stone, they discovered that He Had Risen, Yes He Had.

It's three in the afternoon, and the Osmond Family Theater is half empty, but also half full, with the staple Branson afternoon audience, bus tours. Down from the fruited plains of Kansas. Up from the parched yet fertile bowels of Arkansas. Over from the purple mountains majesty and prairie towns where cholesterol and deep-fried everything are things to be thankful for rather than feared. People come to Branson in groups. Family groups. Community groups. Retirement groups. Church groups. They come with the love of Jesus and the Right to Life and a hatred of gun control throbbing in their plaque-encrusted arteries in time to "The Wabash Cannonball."

It is safe to say that no one comes alone to see the Osmond Brothers, which is why, sitting in the exact middle of the front row between a woman who has seen the Osmond Brothers thirty times and two very small children attached to a plump, elderly, dropsical-looking woman in pink Bermuda shorts and a thalo-green blouse, I am fully prepared to tell anyone who asks that my wife and children were recently killed in a plane crash.

The Crucifixion number is followed by several couples in shiny red, blue, and yellow, vaguely Swiss, silk costumes, tap dancing.

They tap for a long time, faces dilated in robotic grins, with the kind of oblivious energy one associates with amphetamine psychosis. I look behind me. There is a vast bobbing cloud of white hair that slowly separates into individual heads.

Once the Osmonds hit the stage, it's quite impossible to sit still and let the show wash over you. Not because the Osmonds are so special, but because the Osmonds immediately want to know which half of the audience has more enthusiasm. How loud can we clap our hands? How hard can we stamp our feet? Now, let's get to know each other! Shake hands with your neighbor on the right! Shake hands with your neighbor on the left! The woman who's seen the Osmonds thirty times apparently has my number and merely glares at me, though I clap and stomp and smile like an idiot whenever she does, just to see what that feels like. It feels really geeky. I am wearing a dark brown T-shirt and black jeans, a bad choice for a theater livid with pastels and splashy prints. Most clothing worn in Branson resembles daring wallpaper, ethnic restaurant tablecloths, or stuff a motel would use for curtains.

Merrill, Wayne, Jimmy, Jay, and Alan Osmond are all pretty hefty, middle-aged, vocally gifted Mormons. They're wearing white jackets with rhinestone arrows and blue stars and red and white flag stripes, large silver belt ornaments, string ties, and turquoise Indian bracelets. Each Osmond has a little shtick of his own: one fiddles, another one has a guitar thing going on, one yodels Hank Williams covers, another one sings in that froggy Tennessee Ernie Ford baritone, and one brother tells the kind of jokes that used to fly well on *The Lawrence Welk Show*.

There is an inexhaustible supply of Osmonds on stage, in the wings, and on the road with separate acts. Marie and Donny are headliners at other theaters, and often join these Osmonds for a family hoedown, or coven, or whatever you call it, but not today. Instead we have the second-generation Osmonds on various instruments, dancer Heather Osmond, and Amy Osmond, who, somewhere in the middle of the first hour (all shows in Branson run two hours, with a long intermission), provides a spot of Classical Uplift with a Mozart violin piece. She plays well.

As this unexpected fragment of High Culture sends the crowd into awed mutism, I have time to reflect that the difference between Branson and Nashville is something palpable and programmatic, a satanic bargain between performers and audience based on mutual defensiveness. The audience knows that in the world outside, Branson's headliners—the Osmonds, Glen Campbell, Andy Williams, Cristy Lane—are well past their peaks, which, in many cases, were never exactly soaring. The performers know that the audience—solid white, born-again, lumpen middle- and working-class Americans—is profoundly out of whack with the trajectory of American popular culture, which, for all its inanity, is generally libertarian, multicultural, and secular. The performers cater to the phobia-driven inner life of the audience, devoting lavish stage time to the celebration of family, God, and country. (The Osmonds, like several other Branson acts, wind up their show with "The Battle Hymn of the Republic.") In return, the audience treats them as if they were, currently or ever, major stars.

PRECIOUS MOMENTS

At the John Davidson show, the fantastically corpulent ladies on either side of me are getting to know each other and continue talking across me after I sit down.

"Did you ever put up okra with tomatoes?"

"I put up okra with green peppers and onions."

"Well, I like chow-chow. My daughter-in-law went into the hospital last weekend so I'm going to make some for her. I'd like to make raspberry jam, but her doctor told her anyone who munches on seeds and nuts is endangering their colon. She's having half her colon removed. I'm afraid of the seeds!"

"We pay six dollars a gallon for blueberries."

"I'm afraid of seeds!"

Time hasn't been especially unkind to John Davidson, but as with so many Branson headliners he is remarkably thicker and older than one remembers him. It doesn't help that the slide show above the stage opens with a solarized photo of Davidson as he once was, repeated on seven panels. However, he gamely projects a youthful ingenue sort of image to the crowd, which is, by and large, still quite a lot older than he is. When he quizzes married couples in the audience for "the year they fell in love," instantly delivering a song popular that year, the game hits an awkward pause when absolutely no one claims to have fallen in love more recently than 1960.

Davidson works the room like an appliance set to run for two hours even if the roof collapses. He's bent on winning the audience and at the same time seems oblivious to any particular person in it. He's got his material, his fake-opera-with-a-stiff-from-the-audience routine, his sing-along-with-a-Wurlitzer-juke-box shtick, his family-man-who-pretends-to-be-randy thing. This is a low-tech show in a relatively small theater, far from crowded, and Davidson isn't yet really established in Branson. He is not a good singer, yet he sings everything, even his little speeches, creating the illusion that the show has much more music in it than it does. For Branson, he goes rather far. After singing to one dowdy wife in the front row, he imagines her husband telling her back at the motel, "I bet you twenty dollars he's gay."

Later he pretends to arrange motel assignations among strangers in the audience. Having described growing up with a minister father (family photos appear on the slide panels, each with a little story to tell), he does a number in which a ravenously hungry preacher abandons his sermon to devour a chicken that's flown into the church. During a medley of '50s rock covers, he gives a long exegesis of "parking," which was, he says, "all about . . . kissing, since we're in Branson now."

None of Davidson's show would be at all risqué, or for that matter entertaining, outside Branson, but here he fills an obvious void. In a town where fart jokes and speech impediments define the threshold of acceptable humor, Davidson makes fun of religious zeal and alludes to nonmarital sex. The obligatory patriotic finale comes with a slide montage of heroic icons that includes, among several provocative choices, Muhammad Ali and Arthur Ashe. Davidson is, I guess, a safe form of cosmopolitanism.

Shoji Tabuchi is much more identifiably Branson, a cherished local institution. Like Yakov Smirnoff, the Russian comic whose signature line, "What a country!," has congealed into—what else?—the What a Country Theater, Tabuchi functions as an emblem of successful assimilation, of diversity where there is none. A typical story in the promotional literature tells of a veteran who, after hearing Tabuchi's violin, was able "to forget World War II."

Tabuchi is, in other words, the anomaly who refutes the idea that Branson is an intolerant, small-minded, racially exclusive place. It's affectionately noted, everywhere, that Tabuchi is fantastically rich and spent millions on the restrooms of his theater. In this, and many other things, he epitomizes a stereotype of the "good" Japanese: relentlessly industrious, given to grandiose but shrewd expenditures, and, of course, in his embrace of country and western, endlessly adaptive and unoriginal.

Tabuchi's theater reflects a real-world rather than off-world taste. There are glass bricks in the facade and Deco chairs in one of the lounges, and overall it looks like it was built by an architect rather than a cartoonist. The restrooms are something; from *Citizen Kane*, yes. The lobby is packed full of white people spilling out of their Kmart leisure wear, snacking and taking snapshots. Shoji Tabuchi artifacts and refreshments are peddled all over the building. During intermission, kiosks offering videos, tapes, and T-shirts appear on either side of the stage.

The show uses a lot of lasers, 3-D effects, and scrims. Tabuchi's little daughter, a tiny spot on a cavernous black stage, sings "Imagine" as a carpet of stars lights up behind her. A flying sofa flutters down from the wings, carrying her into an Arabian fantasia of turbans and dervishes and the kind of choreography the June Taylor Dancers used to execute on *The Jackie Gleason Show*. This goes on for a very long time. A restless brat sitting next to me turns to his mother and says, precociously, "This sucks."

Tabuchi, who dominates a stage of musicians with the restless physical presence of a grinning, wound-up incubus, has at least as much talent on the violin as Victor Borge had on the piano. He can play anything country, and does, though after a few minutes it all sounds like the same thing. The fact that he plays it at all is the source of Tabuchi's popularity; as a Japanese, his status is that of an idiot savant, an alien who shouldn't be able to do advanced calculus in his head but unaccountably does. Tabuchi's shtick is all about being Japanese on other people's turf: pronouncing things wrong, eating raw fish, scrambling the titles of C&W standards, and in general ingratiating himself with hordes of Christians willing to forget World War II, since he's been willing to learn the "Tennessee Waltz." Behind the shtick is the scrutable smile of a contented millionaire.

HOUSE OF WAX

The mystery of Branson, if there is one, is the quirky way that star worship functions in a repressive microcosm. Maybe because it's compressed into such a small area, Branson is the tightest little cultural sphincter you are likely to find in the United States. There are no shadows in Branson. No whores, no gambling, no drugs, no egregious drinking. There are, ubiquitously, Family Restaurants serving huge portions of the worst food on the continent; "Frito Pie" is a characteristic menu item. Fried chicken, a dish you'd imagine native to the Ozarks, arrives carbonized, like a mutant pork rind.

There are funfairs stuffed with kiddie attractions, bumper cars, water dodgems, convoys of amphibious Duck Boats (something between a cabin cruiser and an armored personnel carrier, "More Duck for Your Buck") that drive passengers into and around the lakes, miniature golf courses, and biblically large families splashing around in heated motel swimming pools flush with the sidewalk along the main drag.

There is Ozarkland, featuring the Koi Garden Oriental Restaurant, T-Shirt Factory, and Basket Man. There is the Calico Cat Country Store, the Hillbilly Inn, Ma Barker's Famous Barbeque, Kenny Rogers' Roasters, Western Sizzlin' Steak House, the D.J. Motel, the Heart of the Ozarks Inn, the Ozark Mountain Inn, Holiday Inn, E-Z Center Motel, the Amber Light Motor Inn, the 76 Mall (Ladies Apparel, Country Fudge, Aunt Minnie's Funnel Cakes). The Outback Steak and Oyster Bat, Outback Outfitters, and Outback Bungee Jumping Platform. Bonanza Chicken Steak, 36-Hole Indoor Golf and 3-D Cinema, South American Llama, the Cottonpatch Quilt's Gazebo, and the Jungle Boy Outlet.

There is, or are, Precious Moments, a species of ceramic kitsch, the type of droopy-faced little figurine you find in Woolworth's for $3.50, priced from $75 to $400, with legends inscribed "God Bless Our Family," "No Tears Past The Gate," "Mommy, I Love You," "Wishing You A Basket Full Of Blessings," collected by Christians with the gravity of Sotheby's bidders. The salespeople in Branson's many Precious Moments shops do not, as you would imagine, talk about how cute these ghastly little excrescences are, but about their value on the secondary market, how to look for flaws, and which items have been suspended, retired, or discontinued. Motels and show tickets in Branson are cheap. The cost of these objects is the real proof of a parallel universe, where a glazed elf is an investment.

And there is, in some processed, Disneyized, gelded sense, the glittering allure of Stars, Show Biz. A parallel universe, say, in which "top flight entertainment" equals Bobby Vinton and Jim Nabors. It's some kind of allure, supplying that ideal of mildness Lionel Trilling described in "The Fate of Pleasure," an easily digested excitement with nothing profane or suggestive in it.

Elvis, for instance, is hailed from every Branson stage as the King, but every Elvis cover is performed without any incitement to lust, or indeed any reference to sexuality. A star, as any American twelve-year-old understands, is someone a great many people would like to fuck. But in Branson a star is a kind of ideal family member, a sibling or parent or child, whose personal life—all details of which are offered from the stage as part of the routine—should closely resemble the lives of ordinary denizens of the Bible Belt.

What the Branson entertainer projects on stage isn't sexiness or eccentricity or extravagance, but ordinariness. Pride in having produced children, in having stayed in the same marriage for many years, in one's own religious fervor, in being as close to some conservative norm as possible, is the acceptable form of overt egotism. "My kid," Wayne Osmond gushes repeatedly after his daughter's violin solo, "my kid." Knowing chuckles from the audience. This is the kind of moist family feeling they relate to. Most performers here mingle with the crowds in the lobby afterward, further proof that they're just like everybody else, only richer.

"The first day I came to work here," a woman selling memorabilia in the lobby of John Davidson's theater told me, "he came right over to me and said, 'welcome to the family.' That's the kind of person he is." She was selling, among other things, John Davidson brand coffee, a John Davidson line of herbal teas, and John Davidson–initialed varsity sweaters, as well as a "geography game" devised by John Davidson to teach youngsters the often confusing difference between, for example, Canada and Mexico. I heard this again and again from lobby people selling souvenirs for $4.50 an hour: the star had actually spoken to them, welcomed them to the family, was "not at all snobby," but "a regular nice person."

Service industry jobs are about all there is in Branson. A young woman who'd recently moved to another town said, "You've got to work two or three jobs just to live here. A one-bedroom apartment is five hundred dollars a month, gas is up to $1.09 a gallon. And tourism is way down no matter what anybody says. For one thing, people think the floods came here, and then other people hear about how crowded it is and stay away."

Unlike Vegas, or Nashville, or any comparable fantasy sprawl, Branson has the provisional feeling of a place that could become an archaeological curiosity in no time at all, like the improvised white flight suburbs of the Northeast that succumbed to mall-and-condo mania in the '70s and '80s. The architecture of Branson's theaters and motels has the Potemkin Village effect of an amusement park, or a studio back lot; a significant percentage of businesses changes hands each year, folds, or goes bankrupt, and the big country stars who "locate" in Branson, like Loretta Lynn, generally abandon the place after one or two seasons. ("She's had so much tragedy this last year," a coffee shop waitress confides to a couple from Iowa, "that she's decided to give up her theater.")

It may be uncharitable to say so, but artists tend to flee places like Branson rather than settle in them, and for anyone with a viable career elsewhere, Branson has to be a purgatorial stop on the road instead of a destination. Of course there is money, quite a lot of it, to be skimmed off the four million tourists passing through every year, and beautiful homes or compounds to be carved from the vegetation around Table Rock Lake, but it's hard to imagine being young and vigorous and talented and not going stark raving mad in Branson sooner or later. The town smells of embalming fluid.

Appropriately, one of its major sidebar items is Long's Wax Museum, in a ranch-shaped building near the Osmonds' theater. A maze of moisture-buckled plywood paneling and display cubicles behind Plexiglas, the wax museum offers an assortment of stuffed, molting avian and mammal specimens, many of them extinct; myriad vintage firearms, in less than mint condition; and an array of rusted or rotted farm tools and primitive household conveniences (icecream dipper, ice shaver, bung hole auger, cabbage cutter, etc.). The wax displays are a weird mixture of celebrity fetishism and campy religious piety, musty sermons in wax epitomizing the Branson ethos.

Along one corridor, we find the plywood pasted over with assassination headlines: RFK, JFK, Martin Luther King. Inside a cubicle is "the '61 Cadillac in which Jacqueline Kennedy drove to President Kennedy's funeral," with an oil-on-velvet portrait of JFK; in the neighboring alcove, wax figures of Mrs. Kennedy, John-John, and Caroline at the funeral; in an adjacent display, his connection to the Kennedy funeral unelucidated, Michael Jackson, with glove and red leather jacket, waves into space, a dozen gold records dangling near his head.

Next, a procession of tableaux from old movies, the figures in decaying period costumes, the skin tones more than slightly off, and, close up, bearing almost no resemblance to the actors they're based on: Mary Pickford on a swing, Gary Cooper surrounded by hostile Indians, Marlene Dietrich in a tuxedo, Jean Harlow and Clark Gable in a red boudoir. John Travolta, looking like Milton Berle; Clint Eastwood, Barbra Streisand, Dolly Parton, and Burt Reynold. Marlin (sic) Brando in *The Wild One*. Mae West in *She Done Him Wrong*. Karloff as Frankenstein. Hedy Lamarr.

The show business figures are mixed in with other ones: John Wilkes Booth crouching behind Mary Todd and Abraham Lincoln at the theater, Judge Roy Bean observing a hanging, Ronald Reagan standing behind a seated Oliver North, Mahatma Gandi (sic) in the lotus position, the Assassination of President McKinley. In an overlit passageway, glass coffins contain dummies of Hitler ("who committed suicide in his private bunker at Berlin . . . so it is reported by captured Nazi officials. THERE IS DOUBT TO ITS TRUTH"), Eva Braun, and Mussolini "as he actually was just before burial in a secret grave." Mussolini is green, leering, and full of bloody perforations; he resembles the Incredible Hulk, who's also replicated a bit further on. On the opposite wall, there is an odd square object with hairs embedded in it. It takes a moment to notice the nipples. It has sarcophagus-shaped,

Egyptian decorations painted on it. Beside it is a wooden spear identified as an "ancient heart stake."

In the depths of this macabre inventory, the Life of Christ appears like a moth-eaten road show, a little melted from travels in narrative sequence—Journey to Bethlehem Nativity, Twelve-Year-Old Jesus in Temple, Baptism of Jesus, First Miracle, Christ at Mary and Martha's, Last Supper (with place cards), Peter Denies Jesus, Pilate Washes Hands, Scourging Jesus, Bearing His Cross, Casting Lots, Carry to Tomb, Ascension.

SALON DE MUSIQUE

I could not face Jennifer in the Morning, or the Jim Owen Morning Show, or Moe Bandy's Americana, or the Pump Boys and Dinettes Theater, all of which, in any case, were plunking and twanging and picking and clog dancing all over the Vacation Channel, along with off-world comedy bumpkins with missing teeth. It was a bad town to wake up in, strangely desolate despite the traffic, and the honorary friendliness of shopkeepers and waitresses seemed to mask a sinister back-narrative, as if they had stepped out of *A Boy and His Dog*.

In one place that resembled a normal, adult-oriented steak house, McGillies, a few sullen young people could always be found drinking heavily on the patio. You could tell they were local and they dressed like kids who wanted to be somewhere else they had seen on television. The patio had pleasant landscaping and a waterfall but for some reason was bathed in green fluorescent lights. One waitress in McGillies claimed that a newly built star theater was sinking in its landfill, and seemed to detest quite a lot of what Branson had to offer. But malcontents were scarce. Malcontents in places like Branson always tell you some new building is sinking into landfill.

I saw exactly three Black people in Branson. Two were in a white panel truck behind McGillies, maybe maintenance men, and one, a boy of about thirteen, was walking down Highway

76 with two white kids. He had a bangee boy haircut and his shirt off, which made him three things you just don't see on the street in Branson. I wondered who this boy was and what he was doing there and wondered if he felt as oppressed and eager to leave as I did.

Inevitably, I went to the Anita Bryant Morning Show at the Ozark Theater.

I hadn't given Anita Bryant a thought in over a decade, except once, over a year ago, when a play I was writing, set in the late '70s, cried out for a line about her. In some glitch of memory concerning the year or two just before AIDS, I had a blurry mental image of Anita Bryant being reconciled with the gay community of Dade County, dancing in a gay disco, something like that, the kind of little "ironic" item you find in the front of Newsweek—but of course it never happened.

What happened to Anita Bryant was, she lost her job with the Florida Citrus Commission, her TV thing, after organizing against a gay rights bill in Miami. Then something else happened to Anita Bryant when she got a divorce: she lost her religious-right constituency, her rabid claque.

Anita Bryant went into the wilderness.

Now she is back, if having your name on a theater in Eureka Springs, Arkansas (the next Branson), and doing a morning show at the Ozark Theater in Branson can be called back. She appears first, in a long white jacket over a beaded gown, a jacket that looks like vinyl and has red and blue Constructivist stripes that also look like vinyl. The entire outfit is covered in sequins that look vinyl. The auburn hair is whisked up in a surprisingly butch do, the face perfectly sculpted, with good bones behind it. She marches right down into the audience, singing what, I don't remember, but the voice, to give her her due, isn't bad.

Anita Bryant's thing is to take us down memory lane while working the audience like a slot machine. This isn't unusual for Branson, and neither are her rapid jumps from bluegrass to Patti

Page covers to the obligatory Hank Williams numbers, "Jambalaya," "Your Cheatin' Heart," etc., which everyone does. Anita also does an impression of Elvis and shakes her moneymaker more than I would have anticipated. She sits down at a dresser on stage, fixes a ponytail into her hair, changes into a skirt and sweater, and relives someone else's '50s girlhood while singing "At the Hop." She gets two musicians into semidrag to accompany her on some Andrews Sisters songs. She selects a tall, bald, befuddled man from the audience to sing a duet with her and cracks surprisingly cruel jokes at his expense. In fact, there's a slightly nasty edge to Anita's act, some evidence that as far as she's concerned she's still the Queen of Show Biz and it's no fault of hers that she has to perform for busloads of geriatric bohunks at ten in the morning.

This may simply be the attrition from the other side of Anita Bryant's act, which contains a lot of spiel, much of it a melodramatic rehash of her glory days and even more of it a deft reinvention of, and apologia for, her Fall.

The word "homosexual" never passes her lips, but Anita refers, often, to her Troubles, her loss of the orange juice contract and the evil boycott that effectively ended her career, though she knows she had only done what was right. Everyone knows what she's talking about, that unspeakable Godmocking "lifestyle" corroding the very springs and shock absorbers of This Great Country. And then—her voice drops, oozing snappily phrased sincerity—even more devastating was that painful divorce, the last thing on earth she ever wanted, and Being Judged by Strangers. Mud was splashed all over her by the media. She felt humiliated and worthless. It's all there in *A New Day*, her autobiography, on sale in the lobby, "the book I said I'd never write." The blacklist. The persecution. The lifestyle that a few people on their AIDS deathbeds renounced in her presence as she Gave Them Succor. The years of songless exile in Atlanta, where, in the depths of the fait accompli, her Depression Became So Great That She Seriously Thought About Taking Her Own Life.

But then a good friend made her pray. Made her pray for the Lord's "tough love" and shoulder her cross and accept and love herself for who she really was. After a long healing process, during which she also realized that she had to become a corporation and put her fag-boycott-and-divorce-devastated finances in order, she experienced "the blessing of total self-forgiveness."

Anita recounts nearly every Precious Moment of her career, with almost defiant panache, as if she had been, before the fags ruined everything, as big as Madonna. She warbles not only her early Coca-Cola commercial but also her Florida Orange Juice theme, ("Orange juice with natural vitamin C! From the Florida Sunshine Tree!") She is, after all, the youngest person and only woman ever inducted into the Florida Citrus Hall of Fame. She regales us with the eleven Bob Hope USO tours, more tours than any other guest performer, the long rewarding years of bringing the gift of song to lonely servicemen on desolate foreign soil. She tells the story of the army jacket she's changed into, a jacket festooned with cloth decorations—more military decorations, in fact, than any other performer has ever received—that has her last name on the ID patch: Once upon a time, she was performing free at an army base, and asked the general there for a fatigue jacket to put all her decorations on. She had four stars from General Westmoreland, and all these patches from all those USO tours, and they brought her this jacket, which already had the name tag, and it turned out that a Private Bryant had donated his.

She didn't meet Private Bryant at the time, but she talked to him on the phone. She sent him some goodies in exchange for the jacket, and they started a correspondence. He was sent to Vietnam. They wrote to each other for a year. He became her special friend. And then, one day, she got a call from the man's wife. Private Bryant had been killed in action.

Anita Bryant then performs the theme song of every armed service of America, instructing everyone to stand when she gets to the song of the branch they served in, or their spouse served in, and behind her, a giant American flag beams across the back wall of the stage. At the end of this medley the whole audience is standing, ready to trample out the vintage where the grapes of wrath are stored. By the end of her show Anita Bryant has pushed every Branson button so hard that this audience would forgive her if she confessed to murdering the Lindbergh baby.

MONKEY DO

Later that night I caught the magic show at the Five Star Theatre. There were lots of young, dancing magicians materializing tigers and sawing women in clear plastic boxes in half, and a long episode of flamenco dancing that featured male and female ingenues with beautiful bodies, some of them distinctly ethnic. The Five Star had drawn out a noticeably younger crowd than I had seen anywhere else, and the dancers led me to imagine some secret disco in the hills where stir-crazy performers under fifty went to party.

There was Bobby Berosini and his world-famous performing orangutans, an act that called upon the orangutans to kiss and clamber around a kind of jungle gym and make farting noises with their mouths. This became more and more horrible as it went on. Later Bobby Berosini appeared in the lobby with "Tiga," the orangutang who costarred with Clint Eastwood in *Every Which Way But Loose*. An endless line of parents and children formed, to have their pictures taken with Tiga. Tiga looked very much like the stuffed Tiga dolls being sold in the lobby, except around the eyes. Around the eyes, Tiga looked extremely despondent, starved for affection, and, if this is possible for an orangutan, bored. Bobby Berosini looked like an enterprising oil slick.

In the parking lot I struck up a conversation with a young couple from St. Louis who seemed to have strayed into Branson by accident. With little prompting they expressed dismay at the use of rare animals for entertainment. They had only caught this one show and were driving home in the morning. We talked about animals and ecology for a long time. At last, I thought, after all this time, real people. The young man had been to New York. He had a friend who lived in Woodmere.

"Now, I've got nothing against the Jewish people per se," he said, launching into a long story I was afraid to follow because his presence in Branson was about to make sense. It was the last night in Branson. I went to McGillies and got drunk.

(1993)

LA PLAYS ITSELF

The Edward R. Roybal Federal Building in downtown Los Angeles is a salmon-and-gray miniscraper two parking lots away from the Museum of Contemporary Art, a Molotov cocktail's toss from Little Tokyo to the south and Olvera Street and Union Station to the north. The structure closest to the Roybal Building has a family resemblance to other postmodern monoliths in the landscape, its pointlessly angled, blocky ostentation garnished by diagonal glass-enclosed ramps with exposed support beams that twinkle at night under evenly spaced flood spots. Razor-slit windows perforate the facade like holes in a computer punch card.

This edifice, connected to the Roybal by a raised plaza with Grecian pretensions, is the Metropolitan Detention Center. It graces the cover of Mike Davis's *City of Quartz*, and is, Davis notes, "the largest prison built in a major U.S. urban center in generations." Its proximity to the Roybal suggests a smooth two-way flow of major felon traffic from one building to the other, a kind of glitchless, architecturally ideal passage from indictment to incarceration. The defendants in the case at hand, *US v. Stacey C. Koon, Laurence M. Powell, Timothy E. Wind, and Theodore J. Briseno*, however, arrive from the suburbs every morning in private cars, playing peekaboo behind the morning's *Los Angeles Times* with a variable number of television cameras.

The defense team and their clients are from Central Casting: the perpetually scowling, high-domed Sergeant Stacey Koon carries himself with the tranquil arrogance of a bulky, dangerous mammal accustomed to pushing weaker mammals around, chomping into them when irritated. His attorney, Ira Salzman, is a tall, long-faced, dark-complected man with no lips, whose cornily handsome features are marred by deeply pitted skin, bad teeth, and an air of insufferable sanctimony. Officer Laurence M. Powell has the jowly potato face and put-upon, porcine expression of a slow-witted high school bully. Michael Stone, his lawyer, is squat, rosy-cheeked, humorless, and wears a bad haircut settled above the cringing mug of a malefic toad. Probationary Officer Timothy E. Wind, the Greta Garbo of the case, is a tall, darkhaired, fairly pleasant-looking Midwesterner whose counsel, the long-winded, basso profundo Paul DePasquale, suggests what the mating of Don Rickles and Mussolini might look like.

Finally there is Officer Theodore J. Briseno, cast against type: Briseno is almost handsome in a sallow sort of way, with nicely cropped black hair and mustache. He is short, willowy, with quick, delicate gestures and eager, hangdog smiles, searching eyes, and a manner so earnest and anxious to do the right thing that the only word that comes to mind is "twitch." Briseno is represented by Harland Braun, a lanky, pallid, bland-looking WASP with a goofy mouth and an oblivious attitude.

We each come into these things with our little preconceived notions, of course, but even if these people were the Greenpeace board of directors, I think I would still consider them an unfortunate-looking bunch. On the other hand, maybe not.

At the Temple Street side of the Roybal Building one finds a two-story Jonathan Borofsky sculpture: four identical, flat, white silhouettes converge on each other nose-to-nose in the attitude of a fistfight, like one big, angry dude who's been squeezed through an egg slicer and tastefully arranged for serving. The figures are pocked all over with holes, as if they've been sprayed in a drive-by. On the plaza side, where wooly bits of vegetation and sprigs of magnolia poke from decorative tubs and containers, a half-circle of marble columns arcs around a fountain whose centerpiece is a reclining marble infant holding aloft a little marble globe; the columns are festooned, Hindu temple–style, with stubbylimbed, vaguely Sumerian figures, naked, wearing expressions of hapless imbecility and bewilderment. These architectural doodles are the work of Tom Otterness, a sculptor who once shot a dog for a little film he was making.

The six o'clock television feeds tend to lead into the day's events in front of the Borofsky, with cutaways to the lunch break briefings of the defense team, which are held on the plaza. The networks file on Eastern Standard deadlines, which shaves off the last hour or two of testimony every day. Amid the first slew of motions in *US v. Stacey C. Koon, et al.*, petitions for better media access raised some artificial suspense in the press room, where, throughout jury selection, all but three pool reporters—invariably, two networks and a major newspaper—were parked around speakers wired to the courtroom two floors above.

Since this is a federal trial, it is not being televised. Recording devices of any kind have been banned from the building. The pool system favors corporate media, which have the time and resources to keep abreast of the shifting whims of the US Marshal's Office, which decides who gets access to the courtroom and on what basis. The starstruck federal marshals will do almost anything to accommodate the *New York Times*, the *Los Angeles Times*, the networks, or CNN. Those of us attending on an irregular basis, on the other hand, have been repeatedly threatened with the revocation of our courtroom passes, thanks to the idle lobbying of the major media jocks (with the notable exception of the CBS reporter) who don't show up every day, either, but want extra seats for Rodney King's testimony and, of course, delivery of the verdict.

During voir dire, at least seventy members of the jury pool are packed into the courtroom every day, so there are, in fact, only a few seats open for reporters. Keeping the bulk of the press in audio contact two stories down produces an odd sort of redundancy or dyslexia, with everybody straining to follow the badly miked proceedings and devising charts to track individual jurors. To further complicate matters, the jurors are identified by number to protect their anonymity, with another number designating their potential place in the jury box. At lunch recess the day's three pool reporters breeze into the press room to offer their impressions: "White male, late thirties/early forties, blue Oxford shirt, faded jeans, beard and mustache"; "Bleach-blond white woman"; "White male former marine, fifties or sixties." (These potted descriptions, emphasis on race and placement in the food chain of Southern California, are disseminated more or less verbatim throughout the country.)

The briefing is followed by a scramble for the elevators and the midday sound bites of the defense attorneys out on the plaza, another pass through the metal detectors, and lunch in the cafeteria, where one can view the defendants feeding at one end and the current crop of potential jurors at the other. Most reporters generously pass along what they believe has happened in the courtroom on any given day, or tell you which person in the cafeteria is Juror Number 531 or 689, but they are quite often mistaken, and the voir dire comes to resemble a protracted game of Gossip, in which rumors spread like brushfires, and are doused at the end of the day by some simple piece of information that's been garbled by the loudspeakers.

The sensation of groping needlessly in the dark for data that should be brightly lit and readily available also suffuses the actual voir dire, which pits each jury candidate against his or her previous responses to a fifty-two-page Juror Questionnaire. (The questionnaire has been a long-tossed bone of contention between the media and Judge John Davies, who has refused several times to provide copies of completed questionnaires to the press; blank ones are available from the marshals.) Several jurors are disqualified when, under questioning, they amend their written answers, or betray a greater knowledge of the case than they've indicated on the questionnaire, or are shown to have more opinions, or claim to have fewer opinions, than they've expressed in writing.

Like so much of the defense's version of the case, and some of the prosecution's as well, this jury selection almost uniquely demands a collective suspension of disbelief, to wit:

It will fall upon the prosecution to prove, beyond reasonable doubt and according to the two counts of the queerly worded new indictment, that the four officers in question, acting on the authority of Sergeant Stacey C. Koon, willfully kicked, beat, and stomped the person often identified in the press as "motorist Rodney King" with the intent of depriving Rodney King of "his right not to be deprived of his civil rights," though even well-informed partisans of the government's side cannot say with exact certainty which aspects of the beating received by Rodney King on March 3, 1991, in strict legal terms, directly violated his civil rights.

It will be the defense's task to demonstrate, as it successfully did to the jury of the previous trial in Simi Valley, that a large drunken man surrounded by more than twenty law enforcement personnel from three separate jurisdictions (the Los Angeles Police Department, the Los Angeles Unified School District, and the California Highway Patrol) was not beaten with excessive force by the four LAPD officers on trial, that on the contrary the suspect exhibited superhuman strength and actually "controlled everything that happened on or about March 3, 1991" by refusing to assume a "felony prone" position and continually threatening to spring up from a "weak push-up position," forcing the officers to continue striking him, when there is ample videotape evidence to the contrary, evidence that has been viewed at least once by all but one juror (a young Latino man, the last juror seated), and indeed by most citizens of the United States with access to a television set.

With respect to the jury, it is tacitly understood by all the players that few residents of Los Angeles County in their right minds want to serve on it, and therefore the three hundred–something potential jurors who have not deliberately disqualified themselves prior to voir dire comprise a small, determined core of Angelenos who desire, for one reason or another, to qualify for this specific trial. Since a strong desire to be on the jury, in this case, indicates an equally strong reason for a juror to be rejected, the voir dire, which in most federal cases is mainly handled by the judge, has been turned over to the attorneys.

Listening for days to the muzzy, halting responses of jury candidates, one can't avoid the impression that each has discerned from his or her predecessors what kinds of answers will fly with both sides, or will at least forestall a peremptory challenge. There are, of course, a number of potential jurors who answer spontaneously, candidly, without calculation, and these people are, sooner or later, bumped from consideration, as is anyone who seems able to form two consecutive thoughts without assistance from the judge or the attorneys.

Expressing any too-developed opinion or feeling about the massive insurrection that followed the acquittal of Koon, Powell, Wind, and Briseno in the Simi Valley trial leads to closer scrutiny, eventually to dismissal, as does any evidence of an analytical or "political" bent—for instance, an Asian woman, Juror 497, who watched the entire Simi Valley trial on television while recovering from neck surgery, makes the fatal gaffe of confessing emotion about the verdicts "because of how I feel about inequalities among poor and minority people." Juror 497 is replaced as Juror 2 by Juror 448, a white male, former Marine Corps machinist, who "had no reaction to the state verdicts last year."

Juror 383, "white woman, 40s, manager of commercial marketing education for insurance firm," sounds as if she's been put in the jury pool for comic relief: she can't stop talking about herself, especially about her job, where "I teach agents to sell, and naturally I always drive the point home..." She has no time, she says, for anything besides work and education. The volume of information she volunteers points to a mild personality disorder, particularly since none of it is interesting. "I'm extremely disciplined, I went to a Catholic boarding school." There follows a long digression about her eyesight, which once had an 800+

correction but is now 20/20, thanks to "historic eye surgery." Exhausted, the attorney questioning her (Paul De Pasquale, Timothy Wind's lawyer) queries: "You won't feel slighted if I don't ask you any more personal questions?" After several other jurors have been questioned about whether they intend, if seated, to publish books or articles about their experience ("I'm a capitalist," asseverates one, "being an American, so naturally we all think of that."), 383 asks to be heard and states that she has no intention of writing a book.

Neither side wants to waste a peremptory on 383, and neither side wants her on the jury, either. Just from her voice, one can conjure an unbearable scenario of eleven decided jurors, for or against the defendants, and one egomaniacal insurance bureaucrat staging an epic filibuster until she gets her own way. The prosecution waits for the defense, defense waits for the prosecution, neither makes a move, and 383 gets seated.

"The mood of the city is uneasy anticipation," writes Al Martinez, a columnist in the *LA Times*, "like that of a child huddled down in darkness, searching for monsters in the shadows... The emotions are not dissimilar. Will morning come before the things in the night leap out and devour us?"

It's a widespread assumption that unfavorable verdicts in what is usually called "the Rodney King trial," or in the immediately subsequent trial of the LA 4+, *The People of the State of California v. Damian Williams, et al.*, popularly known as "the Reginald Denny trial," will trigger another uprising. Although not everyone is clear about what would constitute favorable verdicts in either case, the worst scenario, insurrection-wise, would obviously be a second acquittal of all four white police officers, followed by unanimous felony convictions of the young Black men accused of attacking truck driver Reginald Denny at the intersection of Florence and Normandie last April 29.

The semantics of both trials, and of the events of last April, suggest the agitated mixture of accommodation and polarization existing in LA: "Reginald Denny" figures less in certain conversations than "the trial of the LA 4," or "LA 4+." People who have more than a cursory interest in the subject tend to use "insurrection," "uprising," or "rebellion," while "civil disturbance" and "urban unrest" are the politically neutral phrases used by social service agencies, city bureaucrats, and politicians. The average white citizen of Los Angeles uses "riot" automatically; none of the African Americans and Latinos I've spoken with have failed to make the choice of something other than "riot" an emphatic one.

The child-huddled-down-in-darkness theme is, as you might assume, most disingenuously struck in the gated communities of North Hollywood and the Valley, the Armed Response zones on the west side, white flight netherlands like Palmdale and areas north of Wilshire and west of Vermont patrolled by Neighborhood Watch groups. It is not a theme that plays too well Downtown in the region charted by Mike Davis as the "Homeless Containment Core," the "Narcotics Enforcement Zones" of Central Avenue and MacArthur Park, Koreatown, or in Compton, Watts, Inglewood, Crenshaw, and Florence, where the logic of last year's events is less elusive and shadowy, where people have been huddled down in darkness long enough to know that the biggest monsters don't live in darkness but merely collect the rent on it, and where the terms of the equation are visibly intact. Barely a dime of useful relief money has ever reached South Central Los Angeles.

Peter Ueberroth's "Rebuild LA," however well intended, has bogged down in a morass of red tape. As for the Federal Emergency Management Agency and its multimillion-dollar allocation for LA disaster relief, Cynthia Robbins, the directing attorney of Urban Recovery Legal Assistance, characterizes FEMA as "the second disaster that follows any federally declared disaster."

"We've seen a pretty big share of people who are trying to get emergency benefits," Robbins says. "I think it's appalling that at this date we are still helping people to access emergency benefits as a first shot through the system. It's appalling that many of our clients who did ultimately get help got it in August, September, and October, which means that somehow, through the good graces of friends and relatives and people in the community, they were able to hang on by a thread from early May."

"We also have people who haven't gotten any benefits at all," says Becky Rosenthal, a paralegal at URLA. "We have a lot of recent immigrants, people who aren't sophisticated, who don't have accountants, swap meet people, they don't have safety deposit boxes for their papers, and often what records they did have were destroyed. The place they worked was burned down or their shop was looted or something like that. They're just not able to provide the federal tax forms, a lot of it is usually cash transactions, so there are no sales receipts whatsoever. For FEMA, if you can't produce the kind of documents they want, you don't qualify for the benefits."

"These are exactly the people," Robbins adds, "who were intended to be beneficiaries when this legislation was passed by Congress."

Juror 202, a Hispanic male, has two children and is involved in coaching. He has had a "generally good" experience with law enforcement. He was arrested on a DWI charge at the age of twenty-three. Does he believe police generally catch the right people and do their jobs right? No, he doesn't think so. He is involved with Neighborhood Watch. Though he sounds like a good enough juror, the defense eliminates him on a peremptory.

Juror 488 is dismissed after stating unequivocally that "what they did was wrong": he says this with a winning mixture of reasonableness and disgust, as if he couldn't be bothered to play out the charade of objectivity.

Juror 598, a Black female, works for the US Postal Service. Was she surprised by the outcome of the first Rodney King trial? Yes, she thought there were a lot of facts leading to a conviction. However, she feels that justice was done in that case. She understands that these are two separate cases. In the absence of a defense challenge, she's seated.

A startling number of people in the jury pool have contacts in law enforcement: Juror 574 has a close relative on the Whittier Police Department; Juror 639 has friends on the California Highway Patrol and the Oxnard Police Department; Juror 649 knows a detective and a parole officer. Juror 519's father was a cop in Detroit. Yet another juror's two children had "considered careers in law enforcement." Many, but not all, are rejected. Judge Davies wants to pick up the pace—even for a "sensitive" case, this thing is moving like molasses.

During the lunch recess, Attorney Stone complains about "a volunteer jury." Ira Salzman, the attorney for Stacey Koon, remarks with some asperity that "speed for the sake of speed is bad."

Salzman describes Juror 598, the Black postal worker, as "a perfect juror," a remark that backfires a few days later. Having seated one Black juror, the defense proceeds to exclude on peremptory the subsequent four Black candidates. The strategy seems to be to get the "racial balance" issue out of the way with one token person of color. Prior to the trial the conviction that the threat of Black violence would force a guilty verdict—"It's like telling a juror, 'We put dynamite in your home and if you vote not guilty we're going to blow up your house'"—was publicly trumpeted by Harland Braun, who is known in LA as a "flamboyant" figure, meaning he's an uncontrollable blabber-mouth. For this, he had a gag order slapped on him; it was later lifted by an appeals court, so the defense lawyers can work the press while the prosecutors remain incommunicado.

When the defense moves to exclude Juror 473, an elderly Black man whose voir dire answers are inconsistent with those on his questionnaire, the prosecutors, Barry Kowalski and Steven Clymer, finally invoke *Bateson v. Kentucky*, a federal finding that prevents lawyers from using peremptory challenges to exclude jurors on the basis of race. They proceed to argue that Salzman,

Stone, DePasquale, and Braun have consistently questioned Black jurors differently than white jurors.

The next morning, Judge Davies rules for the prosecution. The defense immediately wants to invoke *Bateson v. Kentucky* itself, claiming that the prosecution has demonstrated a "consistent pattern of excluding on the basis of race and age, only choosing to exclude whites over the age of fifty." Since the jury pool is overwhelmingly white and middle-aged, Davies dismisses this objection out of hand; soon after, the defense claims to have been contacted by an excluded juror with the news that Juror 598, the Black female postal worker, had made remarks impugning the fairness of the Simi Valley trial. Once again, Davies rules against the defense.

The defense has, in fact, shown a pattern of excluding Black jurors. But Juror 473 probably shouldn't be on the jury anyway. For one thing, he never entered his neighborhood on the questionnaire, and has lived in Watts for twenty-five years. If I heard correctly, he also claimed not to have been personally affected by the riots, had no curiosity about the Rodney King incident when he saw the videotape on TV, and in general seemed willing to say anything that would get him on the jury. Moreover, the defense's objection to Juror 473 is being allowed to stand throughout the proceedings and will surely be cited as one basis for appeal.

On the other hand, the government is playing this case very carefully—because of the videotape, the prosecution in the state trial was disastrously self-assured, a condition the defense seems to be suffering in the present case—and no doubt has a handle on what the standing objection will be worth later on. As far as that goes, Juror 473, who becomes seated Juror 3, has at least as much business on the jury as seated Juror 10, a white male in his thirties who, while working as a security guard, apparently beat up two people, or seated Juror 2, the sixty-something former Marine Corps machinist. Despite the ruling, after 473 no more Black jurors are drawn from the pool and 535, the last person called, is also the last non-Anglo person picked.

"The whole question of juries is going to have to be revisited in this country," Congresswoman Maxine Waters tells me one afternoon in her South Central office. "Somehow we're sliding backwards, in terms of jury selection. We must take a look at how lawyers are able to use this process to exclude potential jurors.

"We're going to have to go back and take a look at what it means to have a jury of your peers, and a change of venue, and all that. I'm not only talking about this case, but the Harold Ford case down in Memphis, where the prosecution convinced the judge that Harold Ford was too popular in Memphis to hold his trial there. So they went a hundred miles away to Jackson, Tennessee, bused in potential jurors to choose who would sit in judgment of this man over in Memphis. We got the Justice Department to intervene, to petition the court not to swear them in. The court disagreed with the Justice Department; as of Monday they swore in eleven white jurors, and one Black juror, from a hundred miles away, from a judicial district that's maybe seventeen percent Black, rather than choosing from Memphis, where the population is forty or fifty percent Black, I think."

When the state of emergency was declared on April 29, 1992, the LAPD began assisting the Immigration and Naturalization Service in sweeps of Los Angeles, in direct violation of laws prohibiting the LAPD from detaining persons based on their immigration status or handing them over to the INS unless they have been charged with multiple or serious misdemeanors or felonies. Six hundred and eighty-one of 747 Mexicans detained were summarily deported—eighty-one Salvadorans, forty-four Guatemalans, twenty-seven Hondurans, four Nicaraguans, four Cubans, three people from Belize, one Italian, and one person from Costa Rica. The following are two of many stories collected by the Central American Refugee Center:

"Lucia A., a 24-year-old woman who is four months pregnant, was walking with her husband on Olympic near Alvarado on Monday, May 4, shortly after midnight, when an LAPD car pulled up and two officers demanded to know the pair's country of origin. When they were unable to produce papers, one of the officers said to her in Spanish, 'You're going to be visiting your country very soon and for free.'

"The officer grabbed her by the hair and pushed her up against a wall, referring to her as a prostitute, and then cuffed her tightly with plastic bands. The day after her arrest, INS presented her with a voluntary departure form and told her she could avoid detention and a high fine if she signed the paper. She signed.

"On May 4, about ten LAPD officers forcibly entered an apartment in Pico Union without a search warrant and began seizing items. The police accused three men in the apartment of looting and demanded Social Security numbers and green cards. All of the residents are legally present in the United States. The men were ordered to produce receipts for all of their belongings, including a television, a stereo, and a radio or face criminal charges for looting."

Somewhere during opening statements, Paul DePasquale enters a motion to dismiss the case against Officer Wind. A number of matters bunged up, some to do with internal affairs transcripts obtained by the prosecution, "avoiding taint from impermissibly compelled statements," violation of Wind's due process, and other opaque issues. These segue into a request from Wind to have his trial separated, on the grounds that DePasquale had once been a law partner of one of the other defense attorneys. This is settled in a nebulous fashion: DePasquale will give his opening remarks after the prosecution rests its case, which means, apparently, that Wind's case will be separated from *US v. Stacey Koon, et al.*, but Wind himself won't.

During a recess, when asked if he is worried about a military doctor on the prosecution's witness list who would testify regarding the blows to Rodney King's head, Stone snaps that there were only five blows to the head, "which was less than five percent of the blows," and furthermore there was "no tissue injury consistent with baton blows." He goes on to claim that the police manual's statement that officers cannot force compliance with baton blows is "nonsense": "We know what they mean but they didn't say it right."

The courtroom is packed, and it is quickly evident that the arched ceiling makes the cramped space look very big. Exhibits—equipment checkout sheets from Foothill police station, a map of the Foothill area, etc.—are blown up so large that if they're shown to the jury neither the lawyers nor the judge can see them. So the defense, the prosecution, and the judge all have video monitors planted in front of them, and the clutter at the front of the room resembles the jungle of wires, cameras, and lights that confront the studio audience of a television talk show: you're there, but you can hardly see anything.

Prosecutor Clymer's opening remarks are accompanied in places by the world-famous Rodney King videotape, which is, by the way, in color, though it's usually shown in an enhanced black-and-white version.

Rodney King was speeding on the 210 Freeway in a 1988 Hyundai XL at approximately 12:30 a.m., with a patrol car in pursuit. His blood alcohol level was high. He was on parole for a robbery. He left the freeway at the Paxton Street off-ramp, and pulled off the road near the intersection of Foothill and Osborne.

Powell and Wind pulled up in their car. The passengers in Rodney King's car got out and laid down on the ground. King forgot to take his seat belt off, and his first attempt to leave the car was hampered by the seat belt.

Other officers had arrived. King was given different commands from different locations. He knelt on the ground. He resisted Powell's attempt to handcuff him, knocking Powell off his back.

Koon fired his Taser, a battery-powered device with a toggle switch that, when pressed, launches two darts. The darts won't operate if they land in clothing—they have to connect with flesh. Then, when the toggle switch is held down, the darts send 50,000 volts of electricity into the suspect. (The LAPD trains its officers not to rely on Tasers.)

We see King's muscles convulsing. After five to ten seconds the Tasers wore off.

George Holliday was filming the event from his balcony. On this copy of the tape, the FBI has installed a date- and time-counter in the upper right frame.

Rodney King's car is in the middle of the screen. We see Powell knock King to the ground with his PR-24 side-handle baton. (The LAPD prohibits officers from hitting suspects with batons or kicking them to make them obey orders.) Powell continues to strike him in the face. (Unless lives are threatened, LA police cannot hit suspects in the face or head.) King tries to get up, but Powell knocks him down. Briseno reaches over and touches Powell's baton to restrain him. King falls to the ground and stays there. (If a person poses a threat, officers may use more and more force, but must de-escalate force when the suspect ceases to threaten.) The officers yell for King to put his hands behind his back. King attempts to. Briseno stomps on his neck. King sits up on one of his legs. Wind kicks King as Powell continues beating him with the baton. Powell gives Briseno a set of handcuffs. Briseno throws King from his seated position to a prone position on the ground and handcuffs him.

A blizzard of radio and computer messages between the patrol cars and Foothill station:

Powell describes King as the "victim of a..."

Koon: "... victim of a beating..."

Powell laughs.

Koon sends a message over a Mobile Digital Terminal: "Bigtime use of force."

Powell: "Ooops!... I haven't beaten anyone this bad in a long time."

Rodney King was taken to Pacifica Hospital, but only partially treated there: a doctor going off his shift stitched up the inside of his mouth. At the suggestion of Powell, apparently, the doctor wrote on the medical report that King was on PCP.

Powell and Wind were to transfer King from Pacifica to County-USC Medical Center. They left Pacifica with King at 3:30 a.m. They arrived at County at 5:30. During the two-hour lag, they drove King to Foothill station. Powell left King in the car with Wind, went into the station, and got other officers to go out and look at King.

When Powell and Wind finally got King to County Medical, they told the emergency room nurse the PCP story. Blood and urine samples taken at the time showed that King had no PCP in his system.

Rodney King's right cheekbone was broken in three places. His right and left maxillary sinuses were smashed. His zygomatic arch was broken. He had facial nerve damage. His leg was broken. He had multiple contusions.

The prosecution says that Powell and Wind changed the log at Foothill station to read 4:45 instead of 3:30 as the time they left Pacifica Hospital. That contrary to regulations, Koon never entered a report of the beating on his sergeant's log.

The defense strategy is clear as creek water: Rodney King is a bad person, a convicted felon, who, driving while intoxicated, led the police on a terrifying, eight-mile high-speed chase, and then resisted arrest. Despite the heroic restraint exercised by the defendants, King literally forced them to beat him senseless. Salzman tells the jury that Koon did nothing illegal, indeed he upheld the standards of the LAPD and even exceeded them. True, King's blood test showed no PCP, but police are taught to rely upon reasonable observations, and the LAPD has standard procedures it follows when "objective symptoms of PCP" are observed.

What are the objective symptoms of PCP? Profuse sweating. Rodney King waving at a police helicopter overhead, like King Kong swatting at the airplanes. Los Angeles police officers are tested on how to conduct themselves around PCP users. They must not, for example, go in for a "tie-up," i.e., physical contact. In a tie-up, an officer's weapon is too close to the subject, who may grab hold and shoot him. Salzman cites the "idea of the officer's weapon retention." This is, he stresses, for the safety of the suspect. The beating with batons and the stunning with Tasers—surefire methods of avoiding a tie-up—were done to prevent escalation to deadly force.

Salzman's presentation, and the one following it by Stone, seems designed to conflate the alleged perception of PCP use with the real thing, to convey the idea that Rodney King, though he wasn't on PCP, manifested the supposed superhuman strength of someone on PCP, so he might as well have been on it. The image of the brute Black superman being evoked has heavy overtones of Willie Horton; I'm not sure about the jury, but I remember from the years I lived in Los Angeles how often the PCP defense used to cover all sorts of egregious acts by the LAPD. Back in the mid-'70s, the police shot a naked man on Silver Lake Boulevard, something like thirteen times, claiming that he seemed to be on PCP, struck a karate pose (rendering his body itself a deadly weapon), and would not obey their commands. The man was deaf, as it turned out.

The defense has prepared its own version of the videotape: on one go-round, pan of the screen is masked to "eliminate camera movement." Second time around, even more of the frame is blocked from view to isolate the action. Another time the image has been enhanced for better contrast. In slow motion—we are fated, today, to see the Holliday videotape in every conceivable permutation—the beating looks like an underwater ballet, and the cause-and-effect relationship between the baton blows and Rodney King's reactions unravels visually. At normal speed, though, it looks like a bunch of cops beating up a helpless drunk. Clymer and Kowalski, unlike the Simi Valley team, have figured this out; they also realize that the tape has much more impact if the lights are lowered in the courtroom.

Even better than the doctored video, the defense has worked up a sort of countervideotape, a montage of colorized black-and-white photos, with cars matted in, illustrating the high-speed chase that led up to King's beating; these show the intersections, freeway off-ramps, and other landmarks the chase involved, shot from several angles. The emphasis is on red lights the suspect ran, endangered vehicles along the path of the chase, and the efforts of CHP, the Unified School District, and the LAPD to apprehend King. By dramatizing the duration of the chase and its potential dangers to pedestrians and motorists and depicting the chaotic and uncoordinated movements of the three law enforcement units as a concerted effort worthy of Interpol or the FBI Bomb Squad, Salzman apparently hopes to transform a traffic violation into a major felony.

Rodney King "had a blank stare and just looked through" the officers. He "swayed back and forth like a drunk on New Year's Eve." King was "patting the ground." While Koon "verbalized," King "grabbed his ass"—his own ass—and shook it at a female officer of the CHP, Melanie Singer. King "continued to resist" after being hit with the Taser. In fact, he "stood up and started dancing."

So far we have a Black convicted felon, DWI, possessed of superhuman strength because of the PCP he wasn't on, waving at helicopters as if to pull them down from the sky, who makes an obscene gesture at a lady cop and has the effrontery, or just the natural rhythm, to get up and dance after being electrified. And we have the slowed-down, cropped, masked, and wobble-corrected video that shows, not Rodney King being beaten, but Rodney King refusing to lie entirely flat enough to satisfy Koon, Powell, Wind, and Braun—and twenty other cops standing around watching—that he was truly defenseless. It's rather like seeing the Zapruder film while someone explains how John F. Kennedy assassinated Lee Harvey Oswald.

But the best moment of the day comes when Braun explains that Ted Briseno is "right-footed," and is therefore bracing on his strong foot while resting his weaker foot on Rodney King's neck. Braun then holds up a boot. The boot looks a little like a high-top Nike Air. This is not, Braun tells the jury, the exact boot worn by his client on March 3, 1991, but it is similar, as they can see, it's very lightweight. Briseno's actual boot, however, was even lighter than this boot. It was, Braun says, "almost like a ballet slipper."

Since day one, it's been apparent that the defense feels it did all its work in the Simi Valley trial. Having won once by slowing down the video and adding its exegesis, it has approached the federal case with nothing new. The prosecution, on the other hand, has made several preemptory strikes against the kind of thing that went over with the Simi Valley jury, admitting at the outset that Rodney King was drunk, that in the first few minutes of the incident he did indeed give the officers trouble, that he was on parole for a felony—his fear of going back to jail for parole violation being his reason for not pulling over in the first place—but stressing repeatedly that whatever kind of person Rodney King might be, he is not on trial, and the thing that must be decided is whether excessive force used by the LAPD violated his civil rights. The fact that he was not on PCP, verified by the blood and urine tests taken at County Medical, gets underlined so often in the prosecution's opening remarks that the jury may well view the defense's interminable observations about PCP as irrelevant.

And the prosecution has new witnesses, including Rodney King himself, who does not lose his composure on the stand, sticks to well-rehearsed answers under intense baiting by the defense lawyers, and has lost a considerable amount of weight—he so little resembles the angry giant of legend the defense feels it has to show the jury photographs of King with a few more pounds on him. His uncertainty about whether the officers called him "killer" or "nigger" doesn't damage his veracity nearly as much as the sound of the word "nigger" in the courtroom damages the defense case. And his admission, when asked to read back testimony, that he cannot read, simply makes him seem more a pathetically helpless victim.

The prosecution's claim that Powell brought King to Foothill station instead of County Medical in order to display him to other officers gets shot out of the water by an Officer Gonzales, who turns out to be the only cop who viewed King at Foothill, on his own initiative. On the other hand, the defense's claim that King was taken to Foothill for "remote booking," and that doing so even saved time in getting King checked into County Medical, sounds extremely suspicious—why not simply have County alerted via police radio? Prosecution witness Dr. Harry Smith, an expert in biomedical engineering with degrees in medicine and a background in physics and mechanics, testifies that at least three of King's head injuries were caused by baton blows rather than impact on the pavement as the defense has been claiming. If King had simply fallen as per the defense, his nose would have been broken, but it wasn't.

There is, additionally, eyewitness testimony from neighbors, and from members of a band who passed the scene of the incident in a bus; the Simi Valley trial had no eyewitness testimony. The use-of-force expert produced by the prosecutors, Mark John Conta, is exactly the sort of gung-ho, streetwise cop—he worked in South Central for a year—likely to impress the conservative, mostly white jurors.

But as the Simi Valley verdict proved, you never can tell.

Research assistance: Ed Leibowitz

•

CLOSING TIME

LOS ANGELES—"OK, I live in the Hollywood Hills. So I can be away from all the crap." The woman driving me to the radio station in Pasadena was, like so many people I encountered that week, considering a little vacation. The short-term goal was a little time off just before the verdicts. The long-term goal, maybe depending on how the verdicts played in "the community"—that mythic place where everybody else lives—was departure on a permanent basis. A poll published that week claimed that a majority of Angelenos would move elsewhere if the possibility presented itself.

"A week ago I start hearing gunshots, like, every night, coming from behind the house. And I think 'I do not live here to experience this.' You know? It's either a crime spree in the neighborhood, or somebody doing target practice.

"I visit these friends, and there's a loaded gun on the coffee table in their living room. Their teenage daughter's alone in the house. I said, 'Nicole, what is a loaded gun doing out here?' She said, 'When the shit comes down again we have to defend ourselves.' I said, 'Are you people crazy?'"

In the closing days of the trial of the four police officers accused of violating Rodney King's civil rights, it was impossible to get through a conversation without mentioning the current status of *US v. Stacey C. Koon, et al.* In a surprise move, the defense rested Thursday morning, April 1, without calling officers Timothy Wind, Laurence Powell, or Ted Briseno to the witness stand, leaving the prosecution very little to rebut. The trial suddenly churned into overdrive; gun sales in Los Angeles County hit a peak.

That afternoon the prosecution moved to show the jury a video of Ted Briseno's testimony in the earlier Simi Valley trial. In that case Briseno had characterized Powell and Wind as "out of control," and said Koon had failed to report the use of force as required by the LAPD. The prosecutors had stated their intention to do this early in the trial, but it had been supposed they would show the tape, or attempt to show it, while presenting their case, rather than during rebuttal. Judge John Davies ruled to allow the tape, providing the government confer with him and the defense over the weekend to decide which bits of Briseno's testimony were admissible. As Davies delivered this decision, Briseno's attorney, Harland Braun, popped up from his seat at least four times to object; Judge Davies finally told him that the Ninth Circuit Court of Appeals was right across the street, and that he should go find a judge to overrule him and issue a writ, to "take it off my shoulders."

I was traveling to promote a book. People who interviewed me started with questions about my novel and inevitably swerved to the King trial, and the almost desperate question, "You've been in that courtroom, what's going to happen?" It was useless to say that the atmosphere of the courtroom was one of vertiginous queasiness and crushing boredom, that the jury was utterly opaque and looked like what you'd see if you sliced a crosstown bus in half and peered in, that the prosecutors were extremely competent but had to operate with less than a full deck of admissible evidence.

It was also useless to say that in this case, as in so many others, reality and the law have collided in a way that exposes the contradictions of the system we live in—of any system, really, where masses of people are kept in check by fear of the police and the threat of incarceration or execution, rather than by a shared sense of possibility.

Los Angeles is a city whose gross physical expansion in the past twenty years has been predicated on the segregation of the underclass from the cash nexus. In LA, the white population has become a minority, and the wealthiest part of that minority sees itself embattled in much the same way that the white minority of South Africa does. It feels threatened not only by the jobless young Black men who have left hopelessly underfunded schools in South Central to join gangs, but also by the economic alliances between African Americans, Asians, and Hispanics likely to form in the next decade, if the city itself doesn't further disintegrate into Balkanized war zones.

LA feels as if it's wobbling between halting efforts at multicultural accommodation and Bosnia-Herzegovina. Most of the old power structure seems to prefer the latter. In the mayoral race you have Richard Riordan, a millionaire industrialist, who wants to lease LAX and contract out most of the city's functions to private companies, the way Detroit was sold to private interests in *Robocop*. You have Joel Wachs, duenna of Tribeca and the Valley, calling for the National Guard and military occupation during jury deliberations in the police officers' trial, enhanced security for white homeowners' associations, and the breakup of the Unified School District. Across most of the mayoral spectrum the themes are "putting more cops on the street," diversifying the capital base, and an implicit endorsement of trickle-down economics. In other words, protect our investments with more cops and we'll take care of South Central when LA is out of bankruptcy. Only Michael Woo seems to offer a coalition-building, Clintonian program. He will probably win, but we are already seeing the weaknesses of the Clinton approach. Tom Bradley was good at coalition building, too, and, like Sam Yorty before him, sold out most of his constituencies to real estate developers.

As for *US v. Stacey Koon*, apart from the defense lawyers and the defendants themselves, I never encountered a single person in LA who thought the police should be uniformly acquitted. Most favored a split verdict: conviction for Koon and Powell, a lesser conviction for Tim Wind, acquittal or some mild penalty for Briseno. I did not see how the jury could possibly acquit all four officers. But absolutely nobody thought they would be acquitted in the Simi Valley trial either, so the general expectation is now running the other way. I wanted not to agree with the American Civil Liberties Union that *US v. Koon* constituted a case of double jeopardy (in this instance, who cares?) and at the same time thought that if acquittals came in again, Los Angeles would've been put through a judicial charade, a cruel joke that simply underscored the realities of Southern California: that no white cop ever goes to jail for violence against a person of color, that the LAPD mainly exists to beat up erratic drivers and to keep the 17 percent African American population out of affluent neighborhoods, and that the "wake-up call" of last year's insurrection (which, perhaps more than any other single factor, handed Clinton the backing of the nation's power elite) merely inspired a heavier application of cosmetics to a festering wound. Wake-up to makeup.

Nor did I understand the willingness of people everywhere to assume that widescale rioting would break out as soon as the verdicts were read: surely the riots would come later, probably in August, if the Reginald Denny matter goes from jury selection to verdict by then. The constant flaunting of combat readiness by the LAPD, the National Guard, the CHP, and the Sheriff's Department pointed in the opposite direction, i.e., an unspoken expectation by the Mayor's Office and law enforcement that the likelihood of massive disturbances was small. As many radical members of the African American community pointed out to me, the entire National Guard would be unable to quell another full-blown rebellion. And, given that LA covers over 700 square miles, even the 8,190-officer LAPD seems inadequate to such an event. But in the event of little happening, it could be claimed that the transformation of Los Angeles into a virtual police state had saved the day.

Assignments, however, had already been made by the wire services, networks, magazines, and newspapers: if you wanted to know which reporters would be at Florence and Normandie or down in Pico Union when the verdicts were read, it was easy enough to find out. There would, no doubt, be a few third-stringers assigned, for comic relief, to Frederick's of Hollywood, and some sidebar people reporting from poolside at the Beverly Hills Hotel.

If rioting does follow the verdicts, whatever they turn out to be, one would have to credit the timing of the judicial process itself, and the mass media, though the causes of last year's disturbances—lately blamed, in a revisionist coup among most of the mayoral candidates, on "bad people" rather than hopeless conditions among the poor whites, Blacks, Latinos, and others who participated—haven't changed an iota.

"The model really appears to be the old patronizing thing, corporations coming down, helping out, chipping in a little bit, rather than long-term stimulus," says Ruben Martinez, author of *The Other Side* and a frequent commentator on the mysteries of LA. "It's not like you can see tangible results. I don't think anybody's at work at a single job that wasn't around before the riots because of Rebuild LA. Given that the economic outlook is still piss-poor, and that that's what set people so much on edge, how can you think there's not going to be another riot eventually, whether it's after the trial or some other occasion?"

Attending any trial for protracted periods of time makes one wearily aware that "justice" is a consensual fiction, a haphazard interpretation of Byzantine legal language by lawyers, judges, and juries, all of whom are, consciously or otherwise, deeply biased, in the sense that "bias" is simply another word for human personality.

For example, it was Judge Davies's particular biased reading of the law that kept out of evidence an incident of 1986, "in which defendant Koon lied about and failed to report a use of force incident." On that occasion, LAPD officers pursued a stolen car. The car crashed. The driver and a seventeen-year-old passenger fled. Koon captured one of the suspects at gunpoint.

According to court document 143, "After Koon apprehended the juvenile, Officers Jang and Sharpe arrived on the scene. Officer Sharpe pushed the juvenile against a wall and punched him in the head. While Officer Sharpe was holding the juvenile, defendant Koon kicked the juvenile twice in the chest. The officers then knocked the juvenile to the ground, handcuffed him, and took him back to the location where the car had crashed.

"The LAPD requires that a 'Use of Force' incident report be completed whenever force is used by a police officer. Koon falsely replied that no force was used."

In a related order, Judge Davies excluded from evidence a 1990 incident cited in court document 145, in which defendant Laurence Powell and his partner "detained a juvenile and his companion for jaywalking. When the juvenile's companion ran away, Powell and his partner handcuffed the juvenile, placed him in the rear seat of the patrol car, and drove away in search of the companion...

"Powell's partner hit the juvenile in the chest with his elbow. Defendant Powell stopped the car, opened the rear passenger door, and began to punch the still-handcuffed juvenile with his fist, cursing him as he did so. Defendant Powell struck the juvenile repeatedly, bloodying his face.... At the station, defendant Powell falsely reported that the juvenile's injuries resulted from his own resistance while being handcuffed."

Even Ted Briseno, arguably the least culpable of the four defendants, has a prior history of stomping, also kept out of evidence by Judge Davies. In 1987, a child-abuse suspect named Daniel Foster was restrained in his apartment doorway by two police officers. This incident is outlined in court document 144: Briseno arrived at the arrest scene, "grabbed Foster, forcing the rookie officer to lose his grip. Foster began to resist again in response to Briseno's intervention.... Briseno took Foster to the ground, where Foster was handcuffed behind his back as he lay prone on his stomach.

"While Foster laid on the ground, Briseno struck him twice with the baton. At least one of the blows connected with the back of Foster's head. Briseno stopped striking Foster only after the veteran officer told him to.... Shortly thereafter... with what the rookie officer described as a 'stomp,' or a 'sharp, rapid' downward movement of his foot, defendant Briseno caused Foster's head to 'thump on the ground.' The stomp occurred while Foster lay prone, handcuffed, and unresisting."

The rookie cop was later able to recognize Briseno in the Rodney King video simply because he'd "know that kick anywhere."

For every item of evidence introduced in the trial, there is at least one and sometimes many that've been left out: deleted draft passages from Koon's memoir of the King incidents, *Presumed Guilty*, in which Koon referred to King's apparent buttshaking motion as a potential "Mandingo sexual encounter" between

King and Officer Melanie Singer, for instance. Sifting through the documents of the case, one can construct many alternative cases. But the jury doesn't know that, and as far as it is concerned, Koon, Powell, and Briseno are first-time offenders.

On Tuesday, April 6, Ted Briseno's Simi Valley testimony is duly shown, a day after the Ninth Circuit Court denies the writ requested by the defense lawyers. It's hard to make out the video from any part of the spectator section, since much of it consists of Ted Briseno's hand and arm, in extreme right frame, pointing to sections of the Holliday videotape of the beating: we are watching a monitor within a monitor, the beating tape even smaller and less distinct than it usually appears, with voiceovers.

Dramatic as Briseno's earlier version of events is—Powell's baton strike "was not accidental," King made "no combative movement," Briseno moved to stop Powell because he believed Powell "would keep beating and beating"—and despite its contradiction of most of the defense's case, it's hard to imagine that anyone in this courtroom hasn't long ago reached his or her saturation level. I catch myself looking away from Wind's attorney Paul DePasquale's monitor, to Laurence Powell's father, a stocky, nice-looking man who usually sports one of three differently colored Mickey Mouse ties, but today is wearing one with a sort of Vorticist design. The only jury member I'm ever able to focus on is a big-bellied blond man with long hair on his face and head, who always wears T-shirts and looks like a retired Hell's Angel.

After the lunch break, Briseno's attorney, Harland Braun, attempts a bit of his usual inane humor, circulating an anonymous note that reads, "Judge Davies asked me to give you this so you can be an even bigger prick." Below Braun's scrawl is an ad for a "Male Enlargement" device.

Testimony drones along. Yes, Briseno saw misconduct by Koon. He thought Koon had reported the use of force and only discovered later that he hadn't. Briseno was afraid of Rodney King, who was "twice his size." (True. Briseno is tiny.) He did think

Rodney King might be on PCP. He told Powell to "get the hell off" King, several times.

The defense gets a "sur-rebuttal" the next day, which Judge Davies crops from three to two witnesses in hopes of getting the case to the jury by the weekend. First, we have Daniel Sullivan, a deputy chief of police in the Valley between 1961 and 1986; he testifies that in 1982 the upper-body control hold was "taken away as a police resource." At the time, Sullivan said it was "preposterous to do away with the one tool that prevented having to beat people into submission."

As Sullivan testifies, I notice that a sketch artist sitting in front of me has made a feature-perfect sketch of the entire jury, contrary to the orders of the judge. I'm not sure, but I guess this means he's committing a federal crime. We'll probably get the sketch on TV after the trial closes.

Prosecutor Steven Clymer, a certified dreamboat whose composure throughout the trial has perhaps swayed the jury more effectively than the histrionics and jokecracking on the other side, deflates Sullivan's testimony with a few questions about why the upper-body hold was removed from the LAPD repertoire: too many suspects were choked to death. (And, parens mine, the city had to pay out too many millions in wrongful-death suits.)

The last witness is Sergeant Stacey Koon, who states under questioning by Michael Stone that he placed himself "on the outer perimeter" of the King incident. There, he "could be more objective in my analysis of what was going on." He was about twelve feet away from the first baton blow. His "best recollection" is that this blow connected with King's right clavicle. Koon supposedly yelled, "Don't hit him in the head!" No baton blows hit King in the head.

Clymer, on cross, brings up Koon's memoir, in which he writes that Briseno "gave a false motivation for his own behavior." Koon, however, is now conciliatory, since Briseno has recanted his Simi Valley testimony, claiming that after viewing the "registered videotape"—the one worked up by the defense from the Holliday video—he believes that excessive force was not used. Different officers, Koon magnanimously states, have different perceptions. And that's a wrap. The next day will be taken up with instructions to the jury, followed by closing arguments. As we leave the courtroom the reporter from a great metropolitan newspaper of record asks *LA Weekly*'s Ed Leibowitz if those will be important to cover. Leibowitz, whose reports on the trial have been scalpel-sharp and vastly more insightful than those of the mainstream press, drolly replies that since the jury instructions determined the outcome in Simi Valley, they might indeed be worth dropping in on. (Several of the mainstream trial reporters could be seen on any given day congenially lunching with the defense attorneys in the courthouse cafeteria, which gives you an idea what kinds of stories provided continuing access to Messrs. Salzman, Stone, DePasquale, and Braun.) In closing, the defense is up first. Michael Stone delivers a four-hour rhapsody to the unsung ardors of police work. That his client laughed and bragged about the King beating for hours afterwards is no more damning, according to Stone, than the giggling fits some people experience at funerals. Koon's attorney, Ira Salzman, who delivers a rambling, incomprehensible soliloquy running for three and a half hours, at one point weirdly compares the prosecution's use of Briseno's videotaped testimony to the "my sister, my daughter" scene in *Chinatown*. DePasquale, more or less abandoning any solidarity with the other defendants, paints his client, Timothy Wind, as the hapless rookie who fell into bad company. Just following orders while his supervisors went bonkers.

Finally, Harland Braun, dependably grandiose and sophomoric, compares Ted Briseno to Jesus Christ: two thousand years ago, he notes, another prisoner was brought before a judge amidst widespread rioting, and to calm the rioters... well, as it's Easter Weekend, the analogy couldn't be timelier, or more grotesque. A lucky thing, Braun says, that Prosecutor Clymer wasn't around then—he would've indicted the Apostles!

Prosecutor Clymer is characteristically terse, using the videotape to show that King was not, in fact, charging at Apostle Powell when Powell struck him in the head with a lead baton, something the defense has claimed throughout the trial.

As I write this the case is with the jury, which has picked Juror 5, a real estate salesman thought to be sympathetic to the defense, as its foreman. On its first full day out, the jury requested a transcript of Officer Melanie Singer's testimony—Singer had burst into tears while recounting the King incident. Judge Davies turned down the request, perhaps in the interest of speeding deliberations, instructing the jurors to rely on their memories. (This sounds, off the top of my head, like a fresh basis for appeal in the event of convictions.)

Several jurors have been attending church services. Their priests and ministers have been asked by the US Marshal to refrain from mentioning the trial, the impending verdicts, or the possibility of riots following same. Apparently, the ministers and priests have accommodated this request, no doubt to the complete bewilderment of their congregations. Few pulpits in LA have been addressing anything else for weeks.

By the time you read this, the jury should have reached its verdicts. Whenever they come in, Judge Davies intends to delay reading them, possibly waiting until three in the morning when most people—bad or otherwise—are asleep.

Is LA burning?

(1993)

PIERRE GUYOTAT'S *COMA*

This bizarrely self-effacing and feverishly energized book has few antecedents: Genet's *Journal du voleur*, Augustine's *Confessions*, certain texts that surpass and dissolve the stagecraft of self-presentation (i.e., Schreber's *Memoirs of My Nervous Illness*) with an insistent, pathological engorgement of narrative, a continual demolition of structural elements and distinctions between "I" and others, self and things, places, animals, trees: *Coma* reenacts the physical and psychic crisis Guyotat's writing drives him to, a crisis in which the production of language accompanies the depletion of the author's body, as if the means of writing were his fluids and secretions, continually exhausted and replenished in a febrile state; there is no surplus; Guyotat becomes the stylus and ink with which writing exudes from him, spatters across notebook pages, determined by a demonic economy: the needles of Kafka's torture loom and the body they mutilate are fused like Siamese twins.

The absurdity of memoir as a literary genre is obvious from its recent effulgence. Not simply because the conventional memoir is a tidy bundle of lies, crafted to market a particularized self in a world of commodities (complete with real or invented quirks, cosmeticized memories, failings that mask more important failings, self-exonerating treacheries, sins, crimes); behind its costume of authenticity lies the mercantile understanding that a manufactured self is another dead object of consumption, something assembled by a monadic robot, a "self" that constructs and sells itself by selecting promotional items from a grotesque menu of prefabricated self-parts.

The notion of identity this industrial process takes for granted is one that Guyotat explodes in each sentence. As with Genet's epiphany on the metro, Guyotat recognizes that he is *the same thing as the Other*, the same breathing pustule of snot, semen, piss, shit: this understanding of identity uncovers a truth too intolerable to franchise: that "I" is *nothing special*, and counts as nothing in the chaos of being it briefly occupies and disappears from.

Guyotat's abjection, like that of Simone Weil, is a desire for transcendence that necessarily constitutes a struggle against the body, against physiological need. If this hunger can't be satisfied (how could it?), the animal hunger that chains us to contingency, to our colonization by the social order, has to be ignored, despised to the point of starvation. To nourish ourselves becomes an obscenity if others starve; survival is obscene when the organizing principle of existence is to *kill or be killed*.

I torture because he tortures, he tortures because they torture: Gombrowicz notes that savagery becomes "natural" when practiced by all against all; the atrocities Guyotat replicates in the texts that nearly annihilate him (*Tombeau pour cinq cent mille soldats*; *Eden, Eden, Eden*; *Prostitution*, et al.), the atrocities of Auschwitz and the Algerian War, are the veritable human milieu of twenty-first century globalization, a regression that promises to fill everything and kill everything.

In this situation, Guyotat's "novels" have a desperate and desolate urgency: like Burroughs, Guyotat avoids telling "stories" with escape hatches and oases of safety. He shoves the implacable, documentary reality of the present in our faces. Criticism typically relegates such writing to the slum of science fiction, a specular future that will never arrive—as if the state of emergency we live in can forever be deflected by political delusions and steadily higher doses of cultural morphine.

In Guyotat's case, criticism advises to sample his work in homeopathic doses, as if too much exposure would kill us. In effect, Guyotat's writing operates as a toxin that poisons what's valorized as literature, revealing its emptiness, its uselessness, its falsity. Guyotat spoils the flavor of bourgeois literary writing, like a drug that causes derangement of the senses. If we experience this as liberating rather than terrorizing, we realize the truth of Artaud's declaration that *all writing is pig shit*—an emetic scream that returns language to its original, primal function.

All writing is approximate, all language a substitution; Guyotat's is less distant from what it describes than what readers are conditioned to digest. If we literally can't stomach this language, we should be honest enough to admit it's not Guyotat's failure, but our defense mechanism at work, a deceit we practice in order not to go mad.

But in a reality turned upside down, to paraphrase Guy Debord, it is necessary to go mad to arrive at sanity. Guyotat undermines our relation to fixed ideas and a code of sentiments that literature has inscribed on us since the nineteenth century. This lubricant of the class system is a law of enclosures that invests emotion in accumulation and consumption. It should be the function of writing to expose this corruption of feeling—to destroy alienation, so far as that's even possible any longer. Guyotat is one of the few living writers who attempts this (Fernando Vallejo is another); if he liberally refers to the arduous effort involved, it's less a matter of egoism than a brittle assertion of fact. He doesn't confuse himself with Christ but identifies with what the social order treats as refuse. The journey of *Coma*, if it is one, is a progression toward the prelapsarian, a recovery of what we were before the Fall: something of the world instead of some exceptional thing in it.

This text, which eludes any category of literature, is an unexampled effusion of tenderness that can perhaps only be read through the prism of Guyotat's other texts: the author is present, an immolated "I" existing in what remains when the habitual comforts and distractions of false consciousness have been ripped away: "*a voice that tears off its bandages.*"

Coma erases time as diachrony. A horizontal text, as a comatose body is horizontal, its memories and perceptions available at the same moment. In this condition the torments of life no longer hurt us, we are free to remember what has happened to us without the pain of going on with things, and everything we have lost is present again.

A friend, who later died, fell into a coma for ten days after an operation; several friends gathered every day around his hospital bed, talked to him as if he were listening; they interpreted his nods and eye movements as evidence of his mute but entirely conscious participation in what I considered a *death-averse cocktail party*. I didn't believe what they told me (that he responded to jokes, for instance, or welcomed their embraces), though I know they believed it themselves.

Later, during four months when he was declared "cured" of the cancer that finally killed him, I explained that I didn't visit him in the hospital because, if he couldn't talk *with* me, or communicate in some other, unmistakable way, I had to assume he was unconscious.

He said that, for those ten days, he was completely unaware of his surroundings or the people in his room; he didn't know he was in a hospital, until he woke from what he described as "a dream, with everything that happened in my life swimming through my mind, dead and living people both, *outside of time*"—this occurred five years ago. Six years earlier, when my mother became comatose, in a hospital in New Hampshire, six months before her death, she asked, through the veil of what was palpably a dream state, where my father was (my father had been dead for ten years), and begged me to call *her* mother (dead for thirty years). Guyotat's is the only book I know that convincingly elaborates this intermediate state between life and death.

(2010)

BARBET AND KOKO:
AN EQUIVOCAL LOVE AFFAIR

Barbet Schroeder is a director who prefers the appellation "explorer" to that of "auteur," and again and again his films demonstrate both his intense curiosity about the unexplored and his willingness to allow material he discovers to speak for itself, leaving the viewer to draw whatever inferences this material suggests.

He is not, however, a witness without ideas—if anything, Schroeder's craft reflects an acute awareness of the implications inherent in his films, both fiction and nonfiction. What makes Schroeder a consummately generative filmmaker is his fastidious neutrality, his conviction that it's not his job to make things tidy and comforting for his audiences.

Even the neonoir thrillers Schroeder made in Hollywood, such as *Desperate Measures* (1998), *Single White Female* (1992), and *Kiss of Death* (1995), reflect his aversion to pat moralisms. The characters in these films, like his documentary subjects, reveal his idea that every person is an unstable compound of "good" and "evil," a mixture of negative and positive qualities in varying proportions, which can become catastrophically unbalanced by a blinding sense of being absolutely "right" when we're convinced that others are absolutely "wrong." The seemingly or relatively innocent casually expose character flaws that are grossly magnified in their nemeses, contradictions that seem ready-made to activate the wrath and criminal ingenuity of people they've less-than-innocently fallen in with (consider the massive carnage that Andy Garcia takes in stride while hellbent on securing a bone-marrow transplant for his son from protean killer Michael Keaton in *Desperate Measures*). If the unfolding of these stories turns unimaginably disastrous, their logic emanates precisely from the lack of a rigorous demarcation between "right" and "wrong."

Schroeder's documentary films nimbly avoid pedantry or parti pris, though the viewer can infer his sympathies in *Koko: A Talking Gorilla* (1978), just as one can imagine his amused horror while recording the hair-raising self-portrait he gave Ugandan dictator Idi Amin Dada free rein to perform on celluloid. Schroeder is well aware that life is not a narrative; that we impose form on the movements of chance, contingency, and impulse; that documentaries are notoriously slippery, since what the camera catches never coincides with even the most flexible script, but ultimately determines its own form. In his unpredictable daily encounters with Koko and her teacher, Dr. Penny Patterson, Schroeder foregrounds the quiddity of Koko's situation, in episodic fashion. Scenes of teaching sessions in language recognition, displays of abstract thought, and demonstrations of Koko's ability to recognize human speech as well as sign language carry voice-over commentary elucidating the scientific issues the Gorilla Foundation's experiments address and hope to settle—the most important, in many ways, being a revised definition of "personhood."

This film poses questions about our relationship to other species, discomforting questions most readily addressed to higher primates, whose genetic resemblance to human beings is so close that our descent from them seems indisputable. These questions are raised in the intermittent narration threaded through documentary scenes of Koko's daily activities, and in interviews with other primate researchers. In this respect, Schroeder's technique is not especially unconventional (though the cinematography of longtime collaborator Nestor Almendros gives *Koko* an atmosphere of intimate immediacy unusual in this kind of film). Schroeder's subject, however, is full of idiosyncratic freshness and appeal. *Koko*, in its undidactic way, can be related to contemporaneous investigations of language acquisition, both in academia and popular culture, inspired by the widespread influence of Ludwig Wittgenstein's radical interrogation of "language games" and Noam Chomsky's linguistic theories about innate syntactical structures. Many of these explorations sought further proofs of Darwinian evolution by discovering "intermediate forms of language" among higher primates, while others investigated the alleged development of "private languages" between culturally isolated children, a phenomenon documented by Jean-Pierre Gorin, two years after *Koko*, in his brilliant film *Poto and Cabengo*, about twins raised in Linda Vista, California, in a household where all the adults spoke a mélange of German and English in extremely defective ways.

In Darwin's least-known important book, *The Expression of the Emotions in Man and Animals*, he demonstrates that all animals "talk"; that the higher species all use the same morphologies of facial expressions, the same muscles, to convey emotional and mental states; that the physical motions of dogs and cats, as well as primates, have distinct meanings that can be "read" by one another, by other animals, and, if we study them, by humans as well. Can the mountain gorilla, and other higher primates, communicate needs, wishes, thoughts, in a manner that both they and humans can understand? Can a gorilla trained in sign language and able to comprehend thousands of human utterances transmit this language to other gorillas? Since the outset of Patterson's experiments with Koko, thirty-four years ago, some of these questions seem to have been answered affirmatively (though the Gorilla Foundation's claims about the transmission of human language from one gorilla to another seem at best exaggerated). Yet the quality of this communication, and the highly specialized circumstances in which it has been inculcated, raise troubling questions of their own.

Despite ambitious projects that the Gorilla Foundation has launched in Cameroon and other parts of Africa, the ongoing destruction of habitat and the decimation of gorillas, along with that of most other endangered species (for food, by their capture for zoos, by deforestation of their enclaves), anticipates an imminent future in which the only remaining refuge for these magnificent creatures will be nonindigenous conservancies, such as the seventy-acre Maui Preserve currently under construction. Seventy acres sounds like a lot; however, quite a few of the world's wealthy entertainers, corporate elite, and scions of vast fortunes own twenty times as much pristine, unused property. Without sufficient habitat, any species "preserved" in circumscribed space, in inadequately variegated clans, will eventually exhaust its genetic diversity.

I don't mean to suggest that Patterson and the Gorilla Foundation aren't engaged in a noble endeavor. I fear it may, in time, prove a quixotic one, a worthy bulwark against inevitable extinction.

Schroeder made his film in the early days of Koko's education, when Patterson and her colleagues had already made surprising discoveries about interspecies communication. Koko had, for example, already learned to manipulate a ViewMaster, to indicate her desire for objects that were not visible to her, to use sign language to invent names for actions and things. Unfortunately, female gorillas will only mate when females outnumber males, a situation Patterson hopes to effect at the Maui Preserve. While Koko developed affectionate bonds with Michael and Ndume, males introduced to the limited habitat in Woodside, California, she was unwilling to mate with either.

In an essay I commissioned from Schroeder in 1993, for a Faber and Faber anthology, *Living with the Animals*, the director provided some astonishing observations about his own interactions with Koko: that she quickly understood she was being filmed, and even learned to start the camera, and behaved differently when it was running; she "performed more." Schroeder attributes "real star quality" to Koko, and there's no question that Koko, like Idi Amin Dada—a very different kind of iconic anomaly—is continually fascinating to watch, extravagantly expressive, and even a bit of a ham. Schroeder's first concern as a director is to find a compelling subject, but it's just as important to incarnate the subject with the right "star"; the finished script of *Maîtresse* (1973) languished for almost a decade, until Schroeder found Gérard Depardieu—for him, the only possible actor to play the male lead. With *Koko*, fortuitously, subject and star were the same thing, which was also true of *General Idi Amin Dada* (1974).

Koko can, contrary to popular lore, recognize her own image in a mirror. In 2005, the American Society of Magazine Editors selected Koko's self-portrait, shot in a mirror with an Olympus camera, for *National Geographic*, as one of the top forty magazine covers of the last forty years. She has taken loving care of several pets, including kittens and dogs. Though her first kitten, All-Ball, died in 1984, Koko continues to miss her: "Even thumbing through picture books of cats that look like her kitty, she does react with emotional words like frown and sad," Patterson said.

Schroeder's film is not so much skeptical as grounded in realism. We would need to ignore the evidence of our senses, the evidence of the camera, to believe that no degree of wishful thinking enters into Patterson's interpretation of some of Koko's behavior. It's doubtful, to say the least, that Koko would be "happier" in the San Francisco Zoo, from which she was purchased after extensive litigation. At the same time, Koko's intimate dependence on Patterson over several decades unavoidably raises the question: What would Koko do if her teacher became, for one reason or another, incapacitated or unavailable? Is the highly unnatural situation Koko has spent most of her life in the only one in which she could survive?

For the truth is that Koko has become unique among her species—as the Gorilla Foundation website has it, "Ambassador for an Endangered Species"—and, despite numerous other, similar primate study projects elsewhere, and the presence of some other mountain gorillas at Woodside, somewhat plangently isolated from her own kind. She is a "celebrity," obliged to appear on children's shows like *Mister Rogers' Neighborhood* and to give somewhat dyslexic interviews, with Patterson's help, to internet audiences on AOL.

Of course, the gaudily decorated, shopping-mall aspect of the foundation's website is the necessary, quotidian means for raising money for a desperately needed sanctuary in Hawaii. But the coarse marketing of an extraordinary gorilla to rescue the vanishing wildlife of our planet depressingly heightens the feeling that nature itself is fated for extinction, since only an improbable volte-face, a reversal of the indifferent depredations of the human race, could possibly produce a less than entropic result.

In *Koko: A Talking Gorilla*, Barbet Schroeder takes no pleasure in such meditations, nor does he give explicit voice to the direst of dire scenarios the film, thirty years on, suggests to its viewers. His film is a work of stoic empathy.

At the time Schroeder made *Koko*, he "became a fanatic for gorillas." He went to Africa and saw "the horrible things that were happening," which have become infinitely more horrible still. He wrote to Dian Fossey, hoping to visit her camp, and she answered, "Don't even try to come near my camp; I'll shoot you." "And she was right," Schroeder says. "When I understood what was happening, I agreed that it was the only way to do it. But, of course, that was the last stand. Now things are getting much worse than anything she had dreamt in her worst nightmares."

(2006)

MASTERING THE ART OF SOVIET COOKING, BY ANYA VON BREMZEN

Since the decline of the pastoral lay, food writing, with its single-minded focus on the gratification of a primal urge, has become the genre closest to pornography in contemporary literature. Like pornography, food writing's basic vocabulary relies on an insatiability that has nothing to do with literary taste, but with the instant stimulation of desire.

Rich or poor, Black or white, morbidly obese or in the peak of trim, you too can stuff yourself to orgasmic satiety, in fantasy at least, with perfectly broiled, poached, baked, or fried anything, washed down with an earnest Sancerre or full-bodied Merlot, followed by a crisp salad leaf, the cheese platter, and... maybe a little crème brûlée? That many more millions subsist on nettles and garbage than can ever hope to sample the gourmet fetish cuisine du jour is beside the point, as taxes and utility bills are irrelevant to a triple-X three-way: We can dream, can't we?

Food writing's more glamorous media cousin, the TV food program, has its own constellation of stars, dominated, like porn, by women, with a handful of ubiquitous male old reliables, from the Ron Jeremy of gastronomy, Anthony "I'll eat anything" Bourdain, to the more fey and gigglesome, teen-idolish James Deen simulacrum, Jamie Oliver. These TV personalities dominate the literary end of the foodie industry, which has undergone the same memoirist transmutation that imaginative literature in general has, the memoir having upstaged the traditional cookbook just as it has supplanted all but the most formulaic novels in wide popular interest.

Whole bookstore sections are thick with the confessional lucubrations of practically anyone who ever wrote a food column, enrolled in cooking school, or opened a trendy restaurant; every celebrity chef has a tentacular Brand encompassing a fleet of namesake restaurants and upscale food markets stretching from London to Dubai to Guangzhou, with an accessory line of literary products that invariably includes a heartfelt account of the food freak's unlikely, inauspicious beginnings, an emotionally charged eureka moment that reveals to the gourmand-to-be how essential and spiritually improving first-rate food really is, tales of his or her uproariously accident-prone apprenticeship, and, in the most celebrated instances, the eventual, hard-won outcome of becoming richer than God.

These books are frequently written in the breathless, endearingly self-involved register of the movie star tell-all, but just as often reflect intellectual and literary ambitions the author is in no sense capable of realizing. The flap copy of one still-aspiring restauranteur's recent recollections informs us—all too tellingly, it turns out—that while launching an innovative bistro in Williamsburg, she found time to obtain an MFA in "creative writing" at NYU. Cherchez the rocket salad and the duck ravioli, ma cherie.

In truth, the lives of many people seriously involved in eating, preparing, and/or writing of delicious food are not especially worth reading about, however genial and engaging these people may be off the page. Not to pick on Eddie Huong—a nice guy, reputedly—but his recent attempt at a rollicking, irreverent reprise of his early years before opening his splendid eatery Bao, *Fresh Off the Boat*, is symptomatic of the tone-deaf, overconfident, and frankly repellent zest with which contemporary food memoirs are usually sprinkled.

The high altitude of M. F. K. Fisher is seldom attained by any modern food memoirist, as few seem equipped to connect their passion for food with the complicated eros (and, frequently, pathos, and thanatos) involved in ingesting sustenance. In Fisher's writing this is always linked to other things happening at the same time, to vicissitudes of personal and outer history; the transience of emotionally charged dining experiences, and a sense of the unique situations that made them memorable, are more important than the actual food items consumed. Something as negligible as a radiator-dried tangerine emits as much evocative juice as a sybaritic five-course banquet.

Much of Fisher's best writings describes periods of economic depression and wartime rationing; this gives them an emotional texture and sociological resonance largely absent from contemporary food writing, which is all but exclusively pitched to well-off consumers of luxury goods whose inner lives are presumed to be a centimeter deep, their pockets bottomless.

Calling Anya von Bremzen's *Mastering the Art of Soviet Cooking* a stunning exception to the general mediocrity of current foodie memoirs would sell it considerably short. It is a rare instance of a food writer with an epic story to tell, as richly layered as the kulebiaka fish pie depicted in its opening pages as the Tsarist era's culinary apogee. This family chronicle of histrionically complicated Russian lives crammed into stunted Soviet destinies enfolds a history of scarcity and shortages produced by the planned central economy's mercurial tinkerings, and the barter and black market transactions that virtually defined daily survival throughout the USSR's existence; it illustrates, with limpidity and good humor, Sheila Fitzpatrick's observation in *Everyday Stalinism* that "Soviet citizens attempting to live ordinary lives were continually running up against the state in one of its multifarious aspects. Their lives were tossed around by Communist policies: their tempers were tried on a daily basis by incompetent and arbitrary officials, clerks, and salespeople, all working for the state."

Bremzen's writing is poised somewhere between bittersweet, Chekhovian resignation and Gogolian gallows humor. She strikes the comedic note where many writers would lapse into mournful editorializing—like most people genuinely acquainted with grief, she meets life's tragic aspects with stoical asperity and, if possible, a joke. In an almost parodic sense, *Soviet Cooking* takes its cue from Proust, Bremzen's taste memories serving as what she refers to as "poisoned madeleines"; what she recalls as vividly as the dishes of her childhood are the fantasies they activated about more elaborate, tastier versions of them that she could only read about in classic Russian and French literature.

Her family's kulebiaka "shared only the name" of the heroic delicacy for which Gogol supplies a full, over-the-top recipe in *Dead Souls* ("In one corner put the cheeks and dried spine of a sturgeon, in another put some buckwheat, and some mushrooms and onion, and some soft fish roe, and brains, and something else as well..."); theirs was "a modest rectangle of yeast dough, true to Soviet form concealing a barely-there layer of boiled ground meat or cabbage." One of the author's most appealing qualities is her dauntless hedonism, ferreting out pleasure in the less than wonderful: "It now occurs to me that our Sunday kulebiaka... expressed the frugality of our lives as neatly as the grandiose version captured czarist excess. We liked our version just fine. The yeast dough was tasty, especially with Mom's thin vegetarian borscht..."

Peripatetic, sophisticated, imbued with very Russian, fatalistic hilarity, dreamlike in its summoning of family personalities and their eccentric histories, *Soviet Cooking* is formally organized—a bit loosely—as the record of a recent year-long project Anya undertook with her mother, Larisa, with whom she emigrated from the USSR to America in 1974: a series of meals, serving to friends the culinary quintessence of Soviet life decade by decade, starting prior to the Revolution with "our archival adieu to classic Russian cuisine"—horseradish vodka, caviar, kvass, "an anachronistic chilled fish and greens soup called *botvinya*," and the aforementioned kulebiaka, à la Gogol. According to Bremzen, the first years of the twentieth century saw an effusion of gourmet excess in the restaurants of her native Moscow, a food culture that vanished after Russia's disastrous entry into World War I, becoming a distant memory during the Civil War and the subsequent era of War Communism.

The archetypal meals of each era occasion a freight of reflections, historical illuminations, family narratives; one is immediately made aware of the intimate connection between private life and the State, the daily effects of a hierarchical, realigned system favoring the Party and its members first, obedient urbanites second, and the restive agrarian peasantry—a vast 80 percent of the Soviet population—least.

The Bolsheviks did not place any importance on what they ate, and decided that others could get by with a lot fewer calories than they were used to. Food was considered mere fuel for *Homo sovieticus*—and, after the Revolution, was scarce in any form. Moreover, the brief, early Soviet emphasis on women's emancipation from kitchen slavery had the unfortunate side effect that an entire generation of Russians became contemptuous of culinary effort and basically forgot how to cook. (Only a few years after this liberation, women were expected to hold jobs *and* perform all domestic labor.) Lenin ("Mr. Stale Bread and Weak Tea"), who ate whatever his dreary spouse Krupskaya plopped in front of him, presided over the herding of urban Soviets into communal apartments where any number of unrelated citizens were obliged to share bathrooms and kitchens. Public canteens served set meals featuring "soup with rotten sauerkraut, unidentifiable meat (horse?), gluey millet, and endless vobla, the petrified dried Caspian roach fish."

"The very notion of pleasure from flavorsome food was reviled as capitalist degeneracy," the author notes. Even in the Kremlin the doleful effect of official policy on dining was felt, as the State, like everybody else, "was not supposed to procure from private sources"—though according to Bremzen, in the winter of 1919–20, the black market "supplied as much as 75 percent of the food consumed" in Russian cities.

The "food dictatorship" Lenin declared in 1918 having proved completely disastrous, the New Economic Policy was put into effect in 1921, instituting a parallel economy of heavily taxed private enterprise, consisting of small street markets, food stalls, and private canteens. (Bremzen's maternal great-grandmother operated such a home canteen in Odessa, where Anya's grandfather, Naum Frumkin—a chief of Naval Intelligence during the Second World War—met her grandmother, Liza, in the early 1920s; he seduced her with tickets to *Rigoletto*.) The liberalization lasted until a widespread fear of attack by the capitalist powers resulted in grain hoarding in 1927, which provided Stalin with a pretext to confiscate peasant holdings, and to launch the first Five-Year Plan, ramping up industrialization "at the expense of everything else."

This initiated collectivized farming and what amounted to a war on the peasantry, whom the architects of revolution had always mistrusted and despised despite official rhetoric exalting the sickle along with the hammer. At this juncture, Stalin's whims and paranoia basically decided, with varying severity, the mutations of the Soviet system, the ethnic composition of the myriad Soviet Republics, and which persons got fed and which ones starved, right up until the Genius of Humanity and Best Friend of All Children finally bought the farm, so to speak, in 1953.

The role of Bremzen's family in the world revolution is richly textured, as it included malcontents, sybaritic opportunists, true believers, and everything in between—her paternal great-grandmother, for example, led a doomed effort to liberate Muslim women from the veil in Tashkent in 1927. But life for all becomes especially fraught in the era of High Stalinism, when virtually every Soviet citizen, however highly situated, was expendable, subject overnight to accusations of sabotage, spying, Trotskyite conspiracy, and other crimes against the bushy mustache in the Kremlin.

Ever present in the thickening atmosphere of fear and suspicion was a seemingly eternal Russian anti-Semitism. While Bremzen's predominantly Jewish family eluded the worst outcomes of Stalinism (her grandfather Naum by a hair: he was scheduled for arrest on the day Stalin died), the taint of Judaism poisoned many of their dealings with fellow Soviet citizens in every period. The relaxed emigration policy for Jews initiated in the Brezhnev era allowed Bremzen and her mother, Larisa, who had been bitterly anti-Soviet for decades, to depart the worker's paradise for Philadelphia in the early '70s—with two little suitcases, even fewer than the permitted number. Once arrived, Anya found herself nostalgic for the spritz of soda water sold from a machine at the Arbatskaya metro station, "squishy rectangles of Friendship Cheese," and Russian sourdough bread, while Larisa went into ecstasies over the abundance of her first Pathmark supermarket, Oscar Mayer bologna, and Wonder Bread. Eventually, Anya trained at Juilliard as a classical pianist; a wrist injury diverted her energies into food writing, an unanticipated profession in which she is one of the best.

Soviet Cooking enfolds many intense family love stories, generational frictions, separations, and reunions, interweaving a remarkable amount of political and social history, ranging across the Khrushchev '50s and early '60s (when non-communal, hideous apartment blocks sprang up like mushrooms), the stagnant Brezhnev years, the brief, mummified premierships of Andropov and Chernenko ("Without regaining consciousness, Comrade Konstantin Chernenko assumed the post of general secretary."), through the Gorbachev and Yeltsin eras. The period after 1974 is chronicled through correspondence, telephone calls, and, during and after *perestroika*, visits home; after the transformation of Moscow during the rise of the oligarchs, in the eerily retrograde Putin era, both Anya and Larisa make frequent trips to Moscow, during one extended stay becoming guest hosts on separate Russian TV cooking shows.

Bremzen has a gift for recounting things we think we know about with revelatory immediacy. Anastas Mikoyan, one of the few Politburo members familiar to Americans during my Cold War childhood (if only as a diplomat often shown on TV getting in or out of a limousine at the UN), figures here almost as imposingly as Stalin. Survivor of every purge of the ruling elite from Lenin to Brezhnev, Mikoyan, commissar of Soviet nutrition, introduced cornflakes, ketchup, and the popular bunless hamburger *kotleti* into the Soviet diet after touring the US in the '30s, had his name attached to various food products and factories, and is the putative author of *The Book of Tasty and Healthy Food*, "a totalitarian *The Joy of Cooking*," successive editions of which reflected ideological shifts in the wind.

> Xenophobia reigns in the 1952 *Kniga*. Gone is the 1939's Jewish *teiglach* recipe; vanished Kalmyk tea (Kalmyks being a Mongolic minority departed en masse for supposed Nazi collaboration). Canapés, croutons, consommés—the 1952 volume is purged of such "rootless cosmopolitan" *froufrou* . . . In the next reprint, released in August 1953 . . . surprise! All quotations from Stalin have disappeared. In 1954, no Lavrenty Beria (he was executed in December 1953).

Mikoyan's book remains in print after twelve editions. Bremzen reports that it was so cherished that many emigrants took it with them when fleeing the state that published it. It is immensely readable, easy to follow, replete with gorgeous, if somewhat waxen-looking, illustrations. Its only impractical aspect was that ordinary Soviet citizens could never hope to afford the ingredients listed in the recipes, which were in any case unobtainable in any shops.

Vignettes of meals served at the Yalta Conference cast the not especially appetizing oddity of its participants into vivid relief. Raucous late-night dinners at Stalin's dacha, attended by Beria, Khrushchev, and Molotov, show the masters of the universe in a powerfully miniaturizing light, as sadistic frat boys clowning for the Ultimate Leader's amusement and jockeying for succession. In a hysterical section on Russian alcoholism, Bremzen makes a convincing case that Gorbachev's failure was ensured at the outset by his quickly abandoned but fated campaign to curtail alcohol consumption. The lengths to which the Soviet *alkogolik* would go to get a buzz on were heroic:

> Down the hatch went *bormotukha* (cut-rate surrogate port poetically nicknamed "the mutterer"), *denaturat* (ethanol dyed a purplish blue), and *tormozok* (brake fluid). Also BF surgical glue (affectionately called "Boris Fedorovich"), ingeniously spun with a drill in a bucket of water and salt to separate out the good stuff. Like all Soviet *alkanauts,* Sashka massively envied MIG-25 pilots, whose airplanes—incidentally co-invented by Artem Mikoyan, brother of Stalin's food commissar—carried forty liters of the purest, highest-grade spirits as a deicer and were nicknamed the *letayushchy gastronom* (flying food store). That the planes crashed after pilots quaffed the deicer they'd replaced with water didn't deter consumption.

This particular feature of everyday life was not uniquely Soviet. As Bremzen elucidates, the Slavic love of booze was the very thing that dissuaded Grand Prince Vladimir of Rus from making Russia an Islamic country, and to embrace Byzantine Orthodox Christianity. Vodka runs through Russian history and Russian literature as the Volga runs through Astrakhan, Volgograd, Samara, and Nizhny Novgorod. It might also be said that authoritarian or dictatorial rule has always been a characteristic feature of Russia, something borne out by Putin's tenure in office.

But the Soviet Union encompassed several Muslim regions, dozens of ethnicities, and hundreds of language groups. Its rulers proposed the eventual dissolving of differences among its peoples into one harmonious utopian entity; the Russian Soviet citizen was encouraged to think of all fifteen of its Republics, from Mongolia to Minsk, as part of their homeland. Putin's Russia is again just Russia. Bremzen's book succeeds in painting a comprehensive picture of what it was to be "Soviet" for slightly less than sixty years instead of "Russian"—today, an identity without a country.

(2013)

PAUL SCHEERBART, OR THE ECCENTRICITIES OF A NIGHTINGALE

Reading Paul Scheerbart's fiction instantly summons a period rich in aesthetic eccentricities and unforgettable eccentrics, roughly spanning 1890 to the start of the Great War: a longueur of late Symbolist decadence and Arctic expeditions, Imagist poetry and hot air balloons, angst-ridden Nordic theater and the first Parisian car crashes. For all but one year of his life, Scheerbart lived in a world dismissively described, in retrospect, as frozen for twenty years in the minutes before the disaster—a placid eternity of Chekhov's *Three Sisters* and Bernard Shaw's *Misalliance*, tastefully spiced by *Le Sacre du Printemps* and the Duchesse de Guermantes's *bal musettes*. It was actually the same world that Céline's embittered, brawling, alcoholic families inhabited in the Passage Choiseul, their adolescent sons soon to turn into cannon fodder, the same human swarm busy going crazy in Broch's *Sleepwalkers* and Musil's *Man Without Qualities*, its festering pathology brilliantly depicted in Michael Haneke's recent film *The White Ribbon*.

The First World War is usually thought to have been "unexpected." Certainly its savagery and massive scale were beyond anything the human race had attempted previously. But it would be hard to look at Munch's *Scream* of 1893, or the paintings Kokoschka exhibited in 1910, without inferring a contemporary sense that something large and terrible was about to happen.

In Scheerbart's Berlin, the sudden capital of frantic modernity, his generation of artists was spooked by the pointless butchery of late-nineteenth-century Europe's cabinet wars, leery of the new century's official optimism and society's myriad efforts at self-perfection. Scheerbart's ebullience over novel technologies of the period—the audiovisual components of mass media—invariably sounds its own troubled echo. Stories reveling in scientific marvels often betray apprehension that the same fabulous innovations making life more interesting would likely make death more ubiquitous, bloody, and communal sooner or later.

It's rare that a Scheerbart story omits any mention of war or fails to strike a worried note about it. In "Atlas, the Comfortable: A Myth of Humanity," several philosophers visit the god Atlas (who has licked the problems involved in holding up the world by placing it on columns) with the urgent question of how to end war forever. Atlas advises that "you have to get rid of rich people." This seems straightforward enough. The philosophers benignly choose to ask the rich to get rid of themselves. The rich, improbably, recognize the public benefit of this idea, but keep "postponing the whole business." In the meantime they enrich the philosophers by donating to the cause; the philosophers finally "become more patient." War continues.

> The greater your despair, the closer you are to the gods.
>
> The gods desire to drive us perpetually closer to the exalted ones. And they have no means of doing so other than misery. Only in misery do great hopes and great plans for the future take shape.
> —Paul Scheerbart, "The Perpetual Motion Machine"

The imaginary contexts of Scheerbart's fables and novelettes distance reader and author from direct confrontations with inter-human violence, as Scheerbart's fictions are designed to go down gently and impart their improving messages with the mildness of vitamin pills. His work engages the mind rather than the heart, though the innocent candor of his style is itself touching. At times it suggests the pathos of a writer clinging to naivete and phobic avoidance of adult reality, but this subtracts nothing from his work's exemplary artistry. Like Walser, Scheerbart is blessed with congenital refinement and an impeccable instinct for delighting his readers.

It was believed among his friends that Scheerbart's death in 1915 resulted from self-starvation, a despairing protest against the global carnage that had commenced the year before. This singular writer whose strongest suits are whimsy and an adolescent enthusiasm for bright, hallucinatory futures deserves to be taken seriously, as his alter persona is Cassandra, who didn't warn the Trojans about nothing.

That said, Scheerbart is proof of Jack Smith's aperçu that much of the best art treats existence and its problems with a delicate, nuanced, unpretentious touch—and is relegated to obscurity because Western culture trains us, insensibly, to equate bombast, heaviness, and Wagnerian overkill with importance and seriousness. Scheerbart merits far more respectful attention than the quirky footnote literary history has reduced him to. It's the luck of the draw and a few PhD theses, I suppose, but his disappearance down the memory hole seems a howling critical injustice, in light of the innumerable Festschrifts and revivals lavished on less gifted contemporaries.

On December 27, 1907, I was thinking about composing some brief narratives in which something new—something astonishing or grotesque—would happen. I thought about the future of the cannon as a useful means of transport. I supposed that items fired from the cannon might be equipped with parachutes that would open automatically, allowing the goods to fall back gently to the Earth.
—Paul Scheerbart, "The Perpetual Motion Machine"

The expressive freedom of Scheerbart's writing is uncanny. His imagination ranges over mythic earthly kingdoms, sentient minerals, ancient gods, future cities, Baron Munchausen's visit to China, and talking planets in distant reaches of the cosmos, with the childlike brio of Jules Verne; his verbal peregrinations are gracefully informal and indifferent to convention. Scheerbart's morally attractive sentiments, sly humor, and infectious curiosity radiate from impeccably limpid sentences, which, like those of Patricia Highsmith, have the authentic poetry of plainness. Scheerbart's voice is utterly natural, unshowy, and, in its unassuming way, addictive.

Like the anti-realist works of Alfred Jarry, Oskar Panizza, and S. I. Witkiewicz—and, centrally, Franz Kafka—Scheerbart's stories, novels, plays, and poems have stronger affinities to folklore, fables, and fantastic tales of every period than to fin de siècle and later Mitteleuropean naturalism. They elude genre categories, hybridizing poetry with prose, fiction with scientific treatise, fantasy with reportage. To extravagantly pataphysical tales Scheerbart attaches dry ironies of "visual proof" in the form of diagrams, schematics, and drawings, subtly blurring the line between oneiric reverie and documentary reality. Scheerbart's stories suspend quotidian space and time, evoking the dream world of origin myths and epic, episodic tales such as the *Arabian Nights*, *The Manuscript Found in Saragossa*, the Icelandic Sagas—narratives nested in other narratives.

Set in the allegorical, indeterminate "once upon a time" of the Brothers Grimm, Scheerbart's texts have the floating effect of Klee watercolors or Sufi proverbs. Their metaphysical, synchronous universe is unmoored from historical contingency. The recurring vagaries of the human condition are in one sense "hypostatized as Fate" (as Marcuse, in another context, characterized Heidegger's concept of technology); in a different sense, what Adolf Loos referred to as humanity's "private mess" is subject to improvement, in Scheerbart's stories, when the private mess is placed in the right containers.

> After that, I imagined the entire sky crisscrossed with funicular railways. I was especially attracted to the idea of funiculars descending from very high mountain peaks. I devised schemes

whereby balloons would support railway cables for expeditions to the North Pole. As for land routes, I came up with the notion of gigantic wheels that in my opinion would roll more quickly to a given destination than the little wheels currently in use.
—Paul Scheerbart, "The Perpetual Motion Machine"

Such works, even when nominally self-contained as stories or essays, announce themselves as fragments of didactic, visionary projects whose discrete parts accrue greater significance considered in relation to each other. A utopian artist, Scheerbart's fiercest concern makes the case that social reality and its outcomes are primarily determined by the constructed environment. Uniquely among the arts, this is the raison d'être of theoretical architecture, and Scheerbart is more readily associated with architecture than with any other art, including literature.

This is partly because, at least in the English-speaking world, he is known solely for one book, *Glass Architecture*—a brilliantly speculative, playfully insistent manifesto expounding the limitless possibilities of glass in architectural design. (*Glass Architecture* is dedicated to a fellow utopian, Bruno Taut, whose extraordinary Glass Pavilion in the Cologne Werkbund of 1914 exemplified Scheerbart's theories, a "futuristic" dome that was, at the same time, entirely functional, its ornament devoid of anachronisms.)

But *Glass Architecture* is merely the best-known item of Scheerbart's prodigious bibliography. Despite its frequently ecstatic tenor, a casual reader might not glean, from its passionately practical advocacy of an already popular building material, Scheerbart's obsessive, fanatical preoccupation with glass environments reflected (forgive me) in his fiction. Architectural manifestos—especially those published shortly before World War I until the late 1930s—customarily strike a tone of shrewdly calculated hysteria. For Scheerbart, however, the urgent desire to improve the world (or at least alter the way it looks) implicit in all architectural writing serves as a motor for fictional narratives, a theme, a folly of one or many characters, an unmistakably and sometimes hilariously romantic *fixé*.

Architecture and glass are to Scheerbart's work what food and cooking are to M. F. K. Fisher's: lenses through which all reality is filtered, producing a radically shifted, revelatory perspective. Scheerbart and Taut were virtually collaborators; both mirrored the powerful influence of Adolf Loos's polemics on functional design and his rejection of useless ornament in the commissions he realized in Vienna. Like the great Viennese gadfly Karl Kraus, Loos saw humanity sinking into mental torpor and affectlessness under an ever-growing accumulation of meaningless physical and linguistic artifacts, epitomized by caryatids on modern buildings and the vapid catchphrases of politics and advertising. In this connection, Scheerbart considered glass construction the least gratuitous, least physically obtrusive, most honest feature of the manmade world, and tirelessly proposed expanding its use: ideally, it would eventually make the manmade world itself less obtrusive and destructive of the natural order.

Remarkably, Scheerbart frequently lampoons his own earnest fetishes, bestowing them on obviously cracked and deluded narrators and other characters; in stories like "The Magnetic Mirror" and "The Glass Theater" Scheerbart undermines his cherished materials and pastimes by basing increasingly absurd rituals on them, fashioning them into garishly precious objects, and putting them to work in insanely over-elaborate Rube Goldberg appliances that expend more time and labor than they could possibly save. Scheerbart emits the winning charm of an artist perfectly aware of his own ridiculousness.

> To this end it seemed natural to me to place the car inside the wheel. This in any case was something new.
> —Paul Scheerbart, "The Perpetual Motion Machine"

He is a quintessential artist-inventor of a kind that flourished in the first two decades of the twentieth century, when seismic effects of new technologies rippled through the industrialized West and inspired the science-smitten to devise bizarre flying machines, implausible urban renewal projects, and mechanically driven, Fourier-like theories of how to save the world. Like the raucously satirized inventor Courtial of Céline's *Death on Credit*, Scheerbart was a flume of ideas for labor-saving devices as well as less credible contraptions to relieve ennui and eliminate aesthetic revulsion. Like Jarry, he incorporated his designs for living into works of literature where they feature at a skeptical remove from their overheated point of origin, stories that continue to dazzle the imagination and communicate a very human, humane, and ultimately moving sensibility.

(2014)

UNICA ZÜRN

Unica Zürn has long been a semi-mythical figure. Little known and in many ways unknowable, she is inevitably associated with the Surrealist artist Hans Bellmer, whom she met at a Berlin show of his work in 1953. Obsessed throughout his career with realistic female dolls whose body parts could be endlessly manipulated, penetrated, removed, multiplied, decorated, and otherwise reconfigured to posit flesh and bone as the material of a recombinative fetishism, Bellmer had worked and lived with other women before Zürn. (He'd also been married and had fathered twin daughters.) But upon meeting Zürn he declared, ominously, "Here is the doll."

From that moment on, their fates were intertwined—or, one should say, Unica Zürn's fate was sealed. She was thirty-seven, Bellmer fifty-one, when she moved to Paris to share Bellmer's two rooms in the Hôtel de l'Espérance, 88 rue Mouffetard. There the pair embarked on their own special variation on the Surrealist l'amour fou. They have been described as companions in misery who inspired each other. No doubt this is true. Zürn's life before meeting Bellmer was troubled, to say the least. Born in 1916, she grew up in Grünewald, the daughter of an adored but mostly absent father, a cavalry officer posted to Africa, and his third wife, whom she detested. During the Nazi period, Zürn worked as a dramaturge at UFA, the German film company, married a much older man in 1942, bore two children, and lost custody of them in a divorce seven years later; she then made a meager living writing short stories for newspapers and radio plays.

She also painted and made drawings in the late '40s and early '50s, independently lighting upon the Surrealist technique of decalcomania. Malcolm Green, in his introduction to the English version of Zürn's novel *The Man of Jasmine* (Gallimard, Paris, 1971; English translation Atlas Press, London, 1977), describes this period of Zürn's life as "happy." She reestablished contact with former UFA colleagues, had what may have been an amiable social life, and enjoyed the work she did as a writer and artist.

One has to wonder, though only to wonder, how much of Zürn's life transpired above the threshold of the dissociative states and debilitating depressions that later entrapped her. The writings for which she is best known reflect an excruciating mental state, relieved solely by fantasies and hallucinations; reality, in her description, is unbearably harsh and punitive, a realm of grotesquerie in which, she writes in *Dark Spring* (Merlin, Hamburg, 1969; English translation Exact Change, Cambridge, Mass., 2000), she is "mocked, derided and humiliated." And while the narrator of that autobiographical novel avers that "pain and suffering bring her pleasure," Zürn's inner torment led many times to long spells in mental hospitals, and finally to suicide by throwing herself from Bellmer's sixth-floor window in 1970, when she was fifty-four.

Like Artaud, Zürn possessed penetrating insight into the nuances of madness without finding any way to escape them. If Bellmer's *idée fixe*, amplified by alcoholism, was the female doll, Zürn was focused on what she called "the man of jasmine," a dream lover and/or father figure incarnated in the poet and artist Henri Michaux, whom she met through Bellmer in 1957, and with whom she took mescaline several times.

Zürn's drug experiences with Michaux, apparently, precipitated the schizophrenic episodes that recurred throughout her final years. So she, at least, believed, though being trussed with cordage like a slab of meat for a famous series of Bellmer's photographs may not have contributed much to her psychic equilibrium. As muse for

Bellmer's technically impeccable paintings and drawings as well as his photographs, Zürn underwent innumerable imaginary rapes, eviscerations, mutilations, and monstrous transmogrifications, becoming an emblematic pornogram. Willing to be such, she certainly was; in that long ago time, few women could secure even a marginal place in the Paris art world, much less the Surrealist group, except under the auspices of a male artist. Bellmer instinctively mined Zürn's masochistic psychology in each of its twists and turns.

While prolonged contact with the Paris Surrealists spurred an effulgence of creativity in Zürn, it carried a corresponding toxicity. Given their representation of women as passive receptacles of "mad love," the elegant reification of female insanity in the writings of Breton, and the canonization of Sade as the movement's preeminent patron saint, it seems unlikely that a woman with Zürn's fragile emotional structure could keep her sanity intact very long within the Surrealists' circle, mescaline or no mescaline.

This isn't to deny that Bellmer encouraged her work, nor that the Surrealists promoted her art, including it in many exhibitions. The superb, fantastic drawings Zürn produced, often during her hospitalizations, have distinct affinities to Bellmer's linear finesse as well as Michaux's calligraphic spontaneity. Most specifically, Zürn adopted Bellmer's use of the "cephalopod," a variable, amorphously shaped humanoid form. She gave the techniques she adapted from others a wildness and bite entirely her own, particularly in the rendering of eyes, veins beneath flesh, and colors of lividity and bruising. While Zürn produced tempera and oil paintings during the early 1950s, her preferred mediums were colored inks, pencil, and gouache on paper. She produced many works in notebooks given to her by Michaux when Zürn was at Sainte-Anne Hospital in Paris. Between hospitalizations, she made a quantity of large-scale drawings; while they are always startling, one can't really claim they "develop"—rather, they elaborate an unchanging set of obsessions.

The lubricious energies the Surrealists discovered in the irrational took a harsh toll on many individuals—René Crevel and Antonin Artaud come to mind; it is worth noting, also, that Bellmer and Zürn lived together in conditions of extreme poverty, in claustrophobic quarters, that Zürn seldom ventured outside except in Bellmer's company. Her dependence on him reflected an unassuageable loneliness—an isolation that his companionship did little to relieve.

The literature about Zürn—for example, translator Caroline Rupprecht's preface to *Dark Spring*, Renée Hubert's *Magnifying Mirrors: Women, Surrealism and Partnership* (University of Nebraska Press, Lincoln, 1994), and Agnès de la Baumelle and Laure de Buzon-Vallet's chronology in *Hans Bellmer* (Hatje Cantz, Ostfildem, 2006)— suggests that Bellmer did his best to support her, emotionally, artistically, and financially, but both, at various times, attempted to end their relationship, which lasted seventeen years. Their symbiosis was at once creatively rich and terribly burdensome. They devoted themselves to art that pressed beyond any safe psychic boundaries, Bellmer undoubtedly with greater detachment, Zürn with a fierce identification with the fantasy world she created.

Much more has been written about their relationship, which involved interventions by such figures as the psychiatrist Gaston Ferdière, who had treated Artaud. A close reading of Zürn's texts, including *Hexentexte* (Galerie Springer, Berlin, 1954), a book of anagrams, reveals a brilliant poetic mind, a preoccupation with death, and a yearning for childhood, a time when, despite its difficulties for her, miracles and wonders could present themselves without lethal consequences—benign events not realized in her fiction and anagrammatic poetry.

Zürn's drawings—forty-nine of which have been assembled at the Drawing Center in New York, along with three paintings—example obsessive, skillful weirdness of two varieties of "outsider art," a mode characterized by fastidious excess and disciplined compulsion. Sometimes whimsical and "light," Zürn's drawings depict persons, animals, and other subjects in states of metamorphosis or fusion; dense coagulations of forms; and sentience as multitudes of eyes that stare at the viewer like those of fantastic organisms peering through transparent yet impenetrable barriers. Her pictures do not politely invite us into her private world, but rather pull us into it with angry insistence, demanding recognition of an intolerable state of consciousness. Even Zürn's most playful works embody a disturbance in which seduction and horror battle for predominance.

The Drawing Center show, curated by João Ribas, is the most extensive gathering of Zürn's drawings in New York to date, though her work was shown here at Ubu Gallery (in 2008), Zürn had four drawing exhibitions in Paris between 1956 and 1964, and has been included in many surveys of Surrealist art. At the Drawing Center, several vitrines containing photographs, publications, and letters provide a sense of Zürn and Bellmer's shared milieu. The total effect of the exhibition is one of freakish aggressivity mixed with a daft, teasing elegance.

While "outsider art" usually connotes untrained naivete and beguiling clumsiness, Zürn's virtuosity is that of an artist willing her madness to manifest itself on paper, rather than a mad person exuding symptoms in pictorial form. Her pictures are radically skewed, shattered self-portraits that mimic the splitting of her personality. They duplicate her face and body, or parts of them, amid or inside avian predators, felines, vegetal accumulations; these Unicas sport claws, razor teeth, multiple mouths, extra limbs, several breasts, antennae. As if Zürn has internalized as self-image the profuse, mutant doll parts of Bellmer's paintings and sculptures, replacing herself with the freakish assemblages of her lover's imagination—as if she has *become the doll* and, in retribution, invested Bellmer's reinvention of her with an autonomy and visionary power he withheld from it.

The muffled scream that issues from Zürn's drawings is surely the cri de coeur of a woman denied: deprived the love of her monstrously distant mother and the companionship of her absentee father, separated from her two children, and refused possession of her own body by its transformation into a pot roast, among other things, by Bellmer. Her revenge is assimilation of the deformities these deprivations caused—her adamant presentation of herself as the twisted and manipulated creature that others have imagined.

Of course this amazing, ungovernable being had to be hospitalized, medicated, isolated for her own good. One has only to read Zürn's account, in *The Man of Jasmine*, of what those hospitalizations were like to understand that "for her own good" and "outworn her usefulness" probably amounted to the same thing. She could not go back, in the end, to any "happier" time, and she could not move forward. Her final crisis occurred at the end of 1969, when Bellmer, who had had a stroke, could no longer look after her. She returned to the asylum for a month; discharged, she was offered, Malcolm Green writes, "the option to leave Bellmer and return to Germany or be placed in a mental hospital as a preventative measure." She chose the hospital, for a final four months of institutionalization. Upon release, she could find no one with whom to stay. Bellmer allowed her to return for a few days, until she could sort things out; according to Green, "they spent the first evening in quiet conversation, and in the early morning she committed suicide." It was a death foretold in the suicide of the twelve-year-old girl in *Dark Spring*, in the defenestration of her father's first wife, Orla Holm, in the suicide of her uncle Falada, with whom she describes identifying in *The Man of Jasmine*.

Zürn left us an unnervingly precise record of her time on earth in her writings, drawings, and paintings, and in the work of other artists and writers. Rainer Werner Fassbinder dedicated his 1978 film *Despair* "to Antonin Artaud, Vincent Van Gogh, and Unica Zürn," and rightly so. *Despair*, though based on Nabokov's novel, was in Fassbinder's eyes about the recognition that, after a certain moment in life, the future will only offer more of what has already been, or the options of madness, misery, suicide. For many sensitive souls, the possibilities of self-reinvention are exhausted long before any sort of natural death. Unica Zürn was one of these.

(2009)

MUNCH'S TELEPHONE

In Whole Foods, Union Square, 10:30 p.m.:

... *and the fact is, I had a mental picture of me on this escalator a half hour ago, a sea of luxury produce spreading out below, sometimes the image of a future action makes doing it for real feel redundant, like how sex feels if you already masturbated and came, or like now, greeted by yellow melons, Product of Korea, the most embarrassing detail in that London Review thing that oh god what is her name, lesbian academic, kind of abject like many academics but yes description of the guy in the codpiece, what is Tracey doing right now, it's 3 a.m. there, he "pranced in a codpiece," I think it read, and Elena Markropolis (not her real name) was serving an exotic fruit that stank like, yes, flown in from Borneo, or whatever, if Tracey isn't sleeping she's drawing a picture or getting in a cab in her cowboy boots after a glamorous party, I feel like a zombie, now I remember. But I, I, when I get to it, concerning Brenda (not her real name): I must be very measured and clear in my memoirs about why I'm taking revenge on a dead person.*

... *but I don't have to think about that now. Now I have my Tracey Emin essay, first of all to decide whether to call her Emin or Tracey or Tracey Emin, in an essay—I can't even think of calling an essay a "piece" after reading that tiresome queen in the New Yorker, he's a reptile but it was funny, every dentist hits a nerve now and then—in a formal essay the writer maintains a certain formal stiffness, an imperious yet servile altitude, writing from slightly above the level of the reader but slightly below that of the subject: that was the takeaway from years of hanging around Brenda, I had some ideas this afternoon, if that's what they were, what* is *salsify* exactly, the label either goes with, these brown knobby roots or those green things, my first thought was, *We're different than what we do, I am a person, these are my books, she's an artist, these are her neon sculptures, blankets,* whatever, but you know something, even people who disappear behind their work, and never go out in public, instead of promoting it by winning people over with their personalities, are spoken and written of as if they're identical with what they produce. *"Grace and redemption are familiar themes in Tolstoy,"* or *"In Tunisia, Highsmith introduces us to a quirky middle-aged American."*

It isn't hard to write overfamiliarly about Tracey Emin: her work pulls us into the kind of intimate narrative that usually gets attached to artists posthumously, when the times they inhabit are long gone, their personal histories archived, sifted, and displayed in exhibition vitrines as helpful evidence of thoughts and feelings that channeled into what they made. A considerable part of Emin's work itself consists of such memorial materials—souvenirs, diaries, keepsakes, personal letters, old clothes, family furniture, snapshots, even cigarette butts, empty liquor bottles, used condoms, smears of body fluids and sanitary napkins. The art for which she's known has insistent reference to her lived experience. Emin's life figures so directly in her art that the two are often conflated and written about as the same thing.

I can't think of another artist as well known to the public except Warhol, who was recognizable anywhere but projected such a blank, withholding image that he was known for being unknowable. Emin on the other hand is known for the kind of candid self-revelation that Warhol drew from his superstars on camera, with the difference that Warhol's subjects mimicked the ritual of Catholic confession with a clear intention to shock an audience, for the absolving amusement of their Prime Mover; Emin is her own subject and puts her story forward with the sense that this is her material, the natural source of her work, and therefore not shocking to anyone who troubles to look into it. Something of Warhol's affectlessness seeped into his actors' interminable monologues, conveying their invulnerable coolness; Emin records an opposite vulnerability in her work, and frankly tells us about the things that have hurt and confused her, interfered with her development or pushed it forward (these are, often, the same things), tallies the emotional cost of living with unusual acuity and sensitivity to nuance.

The horrific mishaps and private messes Emin shares with us aren't unprecedented subjects for an artist, though few female artists (with the exception of comics—Joan Rivers, Sandra Bernhard, Sarah Silverman, and others) have dealt with such material in a raw, unguarded way. The real scandal of Emin's work isn't its content—the blatant depictions of and references to shit, semen, menstrual blood, vomit, cunts, penises, drunkenness, bad sex, etc., etc.—but its violation of an implicit taboo, peculiar to the art world in recent times, against sincerity—a quality so widely, insensibly conflated with kitsch, sentimentality, and lack of artistic training that even a few drops of it affect many critics the way holy water affects a vampire. Even partisans of Emin's art sometimes doggedly ascribe an almost Machiavellian degree of strategy to its least calculated-looking examples, to infer a slyly alienated relationship (itself misidentified as "irony") between artist and spectator. Especially, I think, between Emin and the additional "fan base" her work has acquired beyond the art world through her media celebrity, presumed to be a demographic with close affinities to Beatlemania that connects with Emin's art for the wrong reasons. It's possible that the all-knowing, condescending inflection of this strain of academic criticism is unintentional; in any case, it sucks.

The first-person-singular approach of Emin's work runs against the grain of decades' worth of cerebrally distanced, techno-sleek conceptual art, some of it very good, addressed from a disembodied altitude produced by theories of "the death of the author"—a kind of art meant to slip subversively into the image flows of mass media by mimicking the impersonal polish of advertising. (It was no surprise when such work was smoothly incorporated into the design menu of advertising and magazine graphics; nobody expected it to destroy capitalism and establish Utopia.) Tracey Emin's work is similarly calculated in starting from an idea, a set of concerns, a theme, a title; however, what she produces is emphatically personal and hand-made (or, in the case of neon sculptures, hand-written), and more open in the course of being made to vagaries of instinct and intuition. In this respect she is a more traditional or spontaneous artist than many contemporaries, impelled to create things from the stuff of her daily existence, bored and tense when she isn't working: in her writings, Emin provides a hilarious and scary picture of what she gets up to in her off time. Her writing is central to her art and underpins what she's accomplished.

Strangeland is the most compelling artist's memoir of recent years, aimed straight at the heart in both the visceral and metaphoric senses of "heart." Its blunt naming of things and quick, sure evocations of characters, places, and events makes them roll through the mind's screening room with a brilliant economy of means. Not a lot of qualifying adjectives or slinky adverbs—when Emin says she survived on KFC and Pot Noodle you can taste it. Her sinewy, limpid prose travels back and forth in time while steering true to her consciousness at different ages: she remembers very well what she didn't know, and what she learned, and how she learned it.

She lets us know in a few pared sentences what being raped at thirteen felt like, and how a child's world is altered by adult betrayals, rejection by other children, wishes that come true the wrong way. It's important here, as elsewhere in her work, for the re-creation of traumatic episodes to register the confusion and ambiguity of the moments they occurred in, rather than coalesce into adult-identified "issues"—the "issue," say, of abortion, or racism (Emin is half-Turkish), rather than the narrative texture of experience, which is not generic, even when it elicits strong identification and empathy. It would be wrong to say that self-pity never enters into it: there are moments in life when self-pity is the only healthy reaction.

But *Strangeland* is strangely more than a heartbreaking chronicle of disappointments; it reflects the stubborn survival instinct peculiar to working-class children, especially gifted ones. There is just enough joy and mystery around the edges of Emin's complicated youth to carry her through. And when she finally triumphs, she doesn't pretend that success is just a different kind of misery. She wins us over, in part, because she doesn't tailor herself into a monster of rectitude and humility after scrabbling her way out of hell. *I'm better than all of them*, she thinks, after the public shaming described in "Why I Never Became a Dancer." A few pages later, she's drunk on the train.

There is also, wonderfully, an occult thread running through *Strangeland*: suggestions of spiritualism, an attention to oracles and portents, that fits appealingly with her invocation of Margate and the funfair decrepitude of a seaside resort town. Emin's Margate is very like the Brighton visited by Henry Pulling and Aunt Augusta in Graham Greene's *Travels with My Aunt*, with its carnival circuit mystics and clairvoyants—the kind of town where married men with hired companions used to be "surprised" on purpose by divorce photographers. Emin's improvisational early life often seems guided by an invisible hand, by spirits of dead artists and the peasant wisdom of Cypriot ancestors.

She has a natural storyteller's voice that casts a spell over all her work, whether it's talking in pictures or embroidered words, appliqués, neon, or the voice-over of her videos and films. Or the stitch-like script and scratchy lettering in her paintings and prints, which remind me of the furred line of Goya's drawings, or Ronald Searle's—black strokes that score the paper with the trail of an idea, swift and exact, sometimes garbled like a telegram.

(2013)

A CONEY ISLAND OF THE VISCERA

I want to be the owner of my own trouble.

—LOUISE BOURGEOIS

When I met her, in the mid-1980s, it was by way of a mash note she sent in the mail to the paper I wrote for, not so much thanking me for a review but offering something better than thanks: a terse, oddly touching missive indicating that I'd fathomed her current show very well. Soon afterwards, Louise Bourgeois and I became friends.

We met infrequently, however, and seldom by design. Perhaps I should say we bore an emotional likeness that precluded seeing each other with any regularity. We were both intellectually com-bative, anxiety-ridden, insecure, depressive, and wretchedly insom-niac, and we both sported egos prone to inflate like dirigibles, then shrink to pea-size within the span of a sneeze. We wanted love but couldn't stand most people we wanted it from.

My encounters with Louise were always cordial, affectionate in fact, but a spectral nervousness pestered the atmosphere. Her fear of others mirrored mine, and I knew how unaccountably that fear could flip into aggression. I cringed at the prospect of bothering her, making her angry, or losing her respect, and I thought the risk of those things happening would likely rise the more time I spent with her. Few figures in the landscape besides Jack Smith activated this kind of guarded endearment in me. And Jack was scary. Possibly I was paranoid. But there it is.

There was nothing simple about Louise. But unlike the market-conscious artists I knew, she was refreshingly direct and said what she thought without holding back. She didn't waste words, and she used them precisely, in both French and English. Her obser-vations cut through the grease of small talk. She referenced litera-ture, philosophy, and science, all eruditely and with fervor. I didn't know she'd attended the Lycée Fénelon or studied mathe-matics and philosophy at the Sorbonne; finding it out later didn't surprise me.

She was tiny and, by the time I met her, old, though she lived for many more years. Like many old people do to young people, she looked like a peacock feather could knock her over. Once in a blue moon, I dropped in on the Sunday salons she hosted at her Chelsea brownstone—a peculiar mix of international pathologies. Young artists turned up to show off their work and often got a bru-tal recep-tion. Louise was a hilarious terror. She enjoyed getting people drunk to prod secrets out of them. She loved sexual gossip. She insulted strang-ers at whim, ignored their flattery, ridiculed their clothing, acted out.

Her home had a take-it-or-leave-it decrepitude. When she moved there in 1962 with her husband, the art historian Robert Goldwater, the townhouse was newly renovated; after his death in 1973, she got rid of its domestic trappings and turned the whole place into her studio. She had grown up in a Balzacian milieu of high-end artisans, amid external signs of refinement. She didn't want any of that around her. Louise, who used every imaginable material in her work, from steel mesh and Carrara marble to min-iature safety pins and her own ripped-up dresses, was visibly not a materialist in her life. Not a consumer, at any rate. She remained indifferent to pricey creature comforts even when, in later life, she easily could have afforded them. She cooked on a hot plate, in a kitchen smaller than a Hollywood closet. She jotted phone num-bers on the walls, where she also pinned snapshots, invitations, awards, exhibition fliers, newspaper clippings, postcards, letters, little watercolors, and whatnot. She scribbled and sketched on any handy surface—envelopes, scraps of newspaper, torn cardboard, playing cards. She treasured books, mostly paperbacks, stacked and shelved in no discernible order. She never threw anything out.

In those years, she still left the house; we ran into each other at openings. As it happens, I loved her. At her house one afternoon, she fetched the monkey fur she wore in the famous portrait by Robert Mapplethorpe, draped it over my shoulders, and said, "I think you should wear this for a while."

•

In the summer of 2007, Louise's longtime assistant, Jerry Gorovoy, contacted me, proposing I collaborate with her on what became the handmade, sewn-linen book *To Whom It May Concern*, fabricated in an edition of seven. (A larger facsimile edition was later pub-lished by Robert Violette.) Louise had done a gouache series of headless, distorted human figures, some male, some female, their thin red outlines filled in with mottled washes. I could add whatever I liked. Rather than tamper with these risibly unsettling pictures, I decided to write separate prose poems (thirty-seven, it turned out) as verbal accompaniment.

This project took nearly three years. It isn't entirely out of place here to say that when I first met with Jerry about it—in a restaurant, over dinner, in the company of his friend Scott Lyon and the artist Nicola L.—I was so firmly immured in a years-long depression that I nodded off at the table after we looked over the maquettes. I dimly perceived that Louise and Jerry were throwing me a lifeline, but catching it took a supreme act of false bravura.

With copies of the gouaches nearby, I slowly began writing, a process that felt at first like dragging myself over razor wire. I wanted to match the tangled emotions emanating from Louise's pictures, which seemed to fuse antic defiance and saturnine res-ignation. My rough model was the Henri Barbusse novel *L'Enfer*—Hell. That book describes what occurs over an uncertain span in a single hotel room. The occupants change, but each one is in some personal inferno, even during coitus. The stories in *To Whom It May Concern* are the sub-vocal ruminations of name-less people fucking. Coming apart. Disembodied voices brimming with rage, remorse, erotic sublimity, self-contempt, melancholia.

The texts accumulated over many months. My depression lifted, one suspect layer at a time. I then had the bizarre task to sus-tain, for half the book, the tone of psychic extremity I'd started with and had just crawled out of. If you read through the texts now, it's impossible to distinguish between "written from Hades" and "written." Moreover, they're not as bleak as I thought they were. Which tells you something about the solipsism of depression—and by corollary, perhaps, a little about Louise Bourgeois's creative process as well. As she once embroidered on a handkerchief, "I have been to hell and back. And let me tell you, it was wonderful."

While working with Louise, I gleaned a clearer sense of her work's ingenious diversity, its meticulousness, its sources in her lived experience. And with that, a sense of the multiple roles Jerry Gorovoy, whom I'd known for years outside Louise's realm, played in her life: as studio assistant, best friend, nego-tiator, muse, model, lay psychiatrist, exhibition supervisor. He was indis-pensable. Louise lived at the mercy of her moods, except when at work on tangible things, when she could translate her physical and emotional sensations into some form of art. Believing, sensibly, that working held her inner chaos at bay, she never stopped. Inactivity was her nemesis. Jerry kept her as steady as possible, with the sensitivity and patience of Prince Myshkin, for thirty years. "You do the work," he told her, "and I will take care of every-thing else." He did.

•

It wouldn't be flippant to say that Louise Bourgeois devoted a lifetime to excavating her unconscious. She worked with what she dug up, transforming it into art that, in turn, peered into everybody's uncon-scious. Libidinal spillage and rever-berating trauma assumed shapes of mutating bodies, paradoxical architectures and amorphic objects that seemed to inhabit "the world inside this one," a Coney Island of the Viscera that would have been Freud's first stop if he'd come to America decades later than he did.

Keenly introspective, she knew that conflicts stemming from her childhood—fears of abandonment and betrayal, depressive episodes, bursts of rage, wishes for revenge, erotic frustration—were both the primary cause of her neuroses and the vital catalyst of her work. As the poet John Giorno memorably put it, "You got to burn to shine." Memory served and undermined her in syncopation. She struggled to live in the present by somehow repair-ing the past, the way she'd helped repair tapestries for her family's restoration business in her youth. The configuration she incessantly revisited, turning it every which way like a Rubik's Cube, is well known. Louis, the adored, resented, phi-landering father; Josephine, the revered invalid mother; Louise, the daughter alert to mute transactions buried under the family's genteel lineaments. This ensemble cast of a psychic ceremony moved restively through her memories. Sometimes its personnel changed into figures from her second family (husband, adopted son Michel, natal sons Jean-Louis and Alain). If the puzzle pieces never clicked into lasting resolution, Louise explored their every conceivable Oedipal nuance and possible restaging. This is far from the only theme in her work, but it is the central one, the ur-geometry problem, the existential triangle.

In interviews, she often cited psychoanalytic theory. Louise consumed the work of Sigmund Freud, Melanie Klein, Marie Bonaparte, Karen Homey, Carl Jung, Wilhelm Stekel, and many others. She fibbed, on at least one occasion, that she'd never needed treatment herself. In reality, she undertook analysis soon after her father died in 1951. She first saw Dr. Leonard Cammer, who later founded Gracie Square Hospital, then Dr. Henry Lowenfeld, a

A CONEY ISLAND OF THE VISCERA • 241

Freudian trained by Wilhelm Reich, from 1952 through 1982, with diminished frequency after 1966.

The first eleven years of analysis marked a prolonged dry spell in which Louise produced very little art. Her father's loss triggered an unbearable depression. Grief over her mother's death in 1932 had prompted her to abandon mathe-matics and become an artist. The death of her father had an almost contrary effect.

In 2004, Jerry uncovered two metal boxes of Louise's writings tucked away in her house—records of dreams and process notes on loose sheets, created as an adjunct to her analysis with Lowenfeld, for whom she sometimes made car-bon copies. After studying these all-but-forgotten papers, Louise later began to feature statements and phrases from them and from her diaries on lead metal plaques, and in prints and fabric pieces. She often used handwriting as a draw-ing stylus to render spirals, spokes, or snaking lines, in the spirit of Apollinaire's "Calligrammes."

In 2010, Jerry found two addi-tional boxes of writings. Almost a thousand pages in total have turned up. With Louise's approval, Philip Larratt-Smith selected and edited ninety-three of them for the catalogue accompanying his exhibition "The Return of the Repressed," which toured South America in 2011. A version of the show, along with sev-eral of the actual writings, ended up at London's Freud Museum in 2012. The bulk of the psychoan-alytic writ-ings are currently being prepared and annotated by Larratt-Smith for publication by Princeton University Press, in conjunction with his exhibition titled "Freud's Daughter," which will open in September 2020 at the Jewish Museum in New York.

Aside from obvious documentary value, these writings usefully add to the history of psychoanalysis, and also comprise a compel-ling, frequently deranging literary artifact of a very high order. I think their distinction owes a lot to the fact that they weren't intended as literary works, since today so many things intending to be merely ape the idea of literary works. (I'm aware that the latter sentiment was voiced in previous eras but doubt if it's ever been as true as it is now. Today's MacArthur genius is tomorrow's Edna Ferber.)

Louise wrote many things in a conventionally accessible style—artist statements, reviews of books and exhibitions, magazine articles. She wrote about the little antiquities Freud kept on his desk, about Gaston Lachaise, about gender issues, about individual pieces and discrete phases of her own work. She was a prodigious letter writer, and, as previously noted, kept daily diaries. Owing to a lifelong fear of abandonment, she identified with the discarded and the rejected, and hence never threw anything out. (Maggie Wright, the director of Bourgeois's foundation, the Easton Foundation, can attest to the archival vastness of written material Louise held on to.)

The psychoanalytic writings differ radically from other pieces Louise produced. Drastically unfiltered, they emanate from the most defenseless part of the writer's brain. Though meant to be read by at least one other person, her analyst, they clearly speak to the author herself rather than to an audience:

> Week end: chestnut thorns on the outside masochism = thorns on the inside. guilt turned against self return to the symbolism of the bottle play at filling up bottles (hot water) The box shaped like a small coffin. story of the roasted child = a child is killed—Finally the bottle of hot water—The good little girl is laid down in the small coffin. Equivalent to a masochism brought to an expiatory suicide—early religious training—later on, for my mother I will become a prostitute—aggression against children... I listen, unalarmed to the owl that cries (11 am) about— The death which I feared in the house was mine—I tell myself but Louise you are not going to kill yourself it is not necessary, you are strong enough now to push suicide away— (loose sheet of writing, c. 1959 [LB-0230])

These writings don't "explain" Louise's visual art. Myriad things informed her practice: Sartrean existentialism, Fontaine's fables, Pascal's *Pensées*, Leibniz's theory of monads, Molière, René Descartes, Montaigne's essays and Stéphane Mallarmé, to cite only a few literary and philosophical touchstones. Music was also important. Art history, not so much. At least not in the sense that she made anything with an eye to historical antecedents, or even to current art. She never aligned herself with any school or movement; the only contemporary she seems to have spoken of with unqualified respect was Francis Bacon. Louise visited Bacon in the late '50s, later writing that he had a face like a ripe melon. He may be the only peer whose work comes readily to mind when encountering hers. The screaming mouths in her fabric heads echo the scream of Bacon's pope. The writhing figures in Bacon's paintings could plausibly inhabit Louise's *Cells*.

Her dream records and process notes belong to a category of literature that isn't really a category but a threadable array of texts impossible to imitate or classify. Many such writings (though hardly all) perform for the author a purgative or exorcistic function, and reflect a paradoxically winning indifference, even hostility, toward a prospective reader. Their approximation of how thought is conditioned by emotion, the attempt to stop received language from over-determining how we use words—or to say it another way, the struggle to make language record what's really going on in our heads instead of turning it into a manicured lie—is nicely exampled by Gertrude Stein:

> It is not well to doubt the reason why fortuitous is colored in the way that not to think again.
> Thank you.
> Enigma makes Susan do. Separately fall follow through antagonistic.

What is grammar to a hare in running. A grammar is in need of little words. There can be no grammar without and if if you are prevailed upon to be very well and thank you. Grammar is meant to have fairly soften fairly often it is alight in white and makes a goat have a mother and a sister two are mother and daughter when the days are long there is more necessity for distraction and walks are pleasant. Arthur a grammar or manner. (Stein, *How to Write*)

Close mimicries of consciousness, such texts necessarily resist cohesion. They rupture whatever forms they assume, whether novel, play, poem, or fable. Louise's loose pages most closely resemble what Francis Ponge dubbed his "proems," multiform variations on a subject—in Louise's case, her own interiority. Some pages simply list associations around an isolated *fixé*, like a broth reduction:

The analysis is a jip
is a trap
is a job
is a privilege
is a luxury
is a duty
is a duty towards myself
my husband. my parents
my children my
is a shame
is a farce
is a love affair
is a rendez-vous
is a cat + mouse game
is a boat to drive
is an internment
is a joke
makes me powerless
makes me into a cop

is a bad dream
is my interest
is my field of study—
is more than I can manage
makes me furious
is a bore
is a nuisance
is a pain in the neck—
(loose sheet of writing,
c. 1958 [LB-0127])

Ontological present and recollected past oscillate inside her psychoanalytic texts, demolishing boundaries. Vagaries of spelling and grammar, quirky line breaks, and shifts between French and English reflect their fidelity to the ebb and flow of cogitation.

Louise compulsively returns to what she called "the family virus," examining it in a prose Petri dish. Tales are never quite spoken aloud but rather whispered in snippets, intruded upon by the sudden appearance of a boiled egg or Victor Hugo, and then they start telling themselves again, their details abruptly, weirdly recast by baffling changes in the narrator's demeanor. Something similar occurs in the tenseless novels of William S. Burroughs and the oneiric texts of Unica Zürn. In Anna Kavan's novel *Ice*, the narrative's premise begins to dissolve almost as soon as it's established. *Ice* tells a story that advances only by undermining its own logic, going back on its word, so to speak, as the author repeatedly tries and fails to assemble compulsively recurring, fetishized images into a sequence that will rid her of them once and for all. This cannot happen. Like Louise Bourgeois's fixations, they can be expelled only in order for them to return.

At their extremity, the writings I have in mind share instantly legible characteristics: anomalous, organic, elusive, fragmentary, issuing from the soul's depths, and driven by an overpowering and tortuous desire, recognized in advance as futile, to scrape down to the raw marrow of existence. One astonishing example is Sarah Kane's final play—the prelude to her suicide—*4.48 Psychosis*. Another is Antonin Artaud's *The Nerve Meter* (1925):

> I have aspired no further than the clockwork of the soul, I have transcribed only the pain of an abortive adjustment.
>
> I am a total abyss. Those who believed me capable of a whole pain, a beautiful pain, a dense and fleshy anguish, an anguish which is a mixture of objects, an effervescent grinding of forces rather than a suspended point
>
> —and yet with restless, uprooting impulses which come from the confrontation of my forces with these abysses of offered finality
>
> (from the confrontation of forces of powerful size),
>
> and there is nothing left but the voluminous abysses, the immobility, the cold—
>
> in short, those who attributed to me more life, who thought me at an earlier stage in the fall of the self, who believed me immersed in a tormented noise, in a violent darkness with which I struggled
>
> —are lost in the shadows of man.

For much of her life, Louise Bourgeois lived close to the edge. A brilliant intellect and vast artistic gifts inhabited the same body as a medley of ungovernable emotions, a strong self-destructive urge conspicuous among them. Yet she never had to be institutionalized like Artaud and didn't manage to kill herself like Kane; Louise knew how to save herself. "Art is a guarantee of sanity": this was her credo, her unwavering faith, and although it doesn't always turn out to be true for artists, for her it did. Which was very fortunate for us as well.

(2019)

TOUGH LOVE AND CARBON MONOXIDE IN DETROIT

The assisted suicide trial of Dr. Jack Kevorkian opened with a "bombshell" from defense attorney Geoffrey Fieger, who announced that the deceased, a young man named Thomas Hyde, had died outside the jurisdiction of the Detroit court. The bombshell left a residue of herring rather than gunpowder. Fieger, a flamboyant attorney given to cosmic pronouncements, threw the venue issue in as acquittal insurance. Although the Michigan Attorney General ruled, at the request of Prosecutor Timothy Kenny, that the trial could proceed in Wayne County, Judge Thomas Jackson decided to let the jury determine if the place of death was correctly stated in the indictment.

The only witness to Hyde's suicide was Kevorkian himself, who administered carbon monoxide gas to the "patient" in the rear of a VW van. (Before his license to prescribe was revoked, Kevorkian used a lethal injection device he called the "Thanatron"; he now uses a barrel of CO attached to a rubber hose and a face mask.) Whether the van was parked behind Kevorkian's apartment in Oakland County at the time, or on Belle Isle, the Wayne County park where he delivered the body to police, only Kevorkian really knew.

Having raised the issue in the first place Fieger later declared it trivial and flogged the press for "inflaming" it. His ego was at stake. He saw himself as an avatar of a great social movement, the Clarence Darrow of humane euthanasia. "The trial of the century, the most important case that's been tried in American jurisprudence in seventy years . . . and to ask me such banal questions about the goddamn venue," Fieger shrilled at one noon press conference. He went on to cite Article 8 of the Nuremberg convention: "When a duly constituted law is immoral, you have a duty not to follow it." The Nuremberg law cites a duty to disobey unconscionable orders, for instance to shoot a prisoner of war or to perform involuntary euthanasia; its application to Kevorkian's volunteer work as an itinerant suicide helper was, in Fieger's view, too obvious for discussion.

So the banal question hovered, dampening the atmosphere, for if the law was immoral and Kevorkian's defiance of it a heroic deed, why was his lawyer trying to get him off on a technicality? Unlike Gandhi, to whom Fieger likes to compare him, or Galileo, to whom he compares himself (along with Einstein, Thoreau, Nelson Mandela, and Margaret Sanger), Kevorkian seemed unwilling to take the rap for what he clearly, and in his own eyes nobly, had done.

While Fieger enjoyed lecturing the court and the press that "all of us," especially those of us with terminal illnesses, were on trial, one couldn't avoid the impression that Jack Kevorkian and his intent constituted a pesky aesthetic problem that had come to overshadow any larger issue. In the absence of clear medical and legal guidelines for assisted death, a cadaverous-looking retired pathologist and his adoring followers had pioneered a do-it-yourself, try-this-at-home approach to "self-deliverance."

The aesthetic problem is not small. It encompasses Kevorkian's theories, his feverish proposals for statewide suicide parlors ("obitariums"), his vision of a "mature" social future in which the terminally ill would be joined by the mentally ill, the severely handicapped, and condemned criminals as worthy candidates for medical experimentation and organ harvesting as well as medicide (Kevorkian's term). There is his abysmal career, thwarted, in his account, by the primitive, superstitious squeamishness of colleagues toward his discoveries: that you can, for example, transfuse whole blood directly from cadavers to live patients, or fix the exact moment when resuscitation becomes useless by gazing into the eyeballs of dying patients.

A Taylor Mead poem comes to mind: "I had the right idea in the wrong brain." Those who don't oppose Kevorkian on principle may still find something unseemly about buying the farm in a "battered VW van" and having a dead body delivered to the wrong police station like a Domino's order gone awry. Under Fieger's questioning, Kevorkian accounted for a lifetime of quirky, morbid, marginal preoccupations as "the boy in me." As someone who had previously given him little thought, I found this wholly accurate. Kevorkian exudes the excited pedantry of an adolescent autodidact. On the plus side, his sincerity is obvious and uncontrollable.

Seated at the defense table every day in the same white windbreaker and blue sweater, Kevorkian immersed himself during hostile testimony in a textbook, *Reading Japanese*. He traced Japanese characters on the page with a spindly forefinger. Outside the courtroom, he sported a crumpled white fishing hat and regaled his wellwishers with fortifying wisdom: "Ever study the Inquisition in school? That isn't a trial, it's an Inquisition."

His claque (Hyde's family and friends, people connected to previous Kevorkian cases, and right-to-die advocates, joined by the occasional class of high school civics students) sat behind him and off to one side near the jury. They were emphatically suburban, ordinary Middle Americans, dressed, like the jurors, in colorful ready-to-wear, as suitable for a barbecue or a cocktail party as a courtroom. Lynn Mills, the local head of Operation Rescue, sat at one end of the front bench, right beside Thomas Hyde's family, sometimes fingering rosary beads atop her Bible, at other times peering into a book called *Fit or Fat*. (Mills is not fat and bears an eerie resemblance to the young Lee Remick.) She was, aside from the prosecutors, the only Kevorkian enemy present.

One can easily include Geoffrey Fieger in the category of aesthetic problems. A tall, fleshy, beaver-faced man who looks like a tennis scholarship gone to seed, Fieger routinely dismisses even his mildest detractors as "assholes" and "sacks of shit," thinks his long-term client is the Messiah, and spends recesses and lunch breaks extolling his own brilliance to anyone who will listen. Fieger is the type of B actor who summons awe among the semi-educated, a sound-bite lawyer who stirs the illusion of passion in anemic settings. The Detroit Recorder's Court, a fairly small basement chamber with octagonal seating and wan-looking travel posters framed on the slatted walls, had a blasé, laid-back feeling, punctured only by Fieger's histrionics and, at trial's end, by the angry, tearful testimony of Heidi Fernandez, Thomas Hyde's common-law widow.

Fernandez described in grueling detail Hyde's disintegration from amyotrophic lateral sclerosis, or Lou Gehrig's disease. Fieger had, shrewdly, shown the jury an appalling videotaped interview of Hyde by Kevorkian, getting it in during the prosecution case, when its contents were immune to cross-examination. He showed it again during closing argument. Fernandez broke into sobs three times on the stand, making the trial feel like a senseless persecution. Off the stand, Fernandez was a rebarbative presence, warming up for her big moment in a succession of dramatic outfits and hairdos, yacking to friends during testimony, and chawing a big wad of gum, delighted to be, along with Dr. Jack, the cynosure of all eyes. As Laurie Anderson recently said of Barbra Streisand, Heidi's thing was about "Love me or I'll kill you." As lubricant for Fieger's closing argument, which involved a ponderous quantity of sudden hushes, whispered rhetorical wheezings ("Are we not human?"), and grandiloquent allusions to the civil rights movement, Fernandez's testimony was untouchable. Prosecutor Kenny, a gangling, woeful figure with the flair of a rural undertaker, had the bad sense to cross-examine her.

As it happened, *Michigan v. Kevorkian* was not a case in which aesthetics carried much weight with the jury. Suicide has traditionally been informed by a sense of style, but medicide is a

Kmart kind of suicide for a democratic era, when aged and bedfast dependents of even the average joe often find themselves attached, at life's end, to wildly expensive feeding tubes and respirators that keep them technically alive for weeks and months in a state of vegetable oblivion.

All states have given this problem some imperfect consideration, recognizing, for example, living wills, which allow the patient to forgo "heroic measures" to prolong life. These are often ignored by hospitals unless the patient has vigilant relatives or attorneys. The Michigan statute, hastily contrived solely to restrain Kevorkian, does allow physicians to administer potentially lethal doses of painkiller to the terminally ill. Assisting those too debilitated to end their lives without help is either the logical next step or the crest of a slippery slope.

In many ways the Kevorkian trial was a moot issue. No fewer than three Michigan judges had declared the statute unconstitutional; it was before an appellate court. A state commission on death and dying was studying the statute for revision, and the current law was set to expire six months after the commission's recommendations. Now, following the trial, the appellate court has invalidated the law but also reinstated two murder charges against Kevorkian, emanating from two assisted suicides in 1991—a case of the state stupidly ratifying Kevorkian's persecution complex.

In any event, the jurors—mostly youngish, mostly Black, mostly female—could, along with everyone else in the courtroom, imagine themselves in Thomas Hyde's hapless, unbearable predicament. In the videotape he can barely talk, has almost no use of his limbs, and says he wants to die. As Fieger accurately predicted, empathy (compounded by a few side issues) swept away any slavish attention to the jury instructions.

The second theme of Fieger's presentation, intent, opened an absurd yet viable loophole. Once the prosecution rested, the circus of bad faith began. Kevorkian's expert witnesses are familiar figures in Michigan, true believers who step up to the mike whenever Jack ushers a fresh patient into the Great Beyond:

Dr. Barry Bialek, an emergency room physician in Ontario, testified that the Hippocratic oath was actually devised by the Pythagoreans, that he doesn't believe in the Greek gods mentioned in the Hippocratic Oath, and that the final treatment measures he could take with ALS patients would do nothing to relieve their pain and suffering.

Kenny: "Would you use carbon monoxide as a pain reliever in the emergency room?"

Bialek: "Yes, if it were made available to me."

Dr. Stanley Levy, internist, told Fieger "it was a heroic effort by Dr. Kevorkian, heroic in the sense that it was not standard, something others would not have thought of," and that Hyde's death in the back of Kevorkian's van was a form of "New Age hospice care."

Kenny: "Do you consider carbon monoxide a poison?"

Levy: "I consider all therapeutic modalities potentially poisonous."

Kenny: "Why is it that you haven't prescribed carbon monoxide?"

Levy: "I haven't thought of it."

Kenny: "Would doses of carbon monoxide provide ALS patients with temporary relief?"

Levy (without irony): "I think relief would be permanent."

Interspersed with the experts, Thomas Hyde's brother, his hospice care worker, and Kevorkian's associates demonstrated an identical inability to link carbon monoxide inhalation with death. The gas, they said, was administered "to relieve his pain and suffering," pure and simple, a phrase that gradually took on the empty familiarity of a jingle. The rote evasion exasperated Kenny, particularly when it came from Kevorkian himself.

Kenny: "You had an expectation that he would die?"

Kevorkian: "That his suffering would end. I surmised he would die. A surmise is a guess."

Kenny: "It was just a guess, after eighteen occasions? Were you startled, sir, to find out after twenty minutes that he was dead? . . . Did you provide enough carbon monoxide to cause his death?"

Kevorkian: "No. Enough to end his suffering."

Kenny: "And death ends all suffering."

Kevorkian: "Not if you're religious it doesn't. Some people believe you go to hell when you die."

We hear from Neal Nicol, who described himself, Kevorkian, and Kevorkian's sister Margo Janus as a "think tank" that evaluates medicide candidates and follows through on their treatment. Nicol looks like the actor Pat Hingle in *The Grifters*, stolid and steady-eyed. He is a medical technician; Margo Janus is a retired secretary. Far from encouraging people to end it all, Nicol said, the think tank urges them to keep going, especially "if we know about a procedure and medication the patient doesn't know about. We make sure the families are involved. We always suggest they get religious counseling."

"If a patient changes their mind," Fieger inquired, "can they come back to you?"

Nicol: "No, if they're uncertain, it means they have emotional problems."

Nicol's testimony was avidly seconded by Margo Janus, whose role in the think tank includes videotaping her brother's consultations and consoling the soon-to-be-bereaved. Janus was florid and irrepressibly upbeat about her brother's practice; every statement was a testimonial. Kevorkian "tries to contact the doctors whose names are on the [patient's medical] records," carefully documents all meetings "to assess for himself that this is a case of true physical distress and mental competence," and "discusses all facets of a life—the social, the economic, the political if you will." Kevorkian "has to satisfy his own high medical standards." Janus was like an adorable parrot, embellishing her answers with buzz phrases about the "blatant unprofessionalism" of the police, the "serenity" achieved by medicide patients, the "last soft and tearful goodbyes" between Thomas Hyde and Heidi Fernandez. Why, Kenny asked, if Hyde's death took place in Oakland County, did Kevorkian drive the corpse to Belle Isle?

"Because it's a very beautiful isle."

While Margo Janus made Thomas Hyde's final hours sound like an especially heartwarming bake sale, expert witness Dr. David Schwartz, a psychiatrist, preening imperiously on the stand, painted a grim picture of what Hyde's end would have been like had Hyde experienced the choking death typical of ALS patients:

"Picture a moment of choking or strangling to death . . . the person would have to become tremendously angry and psychotic—hateful!—there would have been no positive feelings . . . all the remembrances of living, in a broad sense, would have been taken away . . . his hate for what was happening would wipe out anything good that had happened in his life."

Like earlier expert testimony, Schwartz's was over the top, and an adroit prosecutor would have ripped it to pieces. People do, after all, die naturally from ALS and other ghastly diseases without becoming "psychotic." Kenny, lackluster at best, instead returned to the topic of carbon monoxide, which Schwartz predictably declared of "therapeutic value" vis-à-vis "relieving pain and suffering."

A large part of the defense strategy was to show how assiduously ("that means carefully," Fieger instructed one reporter) Kevorkian limits his practice to the hopelessly ill and how scrupulously each case reflects, at every step, the wishes of the patient involved. A key element of the process, stressed many times, is an absence of doubt or ambivalence. If anyone changes his or her mind, even at the last moment, Dr. K. simply folds his tent and moves on.

None of Kevorkian's "fail-safe" measures has any accepted medical or legal value except as exculpatory evidence. Still, they do represent an effort to organize assisted suicide into a semblance of medical propriety. It's worth noting, then, that the pledge to withdraw assistance from ambivalent patients has been inconsistently applied in certain of Kevorkian's cases.

The most controversial case was that of Hugh Gale, an emphysema victim who used the carbon monoxide technique in February 1993. Mr. Gale died at the home of Neal Nicol. Right-to-life activist Lynn Mills, who believes that God led her directly to Nicol's sidewalk garbage, abducted a large bag of it after Gale's death and discovered inside a form labeled "Michigan Obitiatry Zone-1," "Final Action," and "Confidential." On it, Kevorkian had typed an account of the procedure used on Gale:

> A plastic tent was put over his head and shoulders.... The patient then pulled a string tied to his left index finger, other end attached to a clip, which was pulled off a crimped plastic tube, opening it from the outlet valve of a canister of CO gas to the mask. In about 45 seconds the patient became flushed, agitated, breathing deeply, saying "Take it off!" The tent was removed immediately, the mask removed, and nasal oxygen started.... The patient wanted to continue. After about 20 minutes, with nasal oxygen continuing, the mask was replaced.... In about 30–35 seconds he again flushed, became agitated, with moderate hyperpnea; and immediately after saying "Take it off!" once again, he fell into unconsciousness. The mask was then left in place.... Heartbeat was undetectable about 3 minutes after last breath.

However, a police search of Kevorkian's apartment turned up an altered version of this document. The lines pertaining to the second request to remove the tent and mask had been whited-out and typed over with the exact number of characters:

> moderately increased rate and depth of respiration, and muscular tension without overt action (an exaggerated response seen in cases of marked loss of pulmonary reserve). Agitation abated in 10–15 sec., with unconsciousness, calmer gasping breaths for . . .

Gale's death was investigated as a homicide. But authorities eventually accepted a benign explanation of the discrepancy: Kevorkian had simply typed up the procedure in a state of distraction, mistakenly recording the first "take it off" twice. Still, according to his own stringent protocol, he ought to have desisted after one request.

Kevorkian also says that assisted suicide should only be performed after consultation with the patient's regular physician. Yet he never contacted Hyde's doctor. Questioned on this by Kenny, Kevorkian said that Hyde's doctor "might have alerted the authorities" to Hyde's impending suicide or even tried to intervene himself.

This fear of interference furthers the argument for decriminalizing medicide, perhaps, but also suggests, like much else in the trial, that Kevorkian's need for secrecy preempts the best interests of his patients. He has, for example, told several patients that his access to carbon monoxide was threatened by state officials, which may have alarmed people into dying before the gas ran out, rather than when they wanted to.

In Kevorkian's mind, opposition to his practice is monolithic and conspiratorial, requiring secrecy and guile. The AMA and the Catholic Church are in league against him, though "half the doctors" secretly support what he's doing. At the same time, he insists that medicide is a medical procedure that needs to be regulated by the medical profession, in other words by the same people persecuting him. But since society is "still in the Dark Ages," Kevorkian must go it alone, devising through lonely trial and error the ideal way to give human beings "the same compassion we give dogs and cats." In short, Kevorkian intends to do things his way until a law is passed that allows him to continue doing things his way.

Popular sentiment in Michigan favors legalization of physician-assisted suicide. As the trial proceeded, a Hemlock Society petition drive to put the issue on a state ballot reached the 100,000 signature mark. A somewhat uneasy truce exists between Kevorkian's followers, who view euthanasia as a privacy matter outside the law, and the Hemlock Society, which seeks constitutional protection for the right to die. Janet Good, the head of Michigan Hemlock, scoured the courthouse for signatures during lunch breaks. A pleasant, articulate feminist whose involvement in the issue has nothing of Kevorkian's egocentricity about it, Good saw the trial as drawing energy away from the petition drive but backed Kevorkian firmly. They have common enemies.

Hemlock distributes Derek Humphry's bestseller, *Final Exit*, a book that provides advice on at-home suicide by plastic bag, prescription drugs, and other methods.

"It lists everything," Good told me, "but the fact remains that no matter how much you know, and I've become almost a pharmacologist, you still have to know people's weight, and so forth... if you don't have a compassionate physician, you're still up a creek. People with money and education are more likely to know someone who can dispense drugs. It's a class thing. Like everything else."

It did seem to boil down to class, and style: if *Michigan v. Kevorkian* proved anything, it was probably that "death with dignity" has become an extremely elastic term, especially among lower-middle-class people who rightly fear the lengthy suffering and expense produced by mortal illnesses and technomedicine. Dignity, for Kevorkian's clientele, equals "taking control" of death, rendering it economical and relatively painless.

Kevorkian's services are free, therefore a smart consumer option—a working-class alternative to pricey high-tech hospitals and a drearily protracted end. Those with insurance and/or money can afford hospice care (arguably the best option for most of the terminally ill, though hospices, even for the well-off, are few), and as Janet Good said, the upper classes know how to secure a stockpile of Seconal, or at least how to contact the Hemlock Society. For less adroit, less affluent, or less imaginative people, Kevorkian is a brand name, recognized nationally, proven effective in twenty known cases. For the happy few approved by the think tank, death becomes a shrewdly chosen commodity, suicide a group activity the whole family can, at least to some extent, participate in.

"We needed the jury to look at more abstract notions," Prosecutor Kenny mused when the not guilty verdict came in. But death and suffering are the least abstract of human problems, and the last thing the jury saw before deliberating was the video of Thomas Hyde, a former outdoorsman, reduced to a groaning envelope of degenerating tissue. His fate could be anyone's. In the face of such distress, the hyperbolic, crude stratagems of Fieger's defense looked less ignoble than the state's prosecution of an essentially pointless case.

Yes, where it actually happened was a factor in the verdict. Yes, they acquitted on the specious separation of cause from effect, i.e., carbon monoxide from death. At least one juror offered the thought that people have a right to do this but that Kevorkian is going about it the wrong way. Fieger won, but his whole case seemed ineluctably tainted by a steady whiff of cynicism and contempt: the aesthetic problem remained.

As the huge sales of *Final Exit* a few years ago proved, the way people die in America is unacceptable to millions. Most people want the right to decide when life is no longer worth living, and access to the means to terminate "mere existence." The dangers of abuse inherent in legal assisted suicide may be grossly exaggerated by its opponents; after all, thousands go out that way every year, illegally and quietly, with the discreet help of loved ones, and sympathetic doctors. It seems self-evident that we own our bodies, that no law can tell us what to do with them when we ourselves find staying in them intolerable.

On the other hand, since suicide is a private matter, the depersonalization implied in "regulating" it, offering it as a standardized service, and having specialists in it like Kevorkian roaming the landscape, or presiding over McSuicide Clinics, offers Americans nothing more than another dismal method of jamming life into death, surrendering the last remaining mystery to faceless consumerism. This is hardly a legal argument but simply a question of taste or, to be more exact, tastelessness. Had Kevorkian ever treated Thomas Hyde, or anyone, for anything besides "that long disease," his life, the service he provides might well look like the mercy of a friend instead of the dubious kindness of a stranger.

(1994)

AND RATS IN ALL THE PALM TREES, TOO

Thom Andersen's film essay *Los Angeles Plays Itself* recommends a view that many of us who've lived all or part of our lives in Los Angeles have held as a matter of course: to wit, that LA is a great place to live if you have nothing to do with "the Industry," in which thirty-nine out of forty Angelenos are neither employed nor especially interested.

The film's opening sequence illustrates the bogus and silly qualities of "Los Angeles on film," with footage from B movies like *The Crimson Kimono* (1959), *He Walked by Night* (1948), *Pushover* (1954), *Out of Bounds* (1986), and *The Strip* (1951). These blatant duds unfortunately contribute the few moments of humor to be found in Andersen's film, which relies largely on clips from the worst filmic dreck available that uses Los Angeles settings, and samples better movies to illustrate "fakery" of an ostensibly sinister and misleading type. (A minor portion of the film is original footage shot by Andersen and cinematographer Deborah Stratman.)

The fact that a character exits through a door in Long Beach and emerges at a location thirty miles away doesn't really "denigrate" Los Angeles as a city; yet in Andersen's mind, the exigencies of location shooting are cause for considerable indignation and, frankly, an unmerited elegiac tone that readily segues into whining. The filmmaker, whose monologue (delivered by Encke King) is overlaid on the flow of images, even finds, and illustrates at all too considerable length, an offensive diminution in the term "LA" as a substitute for the city's full name.

Despite some compelling examinations of the cinematic use of Los Angeles' architectural treasures and of the neo-neorealism exemplified by extraordinary movies like Kent Mackenzie's *The Exiles* (1961), Edward James Olmos's *American Me* (1992), Charles Burnett's *Killer of Sheep* (1977), Haile Gerima's *Bush Mama* (1979), and Billy Woodberry's *Bless Their Little Hearts* (1984), as well as fruitful forays into the less camera-trampled regions of LA by Maya Deren (*Meshes of the Afternoon* [1943]), Andy Warhol (*Tarzan and Jane Regained... Sort of* [1964]), and Jacques Demy (*Model Shop* [1969]), Andersen is far more obsessed with movies that "get it wrong" than with ones that get it right, and he's willing to split infinitesimal hairs to show how films ignore, misrepresent, banalize, and stigmatize the city he loves.

Perhaps the most jejune assertion Andersen makes is an emphatic contrast between "films shot in New York" and "films shot in Los Angeles." To his way of thinking, any film shot in New York, any scene, "announces itself" as part of New York: a place of clear-cut outlines, well-focused streets and buildings, absent the eternal haze of LA's smog. But this is silly: Hollywood films set in New York are routinely shot in Los Angeles or Toronto, New York serving merely to supply *some* of the exterior shots.

Andersen's prolonged lament for the disappearance of LA's Bunker Hill neighborhood strikes a nerve. It would have been nice if he'd included, besides footage from lousy movies, some documentation of extrafilmic devastations of the urban landscape to support his belief that LA is, or at least was, a pretty special place. Andersen might have cited the razing of the Nickodell's outside the gates of Paramount, the miniaturization of the Brown Derby into a rooftop garnish on the banal shopping center that replaced it, the metastasis of strip malls all over the city, the simulacrum effect of the cleaned-up Hollywood Boulevard, the mall-ification of the once blessedly fallow real estate around the now-shrunken Farmer's Market, and the transformation of so many of the city's quiddities into Disneyfied tourist traps; alternatively, he could have highlighted the venerable landmarks that remain—like Boardner's bar, Musso & Frank, HMS Bounty on Wilshire, Victor's Deli down by the railroad yard, the Rose Bowl Flea Market, Cantor's, the Pantry on Eighth Street.

Andersen decries the movies' frequent casting of Los Angeles' unsurpassed, innovative domestic architecture as the residences of drug dealers, pimps, and other unsavory types, like the Pierce Patchett character in *L.A. Confidential*. He feels that these locations, thus used, reflect the contempt both the movies and local architecture critics feel for architects like Richard Neutra and John Lautner. There is no mention of R.M. Schindler, whose buildings have appeared in many less "negative" representations than ones Andersen cites; moreover, despite a genuine-feeling riff about LA's dispossessed—slum dwellers, bus riders, the Black family without hope—his architectural survey chooses for especial sarcasm the theme restaurant situated on the grounds of Los Angeles International Airport, virtually the only structure in the film designed by a Black architect, Paul Williams.

A film largely consisting of clips from other films, *Los Angeles Plays Itself* stacks the deck against uncountable excluded movies that have accurately caught defining elements of LA; even several Andersen does include reflect "real Los Angeles," either in earlier times or the present day, more accurately than he claims. Among the ignored: Allison Anders's *Mi Vida Loca*, Stephen Frears's *The Grifters*, Tim Burton's *Ed Wood*, Barbet Schroeder's *Barfly*, David Lynch's *Mulholland Drive*, and Joseph Strick's *The Savage Eye*. And these constitute the tip of a large iceberg. Among the films Andersen excerpts and finds picayune quibbles with: *Chinatown*, *Double Indemnity*, *Mildred Pierce*, *City of Industry*, and *The Long Goodbye*.

To give Andersen his due, *Los Angeles Plays Itself* is a personal essay, and despite something mushy in its structure and unassuageably smartass in its tone, it's quite watchable anyway, and lights up now and then with honorably impassioned reflections on behalf of a city the director cares about, the inexorable ruin of which he resents and mourns. Unique among LA filmmakers, Andersen actually sees the city's underclass and its hideous poverty and treats the slums' usually invisible inhabitants with the dignity and compassion they deserve. It's true Los Angeles and Hollywood aren't the same thing—most people in Los Angeles County haven't the slightest involvement in the picture business. On the other hand, LA wouldn't be much of anything without Hollywood. Without the Industry to give the place glitz, it might as well be Cleveland.

(2003)

ALWAYS LEAVE THEM WANTING LESS

> One thing I miss is the time when America had big dreams about the future. Now it seems like nobody has big hopes for the future. We all seem to think that it's going to be just like it is now, only worse.
>
> —ANDY WARHOL, *America*

> It's sort of my philosophy—looking for the nothingness. The nothingness is taking over the planet.
>
> —ANDY WARHOL, *The Andy Warhol Diaries*

From time to time, Andy Warhol entertained the wish to host a television show called *Nothing Special*, and to operate a cafeteria for solitary diners, The Andymat. A social oddity since his Dickensian childhood, Warhol retained the imprint of not-having and not-belonging into adulthood, acquiring vivid people he didn't much care about, and pricey objects he never looked at. To a society poised to reject him, he presented a facade of detachment from other people's lives, even from his own: in an interview with Alfred Hitchcock, he said that being shot was "like watching TV."

What everybody knows about Andy Warhol: he grew up in the 1930s '40s—Depression and wartime years—in a cloacal, polyglot slough of Pittsburgh. He said it was the worst place he had ever been. As soon as he could form the wish to get away, he set about doing so. It was no place for a gifted child, much less a gifted boy attracted to other boys. Warhol's talent manifested itself at an early age; in school years, his ability to draw helped deflect potential bullying. He was picked on, a bit. He acted girlish. He was sickly. After an attack of St. Vitus's Dance, a neurological disorder, his hands shook and his skin lost its pigmentation. His face always vexed him. In the 1950s he got a nose job, to no improving effect. It's unclear when he first recognized his homosexuality. During his childhood, and for decades afterwards, being queer was literally unspeakable in America, along with things like tuberculosis and cancer. One way to glide past a boy's effeminacy was to call him "artistic." Warhol's talent, and some savings bonds his father left after dying in 1942, got him accepted at Carnegie Tech, where he enjoyed the reputation of an "eccentric." After graduating, he moved to New York. With unusual rapidity he became a prominent commercial illustrator. At an epochal moment in the early '60s, he painted a Coke bottle. The rest is history.

Warhol's life story gets recounted a lot, providing as it does a slightly skewed, Horatio Alger–ish, rags-to-riches uplift: the infrequently true story America likes to tell about hard work paying off, meritocracy, success in the land of opportunity. It also bears a resemblance to those fairy tales in which the happy ending doesn't quite pan out, even when magical events transpire. Granted three wishes, the old woman finds herself with a permanent sausage on her nose. Warhol wanted to be rich and famous more than he wanted to breathe; in hardly any time at all, his wish was granted. But however avidly the world treated him like an enchanted princess, his mirror showed him an ugly duckling. The only unusual aspect of this story is that Warhol had already seen it in a movie a million times.

He craved the company of others, but never knew what to do with them. In the '60s, when he "gave up" painting, he put them in his movies, but the films only enhanced his separation from the people he filmed. Their presence dramatized his absence, their logorrhea his silence. In Bob Colacello's *Holy Terror: Andy Warhol Close Up*, which chronicles the Warhol '70s and '80s, Warhol often appears forlornly isolated in rooms full of ostensible friends, clutching a tape recorder or camera like a magic wand, as if turning life into the memory of life without having to experience it. Colacello also notes that however often people hosted Warhol in their homes, none was ever invited into his own beautifully appointed townhouse; on the rare occasion when he had to let someone in, Warhol grew nervous and brusquely impatient for them to leave. Minutes after they left, he called them on the telephone.

Seemingly incapable of spontaneity, some private calculus forever ticked away in Warhol's head at a different speed than that of normal cogitation. He had a Zen-like receptiveness that enabled him to stare for hours at faces, objects, or empty space. Warhol's art is about time, and death, and perceptual slippages; he heard the terrifying static of existence and operated in a mental space that usually precluded ordinary human interaction. His passivity was grandly open and indifferent to interpretation. His personality was constructed to draw people close but keep them at a distance. He had a horror of being touched, an even deeper horror of emotional involvement. He needed buffers and screens between himself and the world, and in that regard was eerily prophetic of a time when screens would feel more real than reality. A maestro of ironic knowingness, he declared himself unknowable: "If you want to know all about Andy Warhol, just look at the surface: of my paintings and films and me, and there I am. There's nothing behind it." No one, thus far, has excavated anything surprisingly at odds with the Warhol reflected in his work or gleaned from the books he published. Everyone is less and more than their publicity, and much of Warhol's life, like everybody's, has the prosaic quality of nothing special. It doesn't detract at all from his art to observe that Warhol had no imagination whatsoever. His literal-mindedness is his strong suit.

Warhol's loneliness seeps through accounts of his life. Although he treated longing and disappointment as diminishing flaws, to be met with a stoical "so what," he was histrionically alone, epically needy, absurdly insecure. He was dead certain about his ambitions, however, prepared to walk over corpses to get where he wanted to go. His unwavering trajectory cost him dearly in the way of Freud's "ordinary unhappiness." This is not an unusual feature of a famous artist's biography. Egotism, ruthlessness, and manipulation are standard requirements for the pitch of global fame Warhol finally reached. The novelty, in his case, was the wonderful simplicity of his approach. His weaknesses were his weapons. He trained his work on what he liked best, the tawdry pathos of supermarkets and tabloids, Coca-Cola and plane crashes, the very realm of homely kitsch that art was thought to ignore and rise above. He played up his nelly gayness in the Cedar Tavern and the White Horse, saloons where boozy Abstract Expressionists brawled over the size of their spiritual innards. Warhol dislodged a culture of heroic interiority with the freaky, externalized clarity of amphetamine, making America safe for the fey, the ironic, the obdurately matter-of-fact. When a radio host concluded an interview by thanking "Mr. Andy Warhol," the testingly silent artist grabbed the microphone and said, "That's MISS Andy Warhol."

His self-deprecation was a charming pose, but his diaries suggest that he really did think himself an incurable mess, sartorially wrong, his wig crooked, his skin a relief map of rashes and zits. He found his sole relief from everyday anxieties in constant work.

He never expressed a jot of self-importance. He genially agreed when critics said his films and paintings were garbage. He neutralized hostility by refusing to defend or explain himself. Most saliently, he never paused in his production of objects, in such fantastic profusion that they're still being catalogued thirty years after his death. The staggering volume of Warhol's output and cannily preserved residua confounds any notional scheme of valuation.

The critic Dave Hickey once remarked that Warhol had no idea of middle-class life, and that sounds exactly right. We associate Warhol with both the bottom and top of the New York food chain, seldom anything between. That the bottom was Warhol's ticket to the top may have been dismayingly unclear to his early collaborators, who imagined the attention Warhol paid them would naturally, effortlessly, lead them to bigger things. ("What is interesting to me," Valéry wrote, "is not always what is important to me.") One ponderous feature of "the Warhol '6os" is the phenomenon of the Warhol Superstar—what Fran Lebowitz called a private joke that got into the water supply. Some came to believe that holding his attention for a time meant his interest ran deeper than their entertainment value. It didn't. As Colacello makes risibly clear in *Holy Terror*, Andy's interest in other people consisted chiefly in what they could do for him, not the other way around. Warhol discarded people he had no further use for, often through expert applications of gaslighting. This wasn't the case with Valerie Solanas, who claimed after shooting him that Warhol "had too much control" of her life. The opposite was true. Warhol declined to have any control of her life. She wasn't Superstar material. As someone once said about Adolf Hitler, some people aren't equipped to deal with disappointment.

The unimaginable fame and wealth he acquired never impressed Warhol enough: there was always somebody richer, more famous, or prettier in whose proximity he felt inadequate. Abjection was his métier, and an integral part of his charisma. As in timeworn film scenarios, the more famous he became, the emptier he felt. "I knew Andy for twelve years," Warhol's longtime, live-in boyfriend, Jed Johnson, told the biographer Victor Bockris. "He never talked about anything personal to me *ever*." Warhol's attempts at intimacy were few, forever ending in disappointment, foredoomed by his choice of impossible love objects and a gross misapprehension of what intimacy involves, i.e., relinquishing total control of a relationship. The sickly child who cherished Shirley Temple and fan magazines sustained a lifelong fixation on clichés of Hollywood romance. "I've been hurt too many times," he often said, like a '50s movie queen, when he thought he was "falling in love."

A ridiculous person in some key areas of life, you could say, a cross between Joan Crawford and Franklin Pangborn. Also a genius of withholding and apposite timing. At times, no doubt, an irritating creep. Everyone encountered the same Warhol, but each came away with a different notion of who he was. This could only be true of someone deliberately, and not at all insentiently, standing back from the passing circus, taking notes.

•

Writing about Warhol poses inherent difficulties. A fulsome literature already exists: the very thorough, very entertaining biographies by Bob Colacello and Victor Bockris; Wayne Koestenbaum's brilliant book-length study, *Andy Warhol*, Jean Stein's *Edie*, Mary Woronov's *Swimming Underground*, or Viva's *Superstar*—or, for total immersion, Warhol's *a*, a novel, which records twenty-four hours of amphetamine chatter among the Forty-Seventh Street Factory's semi-resident speed freaks. There are countless essays and catalogue texts that examine every aspect of Warhol's life and art. The Silver Factory years, when Warhol conferred celebrity on otherwise unknown people in his ken, compel more attention than others: the Superstars provided the exuberant "personality" that Warhol withheld, in a sense acted as surrogate Andys. After the Solanas shooting, Warhol gradually restricted his social life mainly to the rich, the already famous, and employees. He became less interesting to the kinds of people he wanted to keep away from him anyway. His mordant sense of absurdity remained intact. *The Andy Warhol Diaries* covers every day of his last eleven years and reveals more about his ability to cut through the grease of social relations than whole libraries of exegesis. Warhol kept his fingerprints off his manifestations; even the posthumously published diaries were written down by Pat Hackett. This ghostliness invites all manner of interpretation, but Warhol contrived his work, and his public image, to be taken at face value. As his late Rorschach inkblot paintings made abundantly explicit, what you find in his work is what you read into it. You don't need an art degree to get it.

His ascent and eventual centrality appear foreordained in the post-Warhol cosmos, where Andy Warhol Pocket Planners, Andy Warhol Banana Tote Bags, Warhol Philosophy Pencil Sets, and Andy Warhol's Greatest Hits Sticky Notes are among myriad Andy Warhol provender available on Amazon, but Andy Warhol's success owed as much to good luck, chance, and contingency as it did to brilliance and calculation. Warhol always needed collaborators to support the scale of his activity: to squeegee the silkscreens, sit for his camera, perform in his movies, edit his magazine, hustle the portrait commissions, manage his business, sell the work, and so forth. The Warhol phenomenon had too many moving human parts to ascribe its effects solely to the artist's psychology, or the artist's will. The extreme tension in Warhol's work between meaning and nonmeaning has to do with randomness, accidents, and visual noise carrying as much weight as intentions. Likewise, a lot that happened in Warhol's life just sort of happened, meaninglessly, the way lots of things happen in every life.

This obvious fact, and much else that would occur to most sentient beings, has entirely eluded Blake Gopnik, whose elephantine, ill-written, nearly insensible *Warhol* has now been unleashed, weighing in at nine hundred pages, any two of which suggest nothing so much as an incredibly prolonged, masturbatory trance of graphomania. The book's dedication purports that Matt Wrbican, late archivist of the Warhol Museum in Pittsburgh, "wanted this book to be . . . longer." If so, Wrbican definitely shared Warhol's sense of humor.

A prodigy of research, Gopnik claims to have interviewed "more than 260 lovers, friends, colleagues and acquaintances of the artist"——261? 263?—and consulted "some 100,000 period documents." None of this effort has produced anything resembling a fresh idea. Information available for decades is rolled out as startling news, embedded in a dense lard of fatuous pedantry and vapid generalizations. Gopnik's writing generally reads like boilerplate cribbed from bygone reviews and magazine articles, recast in a squirmy, sophomoric prose that deadens everything it touches. *Warhol* opens with a logical impossibility. It places the artist in Columbus Hospital's emergency room twenty minutes after being shot by Valerie Solanas, then informs us, in the very next sentence, that it had taken an ambulance a half-hour to arrive at his studio. This "prelude" features a graphic, bloody account of the five-hour surgery that saved Warhol's life. "Stories have been told of three or four bullets piercing Warhol's body . . . but Rossi found that a single slug had punched straight through the dying man." It is by far the liveliest scene in Gopnik's book and occurs in the first three pages. It also presages the author's bizarre, recurring conviction that he has discovered something that no one previously imagined, or disproven some widely held, erroneous belief—invariably, something everybody knew, or something nobody believed.

In most instances, the alleged revelation is also something nobody could possibly care about: that Gerard Malanga, for example, misremembered which pop song was playing in Warhol's studio on a particular date, or that Warhol was mistaken to think Edie Sedgwick invented the miniskirt, because "it had broken out a few months earlier in both Paris and London." Gopnik's ideal reader is someone who has never read a word about Warhol or contemporary art, seen a movie, or formed two consecutive thoughts without assistance.

Taking a deep dive into Warhol's childhood, Gopnik parses the family ethnicity at numbing length, citing a "world movement for Carpatho-Rusyn culture" only to chide this dubious entity for presuming to link Warhol's art to "the touch on the Rusyns' hand-painted Easter eggs," whereas "one of Warhol's most notable achievements was to push back against both signature touch and hand painting." No statement escapes pointless qualification: "And while it's true that there is a notable folk element in his early commercial art," this is not "specifically Rusyn," whatever that means, but rather "generic enough to have come out of almost any peasant culture." "Folksy styles were everywhere in Warhol's early years," Gopnik adds with a sigh, "as has now been largely forgotten."

No scrap of miscellaneous data escapes Gopnik's scrutiny or fails to trigger an avalanche of mindless verbiage. Everything that happens happens for portentous reasons, foretelling this or that, or recalling something from Warhol's past, or maybe not—Gopnik can never decide, but assumes anyone reading his book is a moron who needs the benefit of his guesses. *Warhol* would shrink to about twenty pages if he simply said what did happen and left it at that.

Somewhere in the suet of chapter 19, Warhol fails to give Malanga money for a taxi after their return from California:

> There are a few explanations for Warhol's froideur toward his assistant. There had been an incident at the motel in Venice Beach when Malanga had brought a girl home to their shared room and Warhol had exploded.
>
> The refusal of cab fare may also have been Warhol making clear that, after all those weeks in close quarters, the young man who had been "helping out" was indeed more an employee than a friend. For the next quarter century, Warhol was forever trying to remind staff, and himself, of the distinction. They and he mostly managed to ignore it, which was a source of everlasting tension.
>
> But the most likely explanation is that Warhol wanted to save the cab fare.

"Maybe," "possibly," "probably," "might be," and "precisely" operate in Gopnik's prose like maypoles for ribbons of blather:

> Malanga's account . . . might be the source of the words put into the artist's mouth seventeen years later . . .

But despite these complications, or maybe because of them...

Maybe he was predicting getting dumped once again, and the murderous bitterness he knew he'd feel.

But in fact his special treatment probably increased his visibility and impact of his films as art.

Nonintervention was probably his greatest sin.

The role of the A-Men in Warhol's life has probably been exaggerated, mostly for the sake of the bohemian patina they lend it. But that patina is precisely what Warhol was after.

As usual, Warhol had figured out precisely where he needed to be if he wanted to register as being on the cutting edge.

Maybe it was precisely that dual nature, suiting both matrons and mavens, that made the Flowers Warhol's first serious salable wares.

What is new in *Warhol* is an omnipresent species of trivia normally consigned to archives, for the simple reason that it is trivia, the submental detritus of liquor store receipts and electric bills, occasionally helpful in fixing the date when something occurred; Gopnik is endlessly fascinated by this experiential lint and can ruminate for pages on the possible meaning of a laundry ticket. Determined to find significance in any bit of minutiae he comes across, he often achieves an almost sublime idiocy: "In 1961, Warhol's own gum chewing might have been a new pose, but it reflected a genuine and lifelong interest in the worldview and culture of actual gum chewers." "He might have liked frankfurters fine, but earlier that day he'd asked a photographer to treat him to the newest and fanciest French restaurant in town." "But Warhol's striped shirt also pointed to a more recent precedent with just as much cultural cred as Picasso." There are deeper ponderings, too, gleaned no doubt from over 260 interviews: "Maybe the most important thing to recognize is that he came across as your standard secular, gay, lefty, party-going avant-gardist, and that was the image he chose to let loose on the world."

Gopnik's effusions of admiration for Warhol seem inspired entirely by Warhol's fame and success. They sound exactly like contempt, couched in the vernacular of a high school newspaper, circa 1959: "yet another of his zany conceits," "As a good avant-gardist," "with his brilliant eye for the avant-garde," "Warhol's old avant-gardism," "Warhol's movie . . . rambles from goofy scene to goofy scene," "a wacky avant-garde aesthetic," "she refused his goofy, impractical offer," "his patina of weirdness," "seeing some weirdo artist muscling in," "weird and wooly collaborations," "the simple weirdness of that concept," "but the truth is that the whole thing was more goofy than savvy," "Earlier weirdos, like those at the Judson," "his weirdness would always win out."

There's more. Much more. Unidentified quoted material appears, suspiciously often, in support of whatever nebulous point Gopnik thinks he's making. Frequently, named persons are quoted without source references, leaving an impression that Gopnik personally interviewed people who never spoke to him. Gopnik projects his own punitive fantasy of Warhol as a creature from outer space onto an assortment of straw figures—the public, the reader, the art establishment, or whomever—as stubborn "myths" only Gopnik has been brave enough to dispel. "So much for [Warhol] as a film ignoramus." "Warhol often gets described as apolitical, which isn't right." "The myth that Warhol was close to teetotal falls under the weight of evidence." "This fits with a common notion that Warhol was deeply un- or even anti-intellectual, and maybe marginally illiterate or at least dyslexic."

It's unlikely that anyone in America needs Gopnik's lucubrations on amphetamines and their effects, though it may come as news to young people that many different kinds of pharmaceutical speed were easily available in the '60s, all of them more fun than Adderall. To his credit, Gopnik does provide a lengthy description of the gay scene Warhol found in Pittsburgh during the 1940s, though the best one can say is that he spoils this less than everything else. His fondness for anachronisms ("hardly conformed to the era's stereotype of the wacky gay man," "cliched image of a slight and swishy queer artiste," "the light-loafered limp-wristedness," "on the receiving end of his friends' swishophobia," "a brazen self-portrait by an unrepentant homosexual"), even when mobilized in defense of Warhol against "homophobia," reflects the provincial squeamishness that provides the only real hilarity in this book. For a time, Warhol photographed men having sex in his studio; Gopnik refers to this as one of the artist's "more scurrilous projects." He pronounces the crotch shot Warhol did for the Rolling Stones' *Sticky Fingers* album "naughty and daring." Ondine "supplied plenty of naughty gay talk." This nervous, prudish flippancy, native to the suburban bourgeoisie, addresses a constituency Warhol had no use for whatsoever. The most telling example, in its way, is Gopnik's description of *Trash* as a film "about the sexual escapades of a drug addict." The entire premise of *Trash* is that the male lead doesn't have any sexual escapades, because he can't get it up.

This book could only appear at a time when the bohemian mobility, sexual freedom, and cultural ferment of New York in the '60s, '70s, and early '80s are not simply being forgotten as people who were there die off, but becoming unimaginable. A time when New York has become so cluelessly middle-class that someone can actually write, of the back room at Max's Kansas City, that Warhol "behaved more like the cool-cat senior in high school who the freshmen do everything to impress and who looks on with amused condescension." This is the point of view of someone who never, ever could have gotten into Max's.

(2020)

HIDDEN IN PLAIN SIGHT: ROBERT BRESSON'S *PICKPOCKET*

I have an unusually easy way of remembering when I first became fascinated by Robert Bresson's films. *Pickpocket* (1959) was the first one I saw, at the old Orson Welles theater in Cambridge, Massachusetts, in my late teens; it was also the first movie I saw on LSD. (Even on acid, I was never one to enjoy *Snow White and the Seven Dwarfs*.)

Since I hadn't absorbed the truisms about Bresson that even then encased his work in a gelatin of spiritually heroic clichés, I was, after *Pickpocket*, skeptical about the thematic platitudes critics and film writers routinely and confidently attached to him. Some of them were plausible, some undoubtedly true, but many just sounded convincing; once art becomes a religion, you can say any high-minded nonsense about it with utter impunity.

As per standard critical note, *Pickpocket* is obviously "inspired" by Fyodor Dostoyevsky's *Crime and Punishment*. A man commits forbidden acts, gets caught, and goes to prison, where his suffering is ameliorated by the steadfast love of a good woman.

But *Pickpocket*'s central character, Michel (played by the Uruguayan nonactor Martin LaSalle), with his watery, feebly asserted version of Raskolnikov's Nietzscheanism, is merely a petty thief, conspicuously lacking the will to monstrosity of Dostoyevsky's axe murderer. His crimes never rise above the level of common, small-time transgression. They are enlarged to epic scale only by his neurasthenic imagination. His decision to tempt exposure and shame on a daily basis is a difficult one, but not because he wonders, terrified like Raskolnikov, whether he's truly capable of it. It isn't monstrous to steal. Often it is necessary, and its drastic punishment is more wicked than the crime. *Les Misérables*, after all, is about a man implacably hounded by the law for stealing a loaf of bread.

True, Michel could get a job. But stealing has a specific psychosexual meaning for him, beyond fulfilling the simple need to eat. Michel is like a man who knows he can cop an orgasm if he manages to be in the right place at the right time and rubs up against the right partner. His fears are more logistical than spiritual, and also function as aphrodisiacs.

It's unlikely that Michel steals because he considers himself a "superman," in a class of hypothetical extraordinary beings whose unusual gifts place them above the law—though he posits such a theory, abstractly, in his sour, unengaging encounters with the police detective played by Jean Pélégri. Michel steals because it is the only act that makes him feel alive in a world becoming dead—not only dead to pleasure and unprogrammed emotions but, as later Bresson would make ever more explicit, organically dead. Theft reconnects Michel to the flow of life around him, from which he otherwise feels desperately isolated, and which he perceives as pathetically limited in its possibilities.

When he refuses to see his dying mother and answers his friend Jacques's sarcastic reproach "And you say you love your mother" with "More than myself," Michel says the literal truth. This is not because he can't access a profound love he really feels for her but because he feels nothing at all, and loves her as much—in other words, as little—as anything or anyone else. A prisoner of coercive social forms, like all of us, Michel "feels" he should feel what he can't feel, but since he doesn't, he can only offer the empty verbal assurance that he does.

Michel is more like Albert Camus's Meursault than Raskolnikov, but this likeness is nearly as superficial. Meursault's only important act in *The Stranger* is the unmotivated killing of an Arab on an Algerian beach. Michel's thefts, on the other hand, produce an income, require continual refinement, and relieve him of the wage-earning regimentation of the Parisian subbourgeoisie. He sets a trap for himself, but the forces of order that close it on him have no intrinsic worthiness; they simply defend a mediocre status quo that governs the circulation of capital.

The erotic center of *Pickpocket* is not Michel's growing love for Jeanne, the young woman neighbor looking after his mother. Indeed, the shrewdly chosen visage of Marika Green emits expressions of overdrawn humility and neurotic dutifulness. If she wishes to "save" Michel, whose disjointedly angular beauty so closely resembles that of Egon Schiele, this may be the effusion of saintly purity, but if you ignore the austerity of Bresson's cinematography, you can also assume that she wants to save Michel for herself, to secure an attractive breadwinner for her fatherless children, "redeeming" him for a future life of dreary convention.

Far more romantic than his dealings with Jeanne are Michel's encounters with the thief played by the real-life pickpocket Kassagi. Distinctly reptilian, as comfortable in criminality as a rubber duck in a bubble bath, Kassagi is like the lover who, after you've had a few quotidian partners, reveals the astonishing range of pleasures available from someone who actually knows what he's doing.

The "redemptive ending" of *Pickpocket*, cannibalized whole in any number of movies, is also, from a certain angle, specious. Jeanne may well repine while Michel's in prison, sustained by the exalting power of love; Michel, on the other hand, given his good looks and fragile physique, will probably find dozens of lovers in jail to refine his talents as a criminal, and emerge a hardened, masterfully seductive, charmingly predatory thug.

Yes, it's comforting to think otherwise. We would like to believe, contrary to everything we know, that a hopelessly corrupt world offers endless opportunities for rehabilitation. But as the protagonist of *The Devil, Probably* (1977) would put it, rehabilitation to what? Belief is just as toxic as cynicism. Redemption has become a business, a commodity, a lucrative premise for launching an Oliver North or a G. Gordon Liddy as a talk show host. Bresson had to have known this well in advance of the fait accompli, given that *Pickpocket* was made long after Guy Debord and the Situationists had described precisely how our emotions were being turned into products.

The Catholic right loves to claim Bresson as a sort of "Christian atheist," yet his work is remarkably fixated on the death of feeling and the uselessness of Christian faith. To find in it a lamentation for the absence of God is to cheapen the existential toughness of its core. While Bresson adapted material from a protofascist Christian like Georges Bernanos, his version of *Diary of a Country Priest* (1951) presents its clergyman as an insipid admirer of his own earnest masochism. Bresson's real subject is not the priest but the poisonous malice of the provincial imbeciles who constitute his "flock."

Furthermore, before anyone awards Bresson a Jean Hersholt Humanitarian Award for his so-called belief in spiritual redemption through suffering, and in the ennobling, Tolstoyan honesty of peasant ordinariness, we should consider his first great work, *Les Dames du Bois de Boulogne* (1945), and his final masterpiece, *L'Argent* (1983). In the former, Bresson shows us María Casares wreaking an intricate and ingenious revenge, à la Pierre Choderlos de Laclos, on a once potential lover she never wanted in the first place and desires only after she ruins him; frequently described as an anomaly in Bresson's oeuvre, this film is anything but. Leo Tolstoy's story "The Forged Coupon" illustrates through the metaphor of counterfeit currency how the inauthentic spreads destruction through a society; in Bresson's adaptation, *L'Argent*, he bends this tale into a straightforward, horrifically brutal depiction of money itself as humanity's ultimate self-annihilating invention.

Pickpocket, like all of Bresson's films, records the expiration of humane feeling in the modern world, the impossibility of decency in a universe of greed. This is amply illustrated in *Au hasard Balthazar*

(1966), a film about the sufferings of a donkey so painful to watch that if you can see it through without weeping, you deserve to be hit by a Mack truck when you leave the theater. For Bresson, the casual destruction of life, any life, is the damning imperative of the human species. As William Burroughs put it, "Man is a bad animal." This message is spelled out in boldface in *The Devil, Probably*, with its copious footage of man-made ecological disaster.

Critics frequently link Bresson with Carl Dreyer, which is a bit like pairing August Strindberg with Henrik Ibsen. Like Ibsen, Dreyer has a seamless lack of humor and a solemnity that gives his films the gravity of a cancer operation.

In Bresson, however, the absurdity that delicately fringes Strindberg's dark dramas echoes in whole passages of deliberately idiotic dialogue, in actions that speak volumes about nothing but feel uncomfortably textured like real life. Dreyer boils life down to its pivotal moments; Bresson shows that most of our lives are consumed by meaningless routines. This can be startlingly funny, just when you thought a Bresson movie couldn't become more grim.

In *Pickpocket*, the society whose laws Michel breaks is far more criminal than he is—not technically, not legally, but spiritually. This is Bresson's archly comic irony, heavily veiled in nocturnal chiaroscuro. His film's tragedy, which is finally more important, is that Michel would like to feel guilty for his crimes, and would even like to love his mother, or Jeanne. But like the humans of the future that Bresson so clearly envisioned, who are already living among us, Michel can't feel a thing, and couldn't love anyone if his life depended on it. The sad truth is, it doesn't.

(2005)

MOVIE RITES

Even before Robert Bresson died, an elegiac note had begun to sound in various essays and articles written about him. Elegiac not for him personally, but for his whole conception of cinema. The *Chicago Reader*'s Jonathan Rosenbaum, for instance, worried that Bresson's films, in which the meticulous composition of shots and the precise spatial location of sound effects are of paramount importance, translate unusually poorly to home video; and, since video is where today's would-be cineast gets acquainted with film history, the persistence of Bresson's vision is called into doubt. In *Robert Bresson*, Cinematheque Ontario's 1998 collection of essays, Martin Scorsese put it this way: "I have to wonder whether or not young people who have grown up on digitally engineered effects and DTS soundtracks can actually find the patience required to watch a film by a Bresson or, for that matter, an Ozu or an Antonioni. In a way, it seems impossible: it's as though they're from different worlds."

These are not trivial concerns. They suggest larger questions about aesthetic obsolescence, the effects of technology on culture, and precisely what sort of different world we uneasily inhabit now, in contrast to the world of 1960, or even 1980. Complaints of an ever-shortening audience attention span have been heard for decades; we are assumed to live, today, in a state of perpetual distraction, lacking depth or interiority, and I suppose the question really is, to what end? Charles, the protagonist of Bresson's *The Devil, Probably*, provides an answer of sorts when he sarcastically recites a list of consumer products and banal leisure-time activities as the things he would lose if he killed himself.

I think of Bresson's films as residue of an ever-receding moment, or perhaps of a state of mind, an atmosphere, that living in the present makes less and less available. It's something like this: You go to a work of art and hope to be transformed. Quietly, secretly, to be roused from a waking sleep, agitated at some resonant depth in your psyche, shown something you couldn't have shown yourself. Bresson shocks you into reconsidering your whole existence. Not in the cheap sociological way that makes so many current movies "relevant," but in the almost somnolently muffled, self-exasperated way that Sartre's *Nausea* makes you see what is right in front of you as the infinitely strange, unassimilable horror that it is.

It occurs to me that I saw all of Bresson's films except *L'Argent* in the era before home video, when to know about film one had to go to screenings—in other words, to schlep all over the city, in all kinds of weather, at odd hours, to places where twenty-five or thirty other people would have gathered to see the same movie. Those were social occasions as well as aesthetic experiences, and they had something to do with a kind of . . . well, *communion* with other people interested in film as more than idle entertainment, who had also carved out the time in their lives to see something special—something important enough, taking sufficient priority over other things, to claim the particular hours when the theater happened to be running the film.

The VCR/video store (now DVD and streaming) phenomenon has eliminated the sense of occasion around viewing any movie. With the generally welcome convenience of seeing films whenever you wish to, at home, on a television set or computer screen, something essential in the experience of film—I mean the aesthetic experience itself; in short, the entire point of it—has been diminished. Like many technical innovations, home video "saves time," while leaching the flavor out of the time it saves. The idea of the intricately organized frame and its variegated effects, the precise use of sound, the scale of the projected image, everything that could give a film the multilayered, revisitable texture of a novel, has become less important than a kind of documentary immediacy. The expectation of seeing something new, life rendered from a fresh angle, in a complex way has also dimmed: the art no longer "advances" in time, one no longer has to keep up with it, all periods are jumbled together and equally available on a store shelf. The sense that certain movies were speaking to a particular, rarefied constituency, one that possessed a hard-won familiarity with the medium's possibilities, disappeared at the moment when any slob could take those movies home. (Imagine that the only books you could get from the library were expurgated or condensed, or had parts of each page sheared off.)

With respect to Bresson, it seems to me that the things his films deal with are anathema to contemporary filmmaking: the alienation of his characters from quotidian, materialistic modeling of personality; their abject internal revolt against reality; their torturous movements toward grace; their obdurate unlikableness—everything rendered in plain, often metonymic movements, gestures, glances, with gravid silences between laconic bursts of speech, spells of utter blankness, one thing following another with a maddeningly stingy economy, as if "almost nothing" were, for the filmmaker, a theological imperative. And then there is Bresson's breathtaking avoidance of picturing key events; his selective foregrounding of sound over image; his refusal to use stars or even professional actors; his disdain for psychology; his lingering attention to everything that exists between thought and action; his exclusion of anything "theatrical"; the mesmerically even, unruffled tone of his films from beginning to end; and last but hardly least, his unequivocal loathing of capitalism. His films feel necessary in a way that other films just don't. Bresson ruins our taste for the mediocre.

(2000)

DISNEYLAND BURNS

I flew to Paris with the idea of finding something... piquant to write about the Euro Disney resort park in Marne-la-Vallée. It was just a natural for me. For one thing, the various Disney creatures (Mickey Mouse, Donald Duck, Goofy, Minnie Mouse) have always filled me with a high degree of disgust and terror, a creeping fear of idiocy or irreversible insanity that might be brought on by "giving in" to the universe these characters inhabit.

At the same time, I recognize these monstrosities as genuine American archetypes, eerily potent symbols of our culture, about which anybody's personal feelings (even mine!) are utterly irrelevant. "Mickey Mouse will see you dead," as one of Robert Stone's characters says somewhere.

John Berger compares the art of Disney to that of Francis Bacon. He says that the same essential horror lurks in both, and that it springs from the viewer's imagining: There is nothing else. Even as a child, I understood how unbearable it would be to be trapped inside a cartoon frame.

I didn't anticipate a crisis—well, I did and I didn't—that would keep me, for ten days in Paris, skidding along the rim of an emotional meltdown, my own private volcano. "There is nothing else" was never far from my mind. The harder I tried to push this melancholy consideration away, the more fiercely it asserted itself, the more desperate I became to resolve a slew of painful differences between myself and another person, in spite of her absence.

I would decide the implications of recent bad scenes one way, then the exact opposite way a few minutes later, carrying on both parts of a conversation in my head, often while walking up and down the rue Saint-Gilles in Montparnasse, where I frequently killed time between lunch at the Hôtel Lutetia Brasserie and early evening cocktails at the wine bar around the corner. I sat in a little cement park at the end of the rue Saint-Gilles, thrashing through *Le Monde* or the *Independent* with the kind of obsessed urgency typical of the mad, the newspaper pages crumpling messily in the faintest breeze, and telling myself: You little imbecile, you really are insane by this time, no wonder she can't stand you anymore. You've fucking lost your fucking mind. I later read the situation in a totally different way, but that was how it was.

The whole prospect of going to Euro Disney became onerous, dreadful, a kind of supreme insult to the operatic emotions I was struggling with. Could I even do my job under such a blitz of heavy feeling, such hopelessness, such ridiculous idolatry of another person? (And sometimes, like a fresh breeze, the thought would come: If anybody's crazy, it's her.)

It didn't help that the Disney press office, no doubt having figured out what the *Village Voice* was, declined to make company executives available for interviews, and restricted our press passes to a maximum of three days. (I was traveling with a photographer.) The Disney people were extremely bureaucratic, cordial, and uncooperative. I had had the idea of bringing various intellectuals and artists out to the park for their impressions, but it now appeared that to do this I would have to lay out the exorbitant entrance fees myself. In other words, I would be heartbroken and penniless in my favorite city in the world and, worse, not even be in my favorite city but inside a huge American plastic bubble at the ass end of my favorite city, in the Brie region of the Paris Basin. No thank you. Brie, as you probably know, is a type of soft cheese. Suitable, I suppose, for Mickey Mouse.

Several years ago I was on the opposite end of a more nebulous romantic impasse, again with a woman, who, as it happens, now lives in Paris, and has lost her mind, or part of her mind (not over me, thank God). She seems to be getting it back, bit by slow bit, but her mind is still like a loose phone wire and when I spent time with her, I continually told myself: Keep on like you're going and you'll end up the way she is now, half in, half out of the moment, spilling into another dimension whenever there's a silence or a break in continuity. Unless you've known madness it sounds romantic, like Breton's *Nadja*, to wander the Paris streets with a woman in the throes of subacute schizophrenia, who sees signs and auguries in every chance occurrence. In reality it's exhausting and depressing and made me want to blow my brains out with the kind of pistol one can buy so easily in America, but, fortunately or not, not so easily in France.

It took forever to get motivated, plus one final bracing Rémy Martin in the Bar Centrale in the Marais. (I'd read in the prospectus that no alcohol was served in Parc Euro Disney.) Then to the RER train in the giant Métro station at Châtelet–Les Halles, where tickets for Marne-la-Vallée, home of Euro Disney, come in a little folder with a Mickey Mouse silhouette pouch for your return ticket. The train held an unreadable assortment of suburban types, getting off in woebegone places like Bry-sur-Marne and Noisiel, Balzac towns full of hundred-year-old wooden buildings, obdurate necks and ruddy faces, and, on certain RER platforms, huge curved placards featuring the entire family of Disney characters grouped at the bottom, grinning moronically, the legend above them promising, in French: "Where Every Day Is Like Sunday." This automatically recalled the Morrissey song: "a seaside town / that they forgot to bomb." Very few people were headed for Parc Disney, though fifty or sixty debarked at the end of the line, dispersing by bus or private cars into the countryside.

The RER station is all glass and aluminum or glass and steel, all transparencies and streaks of shiny gray; all of modern Paris outside the city's heart favors this Alphaville or Tonka-toy approach to municipal architecture. It is that cheaply durable mall look that colonized Les Halles with strip joints and hamburger shops when the old markets were torn out fifteen years ago. The Marne-la-Vallée metro station sits hublike athwart the various spokes of the Disney wheel, in it but not of it, somehow, like the vaporetto landing at the train station in Venice.

The light was going. I thought it was going to rain. We walked through the gates of the park, into a gaudily landscaped forecourt, the kind of thing you'd find under an atrium at a major Hyatt Regency, with fountains splashing and foaming through a lot of ornamental brickwork. Unhappy children were crying outside the entrance of Euro Disney. For them the dream was over, evidently. A big clock on the front of the main building, with Mickey Mouse hands. A salmon-colored building with little pinpricks of light over every linear surface. The overdone gingerbread effects against the waning, cloud-silted evening sky evoked certain paintings of Paul Delvaux.

Yes, it was late in the day and midgets were casting giant shadows. Really terrible roller-rink music screeched from every imaginable cranny of the simulated rail station, which does in fact have an elevated train passing overhead, but more strategically acts as a barricade to the main park, and functions as a hotel, too, with long ornate arcades at either side of the ticket windows—arcades stuffed with shops selling anything you can think of, mostly bogus 1890s crap, fake memorabilia, fake antiques, globe lamps in frosted glass, old boxing posters, political posters, patriotic posters, anything with a flag on it, everything except that Minnie Mouse fuck doll we've all been waiting for, creepy little teacups, creepy little desk ornaments, things that working-class people might think genteel or precious, those kinds of pathetic objects one wishes could have an aura or sentimental value, but because they come from a place like this, they can't.

Across the RER station, and partially pillowed in a mist that was rising in the twilight, was a shipwreck-looking huddle of aggressively thematic structures called Festival Disney. From the vantage point of the main park, the angular roofs and facades of Festival Disney resemble the Olympic Village in Munich, which Werner Schroeter used, in *The Death of Maria Malibran*, to evoke the infernal factory landscape of Manchester, England, at the dawn of the Industrial Revolution.

Behind the RER station, the private Disney bus line ferries visitors to the five hotels dotted across a densely landscaped corner pocket of the Disney complex. Though it later turned out you can easily walk to the hotels by passing through Festival Disney and down a corny promenade that looks like a backwater marina in Miami, minus yachts, and along an artificial lake ("Lake Buena Vista," what else), new arrivals, weighed down with luggage, naturally opt for the buses, which crawl along a circuit of trafficless internal roads indistinguishable from the "real" rural autoroutes outside the . . . what do you call it—the compound, the corporate property, the Disney—protracting what ought to be a three-minute zip into fifteen or twenty minutes' worth of ennui.

Euro Disney can be depicted within a circle, the "Boulevard Circulaire," in fact, which wraps around the amusement park, the resort hotel complex, Festival Disney, the artificial lake, and the property earmarked for Disney-MGM Studios Europe. Outside this enchanted perimeter lie Golf Euro Disney and Camp Davy Crockett, a golf course and camping site respectively, which properly belong to the extended future Disneyville, Disneymonde, or whatever it will ultimately be called.

It seems that the hypothetical planning of Euro Disney knows no final boundaries, that its American proprietors envision a steady, limitless growth, a Manifest Disney surging eastward across northern Europe, like Borges's map that grew until it coincided with the area it charted—eventually folding in private housing, perhaps transforming the countryside into Disney towns and Disney villages.

Note that the perimeter of Euro Disney contains part of the state railway system, a metro station, and a presently inactive TGV trunk line. The wider realm of Future Disney encompasses numerous public roads. There has been, in effect, a complete interpenetration of the Disney corporation and the state: for instance, the privately franchised newspaper kiosk in the RER station is perhaps the only one in France that doesn't sell cigarettes. Cigarettes must be purchased at certain hotel lounges and Festival Disney bars, at a steep markup.

The Disney person I most wanted to speak with was Philippe Bourguignon, senior vice president in charge of real estate development. But the Disney press office instantly nixed this proposal: I was writing about the park, no? Bourguignon is involved with future projects, of no immediate concern. But of course it's this "future" thing, the vision thing, the prospect of metastasizing all-American amusements transplanted from tropical Hollywood to the damp northern European farm belt that's most arresting and sinister about Euro Disney as a whole. The landmass acquired by Disney in Marne-la-Vallée extends across several towns—Bailly-Romainvilliers, Magny-le-Hongre, Coupvray, Chessy, and Serris, in the corn-, sugar beet-, and wheat-growing flatlands—and is, roughly, one-fifth the size of the city of Paris.

Imagine, if you will, a major Japanese corporation purchasing ten square miles of the Ramapo hills to develop MITSUBISHI LAND USA, a theme park devoted to Japanese comic book and animation characters (and Japanese fast food, Japanese kitsch, Japanese history in broad strokes, and Japanese corporate underwriting), directly across the Hudson from Manhattan—Americans would, I think, burn the place down. (My friend Lynne Tillman thinks just the opposite. "Americans would love it," she assures me. "Besides, have the French—I mean really, when have the French even produced one major rock and roll, one important music group in all this time? They're still going 'ye-ye,' 'ye-ye' . . .")

The French despise Euro Disney—François Mitterrand told a TV interviewer in a withering voice that it was "not his cup of tea"—but, in a jittery economy, look indulgently on anything that promises to bring in revenue. Jeffrey Katzenberg and Michael Eisner aren't in any immediate danger of being hung, even in effigy, in the Place de la Bastille. On the other hand, despite the massive long-term capital investment (you don't open a dry-cleaning shop unless you're prepared to lose your shirt for two or three years, much less a theme park one-fifth the size of Paris), there's a possibility that the whole project will fall on its face. After all, the Ninja Turtles tour crapped out at the French box office, proving that kids are not the same everywhere. So far, Euro Disney isn't getting anything like its projected numbers of visitors or revenue. The *New York Times* reports that the park will lose $60 million in its first fiscal year.

We're at the Newport Bay Club, a kind of puffed-up New Englandy neocon, pomo sprawl with indoor and outdoor swimming pools, a "yacht club" restaurant, and a plaster bust, I swear to you, of Walt Disney, perched at eye level at the top of the sweeping double staircase leading down to the "Cape Cod" dining room, the "Lake Buena Vista" boathouse, the ferry landing, the enclosed swimming pool, and blah blah blah.

Designed by mediocre architect Robert Stern, the place reeks of bogus gentility and class pretension. It evokes the grand hotels of northern New England, like the Balsams, which have long been converted from upper-class spas to petit bourgeois convention centers, or the grotesquely proletarianized restaurants and hotels of Carlsbad, Czech Republic. The only people in here come from an unbearable strain of French bourgeoisie that actually pays for first-class seats on the Métro, and the kind of American and German swine so bloated from excessive meat consumption they move in an alternative universe of obesity. Of course, you also get your svelte grandmoms and a smattering of debs in Laura Ashley gowns, and the occasional young corporate barnacle nursing a

Scotch in the lobby-level piano bar, yearning for a blowjob from his fiancée, or, better, from someone else's fiancée. But mostly you get fat people with fat kids.

The Newport Bay gives off a "subdued" feeling completely at odds with the garish excess people have come here to expose their children to. On balance, however, the room isn't bad. There is, surprise, a minibar, stocked with the standard beers and liquors. The alcohol prohibition, it turns out, applies only to the actual Euro Disney theme park, not to its surrounding franchises. The Newport Bay has 1,098 rooms. Nightly tariff in peak season, Fr 1100, e.g., almost $250. In actual Newport (where, if memory serves, there aren't any hotels) or actual New York, this would buy you a luxury suite. This room is slightly smaller than those in the average college dorm.

After our very brief exposure to the blandishments of Euro Disney, the photographer and I are chugging through the contents of the minibar with what can only be called zeal. On the cable TV, an endless montage of advertising for the very resort that surrounds us! Some of the attractions—big-tit girls in Mylar go-go fringe and twanging country crooners—look surprisingly adult, really. It appears that we're just missing Happy Hour at one of the Festival Disney theme bars. The good news is that something called "the Hurricane" is scheduled to happen after 9 p.m. Also, the bars stay open until 3 a.m. This means there is some sort of grown-up life around here, if you stretch the term "grown-up" a teeny bit. Well, of course, there would have to be: if you had to run Euro Disney according to the ludicrous aporias of "family values," with no chance of at least the head of the family getting trashed and maybe laid by someone not his family-value partner, chances are you would have to locate Euro Disney in Utah rather than France. Naturally, some journalist could easily go to town on Festival Disney, DISNEY'S DIRTY SECRET or what have you.

I am on the phone with the novelist Jean-Jacques Schuhl, with whom I've been drinking and dining in Paris every night. I am under the slightly stoned impression that "the Hurricane" is an actual meteorological event, an artificial storm contrived by those wacky Disney Imagineers, staged in the downtime after all the tubby little snotnosed Mouseketeers have been tucked away in their $250-a-night beds. In my mental world, "the Hurricane" would logically provide the more mature Disney consumer with that reassuring, modern sense of imminent cataclysm.

As it happens, some type of weather is blowing up outside, ruffling the gray gelatinous skin of Lake Buena Vista, where a lonely motorized pontoon boat is ferrying schmucks from the Newport Bay to the Hotel New York (Fr 1600 a pop in peak season, or $320 a night). The New York is a vapid exercise in capital P postmodernism by Michael Graves. A plastics convention is in progress over there, across the "lake." I don't mean to sound like a snob, but I can't help contrasting this dinky artificial pond and these pathetic nouveau nothing buildings, the fake grassy knolls and stubby hills bordering the lakeside walkways, with my first glimpse of Lake Como from the Milan-to-Cologne overnight train, or some of the other sublime aquatic views that Europe and nature provide free of charge. I mean, consider Venice in winter. What I'm seeing from this window is a very dim suburban notion of luxury, the kind of spotless, lifeless municipal space provided by a secure tax base in places like the Portland, Oregon, riverside. Everything psychotically clean and landscaped for optimum surveillance ease, like Haussmann's makeover of Paris itself, though here every blade of grass has been designed by some eminent wastebasket of contemporary architecture.

"Don't leave the hotel room," Jean-Jacques insists. "Only report what you see on the television."

"I'm tempted by that Hurricane, though, Jean-Jacques. Leave it to Disney." ("Hurricane" turns out to be the name of the Festival Disney disco.)

Jean-Jacques clears his throat. "And is it true, out there, they have prostitutes dressed as Minnie Mouse? Wearing large masks and ears? You must put that in your article . . . even if it isn't true. Because it should be true, don't you think?"

IS IT MICKEY OR IS IT MEMOREX?

All day Thursday, slogging through the crowds, we came across life-size Tweedledums, Tweedledees, Captain Hooks, Tinker Bells, the gamut, but no Mickey, no Mickey anywhere. On Sunday, however, we spot the little rodent right inside the park entrance.

"Excuse me, is this the only Mickey in the park?"

"Yes, he's the only one."

Rafik, a young Tunisian security man, warily eyes the mob of frenzied children clinging to the only person in the park dressed as Mickey Mouse: each child's hysteria feeds the others', and even some perky young moms and dads are going crazy. The man in the Mickey costume (I assume it's a man) pretends it's all in the day's work, but he's getting mauled pretty seriously. Rafik says it's a constant problem, people mobbing and molesting the main Disney characters, Mickey and Goofy and so on. Many of the swarming children wear Minnie or Mickey Mouse ears.

"How long have you worked here?"

"We can only have them out for twenty-five minutes. With the heat, they'd collapse."

"No, I mean, you've been working here how long?"

"Twenty-five minutes, then we go in for some time, then at four they will lead the big parade."

"And where's the big parade go?"

"It's here, all along. Main Street, U.S.A., like that."

"You're very beautiful."

"Yes, it's beautiful, very busy, very colorful."

"Do you go into Paris? At night?"

As I try recalling Elizabeth Taylor's exact account of the death of Sebastian Venable a young Englishwoman wails ecstatically, "I hugged Minnie Mouse!" People are circling Minnie, Mickey, and the ravening kids with Canonvision, Sony camcorders, etc. We're all in front of the Ribbons & Bows Hat Shoppe and the Franklin Electric Lighting & Appliance Shop in the "Main Street, U.S.A." area of the park. A Clydesdale-drawn trolley passes on curving tracks. The noise and the people are too much. Rafik and I spin off into separate orbits.

The most striking feature of Euro Disney is the security force, which comes in all shapes and sizes and all nationalities. Everywhere in the park and its environs roam men and women in suits or shirtsleeves or regulation skirts, carrying large Sony walkie-talkies, conspicuous black earphones plugged into one ear. They seem, at every moment, to be reporting through the handset to some magus, some Walt figure behind the curtain. Lower-level personnel, waiters and sweepers and salesgirls and such, are kept under constant surveillance. Anything resembling a potential "incident" is dealt with swiftly, sometimes brusquely, sometimes brutally. The French gendarmes are present as well, empowered to make arrests the security people can't.

We have one report from *Libération* in which a local man was roughed up, then questioned for several hours by Disney Security, for parking his car wrong. He looked suspicious with his shoulder-length hair, had a less than cheery attitude, what have you. The questioning was done in the presence of the French police, who did nothing to protect the victim's civil rights. A mild scandal ensued. As compensation, the Disney people have offered the unfortunate man a free afternoon in the park.

Paris voices, later on:

"I'll tell you, though, the kids love it."

"Kids really go for it. So I guess these stupid stories really do come across for them."

"We might think it's a load of shit, but the kids love it."

"Well, fuck, face it, kids love anything you put in front of them. A Fabergé egg or a piece of cow turd, it's all the same to them."

"I really dread going out there. But I'm sure I'll have to, the kids see it advertised on TV and they want Mickey, they want Donald Duck."

"My son's five, he completely adored it, I have no idea why. You should interview him."

These are the Lands of Euro Disney: Fantasyland, Adventureland, Frontierland, Discoveryland, and Main Street, U.S.A. Like the institutional postmodernism of the resort's six hotels, the superficially varied styles of these lands articulate a heavily overdetermined anachronism, a mode in which any escape from cliché has become impossible.

Adventureland is an Arabophobic and racist pastiche *of The Thousand and One Nights*, complete with "native dancers" from darkest Africa who only lack bones in their noses. Each land has its redeemingly amusing features: Adventureland has "Pirates of the Caribbean," a genuinely fun boat ride through a swampy maze of simulacra (pirate's treasure chests, booming cannons, warring pirates, howling robot dogs, snuffling robot pigs, and dozens of animated skeletons). Really fun, in fact.

Discoveryland resembles the future as envisioned by *Popular Mechanics* back in 1930, "looking ahead" to bejeweled, sausage-shaped spaceships and a world that would represent the ultimate triumph of Art Deco.

Fantasyland is a sort of topiary-and-diorama rendering of classical fairy tales—*Sleeping Beauty, Cinderella, The Little Mermaid*—that Disney stripped of their complexity, violence, libidinal subtexts, and wonder many decades ago, and which are now so much mannerist piffle. At "Alice's Curious Labyrinth," spermy jets of water leap from pool to pool, the pools set atop six-foot hedges. On the hillside at the rear of the labyrinth, there's a floral arrangement in the face of a Cheshire cat. Inside the face, vermilion flowers. The cat's two eyes are rotating in opposite directions; the cat has a little Marcel Duchamp thing going on there, all based on *Alice in Wonderland*, but without the puberty-terror of *Alice in Wonderland*. There are no shadows, no ambiguities or disappointments in a Disney childhood, no sirree bob. Little children are trapped inside this hedge maze, but not really trapped, there's no real chance of getting lost. If I ran an amusement park, there would be real pirates and gypsies and an authentic criminal element on hand to supply a sense of risk.

This is what I really want to say: Don't throw our love away. The best part of breaking up is when you're making up. Since the day I saw you, I have been waiting for you. Hey, girls, do you believe in love? I got something to say about it, and it goes like this. You know you are in bad trouble when the lyrics of popular songs start making you cry before breakfast.

At the end of the Frontierland area there's something called "Phantom Manor," a virtual replica of Universal Studios Tour's "Psycho House." At least the house is identical—I don't know what happens in there. There are maybe a thousand people—well, I don't know, but hundreds and hundreds—waiting in line to go through this house. The nearby riverboat ride is also mobbed, hundreds packed onto the landing stage waiting to go aboard. The Lucky Nugget restaurant is full of people eating barbecue, under little parasols on the old western wooden porch, on the stoop, on the benches outside. Unbelievable hordes of people.

We have no trouble getting on Les Voyages de Pinocchio the first day, but on Sunday it's inaccessible. The line for the carousel, endless. Well, no, I think you could get on the carousel within a half hour. Aside from Dumbo, a fairly conventional whirling-elephant ride just behind it, the carousel is my favorite. These beautiful horses, tricked out in burnished armor, quite noble looking, like all horses, and not much different from the ones in the carousel behind the Châtelet Métro station.

There's a very spooked-out-looking grandmother sitting all alone in one of the chariots. She's wearing a blue-and-white polka dot dress. She really looks like Margaret Whiting or something, very thin, very old, very dignified, here she comes again, now she looks like Max Ernst, or that actor who played Dr. Mabuse in the Fritz Lang movies. She's got a walking stick. "When You Wish Upon a Star" is blaring so loudly that standing here feels like being trapped in the malefic ending of a Fassbinder movie, where you discover all your paranoid fantasies are true.

Flashback. First night in Paris, dinner at Natacha's: Hanna Schygulla remarks that as a kid during the American Occupation, poking around in the rubble of Munich, she did not acquire much of a taste for the World of Disney, which came along with the Occupation in the form of comics and cartoons and seemed to reflect a fantasy life produced by an experiential vacuum. She turns to our mutual friend V., whose childhood was partly spent in refugee camps after her father was hung with piano wire for his role in the 20th of July plot.

"I can't imagine, V.," Hanna says, "that you had much interest in these Disney things either..."

Adventure Isle. That's where these stalwart adventurers are heading, with their bagels, their six-dollar franks, their yogurt ice cream cones. So far, I've only seen one shirtless man, who just walked by, middle-aged, a body that hadn't completely run to seed but not terribly attractive, either. Everyone else seems to have clothes on. Adventure Isle, from this side, has a rock formation with the shape of a giant skull embedded in it, and a very large pirate ship. Now we're leaving Adventureland pretty quickly. Here are the toilets. I've had two attacks of pancreatitis since arriving in France. The first was in front of the Hôtel Lutetia, the second one here, in *Le Visionarium*, a dumb but effective Circle Vision movie about Jules Verne, H. G. Wells, and time travel: featuring Gérard Depardieu as a baggage handler at Orly airport.

Once again my favorite ride, the one I'd most like to go on, Dumbo the Flying Elephant ride, is completely full, you can't get on it. If it took us an hour on Friday to wait for the not-very-scary, three-minute roller coaster in Frontierland ("Big Thunder Mountain," more like Big Thunder Molehill, thrill-wise), it would take quite a bit longer, today, to get on one of the really nice rides. I don't say Dumbo is so special, except that I really love elephants, especially Dumbo the Elephant. I think Dumbo is an uncharacteristically happy and benign Disney creation, nothing at all like the sinister, brainless yet Manichean Mickey Mouse.

We're now in Adventureland proper, just inside the entrance. People cool their hands in a high tublike fountain under a chandelier. We're right in front of the "bazaar." An African woman assiduously sweeps up cigarette butts as they're discarded by the hundreds of smokers passing through. Here's the artificial *hammam*, the public bath, only it's really a tiled trench full of cold water and the space is occupied by both sexes, something that would never occur in Morocco. Allah would strike everyone dead.

The cafés are full, the attractions are full, the shops are full. The stir-fry stand, which was entirely deserted the other day, is now mobbed with people. There's a large line for the sandwiches booth, another empty-on-Friday place. There's a pirate ship that cuts across Adventureland, the line for it's endless . . . you have never seen so much leisurewear in your life.

The commodity on sale at Euro Disney is time itself, leisure time, the time of your life: time to wait an hour for a three-minute ride, time to wait for a restaurant seat, time to stand in line next to other people whom you never talk to, never relate to, waiting for an experience that will be entirely private, even though you have it in synchronization with others. The park has been designed so that however small the attendance, the lines will always be impressively long. In practical fact, there isn't much in this place. You could do everything in two hours, go on every ride, sample every restaurant, buy a piece of souvenir junk in every shop, if there weren't stupendous, numbing lines. Since Disney recommends a three-day visit for families, I assume what they're selling is exactly this alienated duration, the time spent waiting in silence, waiting in obedience to some unwritten code of decorum, waiting like cattle at the abattoir. And nobody talks to anybody.

The other thing John Berger says about Francis Bacon's painting, that's also true about the world of Disney: it presumes a universe in which human beings no longer have any minds at all. Where the human beast really is a hunk of chattering brainless meat. Nothing reinforces this view quite as sharply as a half hour in a place like this. When a small child falls on its face, when another one bursts out in tears 'cause he can't find mommy, I think of hapless defective monkeys, wounded baby seals, that sort of thing.

Festival Disney is sort of fun. If you're straight and eighteen and really, really fuckable, Festival Disney is your oyster, so to speak. Festival Disney is the lubricious side of this didactically family-oriented theme park. It's basically an arcade, something like the massive arcade in Milan that's practically flush with La Scala. But instead of a glass dome, there are silver and red metal-faced square pylons that rise straight up above the various businesses and are linked by thick wire, which makes the ceiling of the complex resemble a vast circus net.

On either side of the wide main walkway are theme restaurants and theme souvenir shops and theme bars, all done with a maniacal attention to detail. Frank Gehry, the only really interesting architect in evidence out here, has inflated the notion of transplanted Americana into a really disturbing *Twilight Zone* effect. Sitting in the Carnegie Deli simulacrum, you really feel you could be in New York, and not in your favorite place in New York, either.

This impresses me as a very deft stage magician's trick, to reproduce faithfully those quotidian, repulsive details of the American everyday, like the license plates and hubcaps nailed to the rustic wooden beams of Billy Bob's Country Western Saloon, or the bowling trophies and framed pictures of athletes on the walls of Champion's Sport Bar.

At least two hundred young cowpokes and their cows are whooping it up in Billy Bob's on this particular evening, jumping, shouting, bumping, and burping to a C & W band so authentic sounding it has to be fake.

Billy Bob's is a macho scene straight out of El Paso, everybody in cowboy shirts, leather vests, and suede chaps, or those Capezio tops any self-respecting set of bosoms more or less leaps out of, tops tucked into Levi's tucked into cowboy boots. Billy Bob's has that crackle of impending violence any real bar for real men offers like a nail scraping a blackboard, and every person in Billy Bob's appears to be clutching at least four mugs of beer and his neighbor's tits, ass, or quiff. Strange to say, for all the noise and booze and confusion in Billy Bob's, it smells like a cedar hope chest in a fresh pinewood closet. Now, a real western bar smells, as we all know, of piss, vomit, spilled beer, and sawdust. A few drinks down the line, I get a waiter in Billy Bob's to confess that they scrub the entire place down every morning with disinfectant, clean everything including the license plates and wagon wheels, and pipe in that chaste cedar-pine scent. Otherwise it'd be just too raunchy to be a Disney thing.

And what is a Disney thing, after all? It is, first of all, sexless, without sensuality, pitched to the zone of warm, sentimental feelings manufactured by "family" propaganda, something cuddly, something huggable, something with no erotic charge, something that has death included in the sticker price, a code of sentiments wherein everybody means well though everybody makes mistakes, where love conquers all in the form of a chaste enchanted kiss, elephants fly and broomsticks sing, where daddy mommy and baby makes three, four, five, even six little replicas, all squalling and picking their little noses. I guess the ideal Disney thing would be one of those fetuses Randall Terry carries around with him, souped up by Disney's Imagineers to crawl around and deliver a tirade denouncing abortion.

One very peculiar thing you notice walking through Euro Disney: you hear the word "Disney" uttered hundreds of times by the visitors, like a kind of charm, or a guarantee of authenticity. This must be peculiar to this Disney facility, which has the novelty of being an American amusement park where the elves and androids and talking teapots speak garbled French. What Euro Disney shares with other Disney manifestations is that wondrously mechanistic complacency about its own effect on people, expressed in publicity that tells you exactly what you will feel about its "heartwarming" characters, "thrilling" rides, and "dazzling," 3-D musical films.

At the same time, Euro Disney's publicity contains a heavy element of defensiveness, since the park's very existence is an obvious expression of American cultural imperialism. It's stressed, for example, that Walt Disney was "of Norman ancestry," a descendant of the d'Isigny family (you all know *them*); furthermore, Walt, too young for the army, became an ambulance driver for the Red Cross in France during World War I. The European origin of the Disney characters and stories is emphasized in all the literature.

At around 10 p.m., I find myself loitering between Billy Bob's and the Sport Bar. The Sport Bar, by the way, has a plausibly European expanse of outdoor tables, full at this hour with every sexually active teen from the area—there are, someone informs me, five men for every available woman, the reverse of the usual ratio—drinking lustily and checking out the babes, rubbing their big peasant crotches, posing and preening for the sparse, discreet, but discernible glances of homoerotic interest. Straight men are so damned obvious.

"What, you want a Minnie Mouse or one of these for a hundred francs? Not really?"

Stephanie's accent is Midlands, I think. She's working at one of Festival Disney's sales kiosks, dealing with some fussy British people considering the purchase of a Minnie Mouse ballpoint pen or a Minnie Mouse doll. Since the customers are people from home, she soon feels comfortable echoing their disgust at the outrageous prices. Once they've moved on, I strike up a conversation of the same type.

"Well," she says, "and who wants to pay a hundred francs for a stupid thing like that? It's an outrage. They get a hundred francs for that and you should see what they pay us. I'm not making sod all, standing here all night with a big idiotic smile, and they want to know where I learned French. I tell them, I learned my French at university, certainly not from Disney's.

"You know they did a big recruitment all over the EEC, they got about twelve thousand of us over here, I think about three thousand have already quit. They promised me six thousand francs a month, but I'm not getting sod all. There's no place to live out here, they put us in this official housing, it's more than an hour away, and they charge a third of my pay for this miserable little apartment I have to share with two other people.

"Not only do I have to stand here, I've got another kiosk to run over there, and besides that, you've got to attend classes at Disney University, where they indoctrinate you with all this Walt Disney propaganda. It's worse than the Nazis."

I'm not making a word of this up, either. A troupe of acrobats juggling skittles comes bouncing and leaping across the perimeter of the Sport Bar's outdoor tables, then jumps onto an elevated stage beside the entrance to Billy Bob's.

"They're not bad," Stephanie tells me, "when they don't drop the skittles." She tells me she's quitting next month. "I've had it. I went all through university and never borrowed a penny from my mum and dad. Now they've got to send me money every month just to make ends meet. We've all gotten screwed, everybody they recruited. And most of us are quitting, too." Disney declined to comment on employee relations or anything else.

I make a date for an actual interview with Stephanie the following afternoon, but she never shows up; the photographer and I speculate that the security people "got to her." There are so many of them peppered throughout Euro Disney that one feels a heady déjà vu of Prague or Budapest before the end of communism.

"We're not supposed to talk to people," Stephanie told me. "Especially not any press people."

At 6:30 Friday morning, the photographer goes jogging. Out the window, the bleary overcast landscape, the postmodern hotels, the greenish-gray "lake," the boathouse, the emptiness... When I pictured what losing her would be like, I saw my heart being scooped from my chest with a serrated grapefruit spoon, like a custard, a blood pudding... The photographer rematerializes forty minutes later. He's somehow jogged through the closed park to the main entrance on the autoroute, discovering that hundreds of tractors belonging to local farmers are backed up to the gate. The farmers have made bonfires from pyramids of rubber tires and gasoline.

Sure enough, out the window, a haze of greasy smoke is settling over the middle distance. I shower, dress, grab the tape recorder. We set off for the main gates but where are the main gates? First of all, the rear entrance of Festival Disney is locked, we have to make our way down to the Hotel New York, cross the indoor swimming pool, go out through the garden, and then through a maze of paths, some of which lead to a carport and only one of which ends at the road used by the Disney buses.

Once on that road, we discover that it bifurcates at a sort of sentry box where the usual blue uniforms and walkie-talkies are changing shifts. One branch of the road wraps around the outer park and passes over the rail lines. Looking down from the bridge, I see that one of the fires is blazing at the distant end of the railway, which looks impossibly far away. To the right of the rail lines, an access road skims several parking lots and a camping ground and extends to a barely visible gate, where it meets the public highway.

"It's there," the photographer says.

"Yeah, but how the fuck did you get there?"

Well, he hadn't expected to run across anything in the first place, so he doesn't quite recall. Beyond the rail overpass, the road abuts an escarpment where several gardeners, all armed with walkie-talkies, are already working on the vegetation. After several false moves and equivocations we decide to split up. I walk back to the overpass and gaze down at the railroad tracks. Out there, at the end of the line, is the public autoroute. It's just a question of getting to it.

I start walking down the access road bordering both the campground and the rail line. The road is unbelievably long. I realize that none of the nonamusement space within Euro Disney is meant to be traveled by foot, or traveled at all: it's like Los Angeles without a car. When the guards at the sentry box see me plodding back to the hotel road from the rear of the park, they demand to see my Euro Disney Pass, and look at me as if I'm obviously demented for wanting to walk around.

Five Black Marias are parked halfway between the sentry point and the gate at the end of the access road. Inside the Black Marias, French soldiers are listening to rap music on the radio. One soldier is taking a leak behind his vehicle. He smiles at me and shakes a little urine off his dick, starts to ask what I'm doing there, then shrugs and gets back in the van. The campground looks empty. The large parking lot around it is dotted with cars, whose cars, who's to say?

The road is at least a mile long. At the very end, a security station, something like a toll booth, and a small white van designed like a police wagon, with an iron grille over the long rear windows. A tall, broad, ugly German in a brown suit stands before the green metal gate, flanked by two Spanish men in unidentifiable, vaguely military uniforms. They all examine me with mild, reflexive contempt.

Well, OK, this big, fat German of the authoritarian type I've run across a million times in Germany, the stout-hearted Brown Shirt type, the former Hitler Youth type, the beer-hall type, yes,

I stare into his mica-blue Aryan-from-Bavaria eyes and he stares into my deep brown one-quarter Jew eyes and what can I tell you, anything but kismet.

"Can you let me through?"

He understands English perfectly but says nothing, just smiles a lipless little smile and shakes his burly head.

"Listen, I'm a reporter, I've got to get onto the main road."

"You have a press card?"

I show him my press card.

"He wants to see the farmers," Adolf Eichmann announces to his Spanish flunkies. "I'm sure, you like the farmers, isn't it?"

"Will you let me through or not?"

"You want to go out? You can go out that way." He points to the auto exit, a fork in the road that goes off a mile and a half in the wrong direction.

"You mean you won't let me out of here? Onto the public road?"

Eichmann replies that if I want to get to the main gates, I'll have to retrace my steps, back up the access road, back to the sentry box, right on the road that goes from the hotels to the park, around the curve where the gardeners are transplanting Serbian spruces and probably planting surveillance bugs in the topsoil, then through the park itself.

There is no percentage in standing here, so I do exactly as he says. It takes a half hour, and once in the forecourt of Euro Disney, I still can't get across it to any of the autoroute entrances. All of which are currently on fire.

The farmers are protesting the current GATT agreements, which mandate huge cutbacks in French agricultural subsidies—supposedly in conformance with uniform EEC policy, but in fact because of egregious pressure from the Bush administration, which views the French farm subsidies as "unfair" to American markets. The Reagan-Bush gang, you may recall, crippled small-scale American agriculture by abolishing our own subsidies, and now wants to "level the playing field" by screwing the farmers of Europe.

A week earlier, the same farmers dumped tons of vegetables onto the autoroute and set them ablaze with gasoline. One of the lead tractors in today's protest is mounted by a farmer effigy with a pitchfork stuck in his stomach. There are three fires going, two at the side gates, one at the main entrance, and another pyre soaked in gasoline that the police stop the farmers from lighting.

I return to the Newport Bay. Festival Disney is still closed, but now the gate's open so I cut through there to Lake Buena Vista etc. The air stinks of burning rubber. The wind blows sheets of thick oily smoke through the air. I realize, suddenly, that Euro Disney is modeled like a concentration camp. Each discrete section of the compound can be locked, and by sealing a few strategic routes, security can make it impossible to move from one part of the place to another.

In the "Cape Cod" breakfast room, as I'm writing up notes, an enormous dwarf of some kind, some creature in a big plastic head mask and gaudy costume, whisks the pen from my fingers and apes writing something on its other gloved hand. Giant chipmunks waddle around the restaurant, goosing people, bringing joy and merriment to the hearts of obese brats and their parents, who favor the windbreaker-and-docksider look in the breakfast room. The children all have very spiffy yellow Mickey Mouse rain slickers (Fr 40, a bargain). Meanwhile, out the window, plumes of smoke roll into the atmosphere behind the amusement park, and the stench of burning rubber snakes along Lake Buena Vista, seeping into the somewhat bleary festivity of the "Cape Cod."

The farmers' blockade has left the restaurant, and indeed all the Euro Disney businesses, severely understaffed today: what we have, evidently, is Skeleton Disney, a condition many Disney employees seem amused by, while others are frankly pissed. A guy who works for the Orly-Euro Disney bus line, for instance, tells me that "two hundred farmers are insignificant compared with the thousands of jobs they've created here," though these jobs, I point out, aren't strictly French jobs, but seem to've been filled by every conceivable nationality. "Well," he retorts, "it's good for the EEC." He also claims that the GATT agreements "have nothing to do with the US, it's a European problem."

We are in the Sport Bar in the middle of the day, and I am buying the bus driver large mugs of beer, to "draw him out." He's a small, nervous man with male-pattern baldness and a disconcertingly obvious homo streak in spite of the wife and children; he keeps trying to get me into the bathroom with him.

"See, what the French resent," he informs me, "is that Disney took all these stories, all these fairy tales we had here already, and figured out how to make money with them. We resent the ingeniousness of the Americans."

I keep him soaking up beer, talking, talking, expounding his philosophy of everything, I don't challenge a word, but some kind of internal movement occurs, some shift in his inner wind, maybe his nerves are touchy because of the fires, his buses aren't running, it turns out he hates living out here, he's from Normandy, he'd like to move back there before he dies.

"It's great making money, yes, I admit it," he sighs, completely drunk. "But I have to say, with all due respect, you Americans have got no class whatsoever."

(1994)

DANIEL SCHMID'S *LA PALOMA*

A casino in the south of France. A suicide at the blackjack table. A magician fanning a hand of cards. A hermaphrodite in a laurel wreath and toga reclines on a Recamier couch, with back titles: *La Force de l'Imagination*. An ancient party, her feathered headdress vibrant against the velvet theater curtains, sings: "You came along, from out of nowhere... Beautiful dreams, beautiful schemes from nowhere..." And then, through the mists of desire, Viola appears, the chimerical essence of *fatale*.

An epicene young man, alone at a table with his glass of champagne, falls in love with the mysterious singer. She has tuberculosis. They marry. A honeymoon at various spas, where she is cured. On a train to the races, he looks up from his newspaper and tells her: Eva Perón is dead. Oh yes, she sighs.

At his family chateau in Switzerland, boredom sets in.

She has an affair with his best friend, who refuses to run away with her. She becomes spectral, withdrawn. A year later she is dead. The two men read her will together. Viola poisoned herself, slowly. She wishes to be exhumed, her remains to be put in an urn in the family crypt. They dig her up. The poison she took preserved her body exactly as it was in life. The widower is forced, then, to slash her corpse into small pieces. We are whisked back to the casino, where he still sits with his champagne, watching her sing: "Shanghai, Shanghai, longing for you, all the day through..."

In the blink of an eye, a magnificent and terrible romance has blossomed and died: what we would call a great love. When you want someone crazily, whether it's based on his looks, the way he behaves, his smell, whatever, and the person is one you cannot, finally, have, even if you come to possess him for a time psychologically or physically (but especially if you don't), you can fill the world with this desire: enough, at least, that when it ends you have a story with a legible arc, one that will feature myriad exalting and pathetic details.

La Paloma is a story every human person lives at least once. If I return again and again to this early film of Daniel Schmid, it's because I have lived this story a few times, irrationally, against my better judgment. I recognize the delirium of the process this film describes as identical from person to person. The warp of an obsession, the way it grabs its victims out of the current, so that any conversation becomes a pretext to discuss the Loved One, is boring. Only the details are intriguing: the small scar below his right ear, for example. For the lover it's a question not of interest but of necessity.

La Paloma contains the voluptuous plenum of romantic madness as well as the deflating revelation that losing yourself in another person is always a story that happens in a champagne glass, in the blink of an eye.

It's possible to be a citizen of this age, to approach all human problems in entirely existential terms, and still succumb to the feverish solipsism of desire. As the advice of perfection, one can say that *desire* is bad, pleasure good. Certainly yearning becomes an unattractive state when it becomes utterly unreasonable; having said this, I must add that the person who has seamlessly rationalized desire into wishing only for what he can definitely have is, in a sense, already dead.

La Paloma is essentially the same story as Gus Van Sant's *Mala Noche* (1986) or Paul Vecchiali's *Drugstore Romance* (1979) or my novel *Horse Crazy:* a story that mimics conventions of nineteenth-century opera, in which the heroine is inevitably sacrificed in the fifth act, and the hero is left with a story to tell. These recent works are compromised by modernity, contemporary consciousness; one doesn't die for love anymore, except in fantasy, and soon emotion itself will seem a ridiculous extravagance, a relic like *Tosca*.

Eva Perón is dead. Outside is the bitter truth of events, mortality, duty, wars, our bodies in the world, systems that control our choices. Inside are feelings: the craving for maternal warmth, our childhood dreams and wishes that we cling to and fight for at the expense of all else.

I like Daniel Schmid's idea that we are all private radio stations transmitting on our own frequencies, sometimes audible to each other, sometimes not. Personally, few blue-ribbon cultural products occupy my consciousness with anything like the force of my own imagination or experience, and those that do, like *La Paloma*, seldom belong to the upper reaches of any established canon. I am indifferent to any argument that a "greater" work should affect me more profoundly, or that there exists a legitimate authority to declare one thing "major" and another "minor." In the end we have only our experiences and we feel them with the particularity of monadic creatures.

Why this film and not another? The intense perfection of its metaphor, possibly; something gorgeous in its refusal to coalesce around a conclusion that is less than hallucinatory; the sublimity of Ingrid Caven, whose voice and persona have always evoked for me the most sardonic and melancholy reflections.

Romance involves us in abjection and absurdity. Beyond a point we have no choice about it. We do violence to ourselves by pursuing it and equal violence by squashing our feelings. It's a souvenir of the last century, and not the worst one. The protagonist of *La Paloma* is a dull man who becomes interesting through his infatuation. For one moment in his life he is truly alive. I can't answer the question of whether his fixation is "worth it," and because I can't answer it, *La Paloma* continues to haunt me as the paradigm of certain disappointments.

(1993)

CAVIANI'S RIPLEY

Patricia Highsmith's Tom Ripley is a seminal creation of American literature, as reflective of a strong current in the post-WWII national character as Ahab and Huck Finn were of their eras. Ripley is the "other directed" hollow man of David Riesman's landmark 1950 sociological study, *The Lonely Crowd*, the sociopath in the mask of sanity, but with something owing to Dostoyevsky's underground man and the Nietzschean transvaluation of values: the setting he conforms to isn't an office cubicle but rather a continental, bourgeois-bohemian milieu, where he cultivates an aura of danger and is nervously patronized as a "colorful character" by people with fractionally fewer moral warts than he. Over the course of several novels, Ripley assumes all the outward trappings of a legible personality but remains, underneath, terra incognita.

Ripley is far less predictable than Hannibal Lecter, who pales beside him as a literary creation—Varney the Vampire as a wine snob in Harris tweeds. And he is less foamingly compulsive than Brett Easton Ellis's Patrick Bateman (another aesthete in his way). Ripley isn't a sexual psychopath in any usual sense, and though he enjoys the act of homicide in the same way that he enjoys harpsichord music, he only commits it when he "has" to, to avoid exposure for previous crimes or some other well-rationalized necessity. The truly subversive game Highsmith plays is to mobilize the reader's sympathies with a deeply amoral protagonist who always gets away with murder.

Numerous directors have taken on Highsmith's enigmatic and contrary antihero. Until now, René Clément's 1960 *Purple Noon*, based on *The Talented Mr. Ripley*, has remained the definitive Ripley film. Alain Delon's subtle creepiness in the title role could only be achieved via the actor's contrastingly matchless physicality, an effect Delon went on to perfect in the films of Jean-Pierre Melville. Wim Wenders's *The American Friend*, extracted from the novel *Ripley's Game*, inhabits a different universe than Highsmith's. At times it could pass as a bad version of *The Player*, with so many coy little cameos that the recognition factor hobbles the film's dramatic intentions. That said, *The American Friend* has the fascination of a deformed fetus pickled in formaldehyde, and Dennis Hopper, while far from being anything like Tom Ripley, casts a certain psychotic spell simply by playing himself.

Then there's Anthony Minghella's *The Talented Mr. Ripley*, which could have been a magnificently loyal rendering of Highsmith's first of the series. It has the perfect cast and, up to about page sixty, the perfect script. Matt Damon ought to have been the perfect young Tom Ripley, palimpsest and chameleon, and, until the killing of Dickie Greenleaf, he is. Then the film spills into such dreary homoeroticism that the intricate gambits of concealment and the donning of personas Highsmith employed to avoid easy explanations and generate suspense turn into little more than nicely orchestrated clichés.

Few directors would seem less likely to capture the essence of Highsmith than Liliana Cavani, and one could say the same about John Malkovich vis-à-vis Ripley. Cavani has a flair for the obvious and the cosmetology, rather than the real flavor, of depravity; like Dennis Hopper, Malkovich is one of cinema's sacred reptiles (I mean that as a compliment), a florid archetype as archly intractable as Clifton Webb. His approach to acting is glacially intellectual and exteriorized. He is utterly without charm, and Ripley is heavily about charm.

Startling, then, that Cavani has crafted the most enjoyable and subtly textured Ripley film since *Purple Noon*, so much in the precise psychological key of Highsmith that the many little alterations she's made in the story seem perfectly unobtrusive, logical, and justified. Ripley lives in Italy, in a vast Palladian villa, instead of the more modest Belle Ombre in the French village of Villeperce; his relations with Reeves Minot, an occasional partner-in-crime, are more pointedly antagonistic than they are in the Ripley novels; Jonathan Trevanny, whom Ripley sets up as his surrogate hitman, volunteers to help Ripley in the movie's penultimate showdown between the bad guys and the even worse guys, whereas, in the book, Ripley obliges him to; and so on.

None of this matters at all: from the sudden grisly anarchy of its opening sequence, *Ripley's Game* yanks the viewer into the queasy, hyperkinetic ambience that Highsmith so uniquely evoked in literature, that quality of hungover propulsion through progressively uglier complications, involving endless trains and airports and implacable adversaries, alternating with a silken, strangely nauseating comfort zone of connoisseurship and high-culture accoutrements.

Malkovich plays Ripley a good deal weirder than his predecessors, yet perhaps this very weirdness, which Matt Damon caught quite effectively in his "mirror scene," is how Ripley has to be manifested for a camera. Moreover, what has always been absent from other attempts at the character—the element of abrupt, obscene, psychotic violence experienced as pleasure—Malkovich incarnates to stupefying perfection. And, happily, the film isn't all about him: Ray Winstone makes Reeves more complex and vivid than he is in the novel; Dougray Scott renders Jonathan Trevanny's improbable mutation from wimpish picture framer to jittery contract killer with terrific credibility; and Lena Headey, as Sarah Trevanny, and Chiara Caselli as Ripley's wife give *Ripley's Game* an unanticipated emotional edginess and ambiguity. Cavani's film sets the bar for future Highsmith adaptations extremely high; Malkovich is Ripley's Gielgud.

(2002)

THE SERPENTINE MOVEMENTS OF CHANCE

> Of the various insects that like to make their home in our houses, certainly the most interesting, for her beautiful shape, her curious manners, and her wonderful nest, is a certain Wasp called the Pelopaeus. She is very little known, even to the people by whose fireside she lives. This is owing to her quiet, peaceful ways; she is so very retiring that her host is nearly always ignorant of her presence.

In the library of Luis Buñuel's house in Mexico City, there were two bookshelves that bore evidence of considerably more frequent consultation than the others: one held the works of the Marquis de Sade, the other the writings of Jean-Henri Fabre, whose volume on the Mason-Wasp is quoted above.

Fabre's *Souvenirs Entomologiques* was the delight of my childhood, though Fabre did not write for children, and I suspect most very young people reading him would be scared out of their wits. "The Homer of Insects," as Darwin called him, describes the lives of the glowworm, the cricket, the cicada, the praying mantis, and myriad other tiny creatures with an empathy and keenness of observation that makes the reader love them as much as Fabre did. All the more horrifying, then, when the great entomologist, a scientist before all else, relates how his characters come to their end:

> I once saw a Bee-eating Wasp, while carrying a Bee to her storehouse, attacked and caught by a Mantis. The Wasp was in the act of eating the honey she had found in the Bee's crop. The double saw of the Mantis closed suddenly on the feasting Wasp; but neither terror nor torture could persuade that greedy creature to leave off

eating. Even while she was herself being actually devoured she continued to lick honey from her Bee!

Buñuel's movies almost always feature insects—the bee Fernando Rey rescues from drowning in *Viridiana*, the deadly scorpions of *L'Age d'or*, the wasps that devour the dead mule in *Las hurdes*, the fly in the martini in *That Obscure Object of Desire*. In *The Phantom of Liberty*, Buñuel's penultimate film, Jean-Claude Brialy's character disrupts the arrangement of his mantlepiece with a large spider in a glass frame: "I'm sick of symmetry," he announces, a line that could serve as an epigraph for this film. In it, the director gives the aleatory ordering of dreams and the role of chance in waking life equal weightlessness. Indeed, it could easily be titled *The Dream Life of Insects*.

Fabre's genius, and Sade's for that matter, consisted in evoking the human being's inextricable connection to nature (in the unameliorative sense of "the food chain")—Fabre anthropomorphized the insect world, while Sade insectomorphized the human. Reading either of Buñuel's favorite authors reminds us that nature has no morality, and the kind we cook up for ourselves is completely arbitrary. (As Witold Gombrowicz put it, if you want to know what human morality is all about, take food away from people for three days.) Buñuel, too, never lost sight of the primacy of instinctual drives. And also like Sade, he was, essentially, a satirist of human folly. His characters often resemble "the Divine Marquis's" instinct-driven monstrosities. But they also have the affectionately rendered charm of Fabre's insects, who combine ingenuity and intelligence within their narrow ken and complete imbecility vis-à-vis their actual position in the food chain.

The semi-incestuous passion of the aunt and nephew at the inn, the similar *fixé* of the police commissioner for his deceased sister, the gambling addiction of ascetic monks, the autograph seekers swarming around the convicted (and simultaneously released) mass killer, the massacre at the city zoo—a few of *The Phantom of Liberty*'s nonstop, straight-faced absurdities—indicate how readily the human animal maintains an existence utterly contrary to its moral code as well as to its much-advertised ability to reason.

The Discreet Charm of the Bourgeoisie much resembles the ghostly masterwork of Mexican picaresque, Juan Rulfo's *Pedro Páramo*. Another oneiric likeness can be found in Jan Potocki's *The Manuscript Found in Saragossa*, a book Buñuel often spoke of wanting to film, an epic of ghosts and revenants, stories nested in stories, digressions that overwhelm the ostensible plot.

The *Phantom of Liberty* proceeds as if its sudden detours into unanticipated places were determined by rolls of the dice, and it was assembled in a comparable way, by Buñuel and his longtime co-writer Jean-Claude Carrière telling each other their dreams every morning. It follows the specific pattern of a less chaotic kind of narrative than the picaresque, the earliest example of which may be Tolstoy's "The Forged Coupon," the inspiration for Bresson's gorgeous film *L'Argent*. Tolstoy's story follows the career of an altered item of currency and shows its effects on a succession of people who accept it as cash and then pass it along to the next person. Another such work is André Gide's *Les Caves du Vatican*, a novel Buñuel tried to adapt with the author in the 1920s, abandoning it after three days. (The structure is rarely used, and a few recent films that have tried it are strangely inept.)

Buñuel's own description of his approach suits as well as a synopsis of Gide or Tolstoy. In published conversations with José de la Colina and Tomás Pérez Turrent, Buñuel mentions that he doesn't especially care for Dostoyevsky's *Crime and Punishment* and thought it would be a far more interesting book if, as Raskolnikov ascends the stairs to murder the old pawnbroker, a boy on his way to buy a loaf of bread rushed past him and suddenly became the focus of the narrative instead of Raskolnikov.

As in *The Milky Way* and *The Discreet Charm of the Bourgeoisie*, *The Phantom of Liberty* shifts attention not only from a central character to a minor one, who then becomes central, but also from one time period to another. The film opens in Toledo during the Napoleonic occupation, as a costume drama involving executions and drunken French soldiers desecrating a church, a statue that comes to life, an exhumation. As the story reaches its climax, we hear the voice of Muni, a plump, antic actress who appears in many Buñuel films, reading the story aloud and next see her sitting with a friend on a park bench in present-day Paris.

Muni leads us to the prepubescent daughter of Brialy and Monica Vitti, who leads us to them. Brialy goes to his doctor's office; during his examination, a nurse, played by Milena Vukotic, gets word that her father is gravely ill and leaves to drive to a distant hospital. The film follows her as she drives into a rainstorm and seeks refuge at an inn, where several monks stranded there rope her into a poker game; they're eventually joined by a young man and his aunt who've just arrived and a flamenco dancer and her husband. It would be criminal to go on, and silly to relate the "plot" of *The Phantom of Liberty*, since the film is a compendium of surprises. Like Dostoyevsky's novels, *The Phantom of Liberty* retains its surprise quality even when experienced a second, third, and fourth time: you find yourself intensely wondering what happens next, when you know perfectly well what happens next.

What does it mean? Phantom of Liberty? Buñuel joked that the title was a collaboration between himself and Karl Marx. It also seems jejune to suggest interpretations, since Buñuel deflected all incitements to explain himself and insisted that nothing at all in his films was symbolic or had the significance people attached to his recurring motifs. He liked the appearance of a peculiar bird—I think it's called an emu—so he put one in. When he cast two actresses in the role Maria Schneider had been fired from in *That Obscure Object of Desire*, Buñuel merely threw the idea out to Serge

Silberman, his producer, as a joke. Silberman thought he was serious, that it was the perfect solution—and that's what happened.

At the end of his life, Buñuel had achieved such fluidity in his filmmaking that he could take *Phantom* in any direction that occurred to him, along the path of the previous night's dreams, fantasies from childhood, premonitions of approaching death, or, if he'd cared to, into outer space. To call him a film director is like calling Einstein a mathematician. There was no artist like him ever, and there will never be another. He didn't simply direct a film called *The Phantom of Liberty*; he *was* the Phantom of Liberty.

(2021)

NOTES ON SAM

About Sam McKinniss: he is so out of the ordinary, and so unusually well equipped to write about himself if he cared to, that writing about him feels presumptuous, knowing in advance that all I know of his art is destined to become a small piece of an expanding aesthetic voyage. And truthfully, most of what's been written about my own work, including by me, has always seemed alien to what I had in mind. How something is made, and why something is made, are matters that often get lost in the public reception of that thing. Quite often artists forget why they made something: it just seemed like the thing to do at the time. I don't understand Sam's work in any secret way, and feel no particular competence to interpret it, as it seems complete without any sort of exegesis. I couldn't say what Sam's work is "about." Nothing is ever about one single thing, and impressive works of art are often about nothing at all except the process of making them, though I think McKinniss has said his work is about—I've forgotten now, something and power. Discomfort and power? Beauty and power? Power, at least, plus something else. He works with images that have inbuilt cultural power, there's that; he makes them ... more powerful, more expressive, more ambiguous. At least some of his work is about America and its sensory ambiance, its compulsively spun narratives, and "the darkness at the edge of town," cf., *Sandy*, *Lord of the Flies*, and, for that matter, *Death Valley*.

Regarding a swan, a lamb, and Brian Slade. McKinniss's paintings range from the size of a piece of copy paper to the imposing dimensions of a royal portrait, rendered freehand, without using grids or projections. Close up, his figures and faces shed their resemblance to photographs and break down into mottled patches and veils of color, legible brushstrokes, the overt paraphernalia of illusionism. Often the subject nearly fills the entire canvas, with a spare, indeterminate background space setting it off; McKinniss invests faces with high drama, suspenseful in that the viewer naturally imagines the next moment and the moment before, and can't quite define the vaguely troubled emotional flavor of the moment at hand. Eyes do a lot of work in Sam's paintings; so do hair and spiky things, like the daisies in Drew Barrymore's hair, the white stitches of Catwoman's costume, Edward Scissorhands's hands and hair, the garish feathers surrounding the crypto-Bowie of *Brian Slade*.

Sam's work arouses thoughts about the Leibnizian fuzziness between fiction and documentary reality, about concealment and revelation, about forms of masquerade, the mutability of memory. His paintings evoke a waking dream reality where figures of fiction have real metaphorical force, on furlough from their narratives. Celebrities are fictional, whatever else they are; Sam's pictures of them are layered in artifice, approximations of "perfect moments" in the careers of certain images.

Power requires the acquiescence and complicity of multitudes. The cultural power of McKinniss's subjects is much like that of Josephine in Kafka's story "Josephine the Singer, or The Mouse Folk." Although Josephine has no singing talent whatsoever, her social function is the same as that of Rihanna or Drew Barrymore or the characters in *Star Wars*, i.e., as a cynosure of public attention, a casting of spells, a spray of bedazzling, mixed messages. Josephine holds the mouse folk spellbound *because something has to*. The ritual space she occupies can be occupied by almost anything from the most excellent to the most gruesome and tawdry, but it can never be vacant. This is more or less the raison d'être of the culture industry.

Fantin-Latour, whose flower paintings McKinniss frequently copies, has been called "a traditional painter with avant-garde sympathies," which could apply to contemporary artists like Dike Blair, Billy Sullivan, and Sam McKinniss, who are realist painters of no discernible school, very different in styles, innovators in subject matter and formal design; Alex Katz might fit in here, too. However traditional their techniques, their works are recognizably of our time, informed by the convulsive history of modernism and the wider movement of history. Even Sam's atmospheric copies of Fantin-Latour have a Pierre Menard kind of postmodernity; we see them through the filter of the past hundred years.

What Fantin-Latour represents for McKinniss is something close to perfection in paint, the apogee of particular skills and sensitivities that McKinniss also has in abundance. I could be mistaken, but I think Sam's embrace of Fantin-Latour is also his way of telling us he isn't running for flavor of the month. Both artists intoxicated by music.

"Who am I? If this once I were to rely on a proverb, then perhaps everything would amount to knowing whom I 'haunt.'" André Breton begins *Nadja* by invoking, and slightly disowning, the ghostly part he plays in the twilit labyrinth of marvels that follows, in the streets of an enchanted city. "Who am I?" is an unreasonably cosmic question, though making art can be an extravagant way of answering it or posing it to other people. Artists are more defined by what they do than most people. "Haunted" may be too passive and filmy a word for Sam McKinniss's relationship to the pictures he makes, though they're full of manufactured ghosts, phantoms with fanbases, screenshots. One feels the artist greets these images with orgiastic enthusiasm rather than melancholy. They come from a different sort of labyrinth, with no fixed or physical location, a cull of pop culture from its virtual storage space. Real people in masked situations, sort of, theatrical animals and landscapes, a very picky harvest of stuff preserved on the internet in .jpegs, stuff current in the recent past or newsy the day before yesterday. Like *Nadja*, McKinniss's art is a search for the marvelous, investing pieces of the cultural commons with their due grandeur.

Time moves much faster than it did before "personal" computing. Everything in our lives has accelerated. Some things in mass culture have sticking power, others don't, but we carry in our cells a terrific amount of eidetic residue from every trip we've taken, every movie we've watched, and, though it really ought to be unthinkable, everything we've ever seen on television, computer, phone. Not whole memories, but sunspots. Sam is a gleaner of sunspots in the refuse heap of collective memory.

Sam's recent paintings suggest a deft, saturnine, facetiously sincere autobiography of taste and tastelessness that reveals less about the artist than the spectator, though in this case, the artist is the spectator, too. These paintings—in shows, where there's more than one—are really unlikely things, samples from the blazing horror vacui we inhabit as alleged global citizens, ergo very familiar, but suffused with pathos, even suffering, as well as flash and comic incongruity. They suggest an unarticulated aesthetic argument, though it would be hard to say exactly what it is; their personae feel connected in elusive ways, like frames arbitrarily snipped from a movie that only makes sense when you see the whole thing. They speak of the odd simultaneity of everything that's happened, the collapsed time of the past ten or twenty years, and the speeding shuttle of celebrity culture that enfolds JonBenét in her beauty pageant bijoux and Princess Di's crashed limo along with Joan Didion and Flipper. (Or, as Johnny Mercer put it, "anyone from Shirley Temple to Aimee Semple.") Because we recognize the figures in Sam's paintings, our initial reaction—i.e., whether we "like" them or not—is also the most trivial, since these images have passed through us repeatedly, even when we weren't aware of them. Anyway, what's not to like? These are filaments of consensual reality, elements of a public sphere that has shrunk to the size of our desktop computers. In another sense, it doesn't matter at all where they came from.

Nearly everything that has ever been pictured, created by one process or another, is reproduced somewhere on the internet, tucked into informational crevices, sprinkled on websites, grouped with similar pictures. McKinniss exfiltrates the ones that make sense to him, that give him a rush, that reflect emphatic ways of being in the world and indirectly echo his personal repertoire of moods and mental weather, reporting haze, cloudy conditions, drizzle, lightning strikes, sunshine. He uses images of people and things we consume on an ongoing basis, images we have already seen, though not at all in the same way, reconstituting little .jpegs as if releasing them from compressed previousness, like paper flowers that bloom when you drop them in water.

For me the most effective of Sam's paintings express exuberance and dread in equal measure—the very large *Swan II*, where the elegant form of the swan is its only visible aspect, centered in a dwarfing expanse of gliding, possibly toxic, nighttime riverine colors, and the strangely sublime *Flipper*, in which this lovable aquatic mammal, completing a dive, leaves a trail of spectacular bubbles and looks both joyous and—what we unavoidably bring to this picture—doomed. McKinniss is well aware that any depiction of innocence, in our era, immediately evokes the prospect of violation, which gives a painting like *Lamb*—an adorable lamb sniffing a jonquil in some high grass—a certain desperate edge.

There are surely private conversations between the works Sam puts in his shows. I don't know what they are. His paintings throb with telltale-heart urgency that is drastically sincere and archly ridiculous. Many famous people, actors, singers in Sam's paintings look stressed out, apprehensive, frozen at a fraught moment in the drama of being constantly seen. Everything is just what it looks like, just how we remember it or don't, but amplified and dramatized, given weight, taken seriously. This is Prince on his great album cover and motorcycle. Here is Snoop

Dogg with sinuous braids and a ferocious profile. Lana Del Rey in a pensive longeur with flowers. Beck, famously clear-eyed and extraterrestrial from Scientology. Whitney Houston in a pause of *"The Star-Spangled Banner."* The actors usually identified by the names of their characters in whatever movies, *Batman Returns*, *Beetlejuice*, *Velvet Goldmine*, etc., and logically so, as nicely removed from their real identities as the artist is from his paintings. Usually their faces are framed in close-up, or medium close, though one very funny piece is a painted long view of Thelma and Louise's '66 Thunderbird whizzing off the rim of the Grand Canyon, into the abyss that awaits us all.

(2018)

HANNAH AND HER SISTER

*Between Friends: The Correspondence of
Hannah Arendt and Mary McCarthy, 1949–1975*
edited by Carol Brightman

In her introduction to *Between Friends*, editor Carol Brightman tells us that Hannah Arendt and Mary McCarthy did not hit it off when they first met. At a party in 1945, McCarthy made a characteristic gaffe by saying she felt sorry for Hitler, who, in Brightman's paraphrase, "was so absurd as to want the love of his victims." Arendt replied, "How can you say such a thing in front of me—a victim of Hitler, a person who has been in a concentration camp!"

It goes without saying that McCarthy didn't feel any sort of pity for Hitler; she was just being Mary, provocateur of the then-Trotskyite martini set. And Arendt had never been in a concentration camp; she'd been briefly interned in France. What glitters in this anecdote, for a writer of my generation, is the fact that it happened "at a party": there were so very many well-chronicled parties during the seemingly endless tenure of the *Partisan Review / New Yorker / Politics / Commentary / New York Review of Books* literary coven, so many confabs and cocktails shared by Cal and Lizzie and Philip and Dwight and the dreadful Trillings and Saul and Alfred and Harold. They lived in a time when literary people and their parties had some palpable connection to the great events of the day; they were taken seriously by presidential advisers, ambassadors, even heads of state. Thanks partly to their clannishness and partly to the invention of TV, the very idea of a literary party now has a ring of quaint anachronism: who, pray tell, would attend?

Theirs was, alas, the last, or perhaps next-to-last, generation of writers who could safely assume that their correspondence would be collected, or for that matter exist in sufficient quantity to be of interest. The telephone has made such communications rare and vaguely suspect: we live in an age that privileges the instantaneous outpouring of unmediated "feelings" over more delicate, dilatory sentiments. (The recent suggestion in *Newsweek* that faxes and email might revive letter writing is faintly absurd, since these pushy forms of human contact tend to demand immediate response, just like the telephone.) The McCarthy-Arendt correspondence has a solid, crafted thereness to it, the force of fluent prose applied to the business of daily life. The quick, sloppy missive is acknowledged as such: "Dearest Hannah: The next mail leaves in forty-five minutes, and I'm writing you this note for purely selfish reasons: because my heart is full of emotion and I want to talk." "My dearest Mary—I am writing not to write a letter but to do everything required to receive one."

But nothing here is truly sloppy—a certain lopsided urgency is the sole, rare infelicity—and most of the letters are fulsome, funny, keenly descriptive, written with one eye darting to, though happily not fixed on, posterity. There are so many things one can write about people, knowing that one will be safely dead by the time they read it, or that they will be dead by the time one publishes it. Arendt: "I was away from New York, an idiotic affair at Baltimore, honorary degree together with Margaret Mead, a monster, and Marianne Moore, an angel . . . Mead (one better call her only by her second name, not because she is a man, but because she certainly is not a woman) . . ." And McCarthy:

> [Hans Magnus] Enzensberger's letter (the famous Wesleyan resignation in protest over Vietnam) is causing a great stir here. . . . The

fact is, far from being in Cuba, he is in California giving lectures. . . . From there he goes on to lecture in Australia, then to Tahiti and other pagan paradises, then back to West Berlin. His wife is staying with Nathalie Sarraute, which is how I know all this. Nathalie thinks it is a rather dishonest comedy. But don't repeat that. She gathers that what happened is that Masha, the young wife, got bored in Wesleyan; "Magnus" too.

Arendt was the ant, McCarthy the grasshopper: Arendt remained married to the same man, and pretty much rooted in New York City, throughout the span of the letters, while McCarthy had affairs, divorced Bowden Broadwater, and married James West, traveling incessantly for one reason or another. (This perfectly suits the separate natures of the philosophe and the novelist.) Comparing these letters with Arendt's to Karl Jaspers, one gets the impression that McCarthy brought out the bitchier side of Arendt, while Arendt had the opposite effect on McCarthy, who frequently sounds humble, awed by Arendt's intellect, and, like an assiduous graduate student, eager to win her approval.

As years go by and life delivers its usual insults to the heart and brain, both women's letters become increasingly tender, fretful, solicitous. McCarthy's dreadful remarks about "pansies" and "fruits," usually in relation to Auden or Spender, do little to allay the impression that her friendship with Arendt was the major love story of her life. A friend of mine who is an authority in these matters assures me that most of the raging neuroticism of the *Partisan Review* crowd sprang from repressed homosexuality—"Rahv, Macdonald, Lowell too for that matter," he says—and perhaps the same is true for the distinguished authors of, respectively, *The Life of the Mind* and *The Company She Keeps*. At any rate, McCarthy was vigilant about possible Sapphic rivals for Arendt's affections: "But I read that Susan Sontag was arrested [in an antiwar demonstration]. And what about her? When I last watched her with you at the Lowells', it was clear that she was going to seek to conquer you. Or that she had fallen in love with you—the same thing. Anyway, did she?"

Arendt was forty-three, McCarthy thirty-seven, when the letters began with a short note from Arendt praising McCarthy's recently published novella, *The Oasis*. There is a lapse of two years before the next—McCarthy's to Arendt, on *The Origins of Totalitarianism*. Letters have been lost, and there are sometimes months of epistolary silence between the two followed by blizzards of communication. Because they told each other "everything," *Between Friends* has the narrative pull of a novel. At times it reads like the kind of novel McCarthy wrote, though it has more in common with the works of two writers she admired, Ivy Compton-Burnett and Nathalie Sarraute: oblique, elliptical, proceeding as much by inference as by direct description. A rich cast of recurring characters glimpsed first from one protagonist's view, then the other's, floats in a kind of annotated historical broth, while the actual meetings of the two heroines occur off-stage and swim into our peripheral vision as afterimages when the letters resume.

The vigilant politics of the principals gives this book one kind of momentum; we go from the McCarthy era to the Kennedy years to Vietnam and the civil rights movement, the student revolts in Paris, Watergate, up to the mid-'70s proliferation of terrorism that McCarthy treated in her last novel, *Cannibals and Missionaries*. Another current carries the personal dramas and daily trivia—the struggles with work, planning of travel itineraries, McCarthy's intricate negotiations for her divorce from Broadwater and James West's even more tangled dealings with his ex-wife, McCarthy's long spells in Venice and Florence, Arendt's conferences and classes, and, as time passes, the deaths of Arendt's husband and many mutual friends, illnesses, and other losses.

The personal intersects often with the public, most dramatically when *Eichmann in Jerusalem* and *The Group* appear a few months apart in 1963, bringing both writers wide fame and violent controversy. It would be too simple to say that McCarthy's response to events was to *do something*, sometimes recklessly, while the more sedentary and reflective Arendt tended to mull things over and often to let them go. But the Eichmann controversy does seem illustrative. Arendt, attacked by Jewish groups for describing the role of the Jewish councils in organizing deportations to the death camps, decided to wait until things had calmed down to respond to her critics. McCarthy found the hysteria of the attacks an intolerable provocation, especially Lionel Abel's *Partisan Review* piece ("The Aesthetics of Evil: Hannah Arendt on Eichmann and the Jews"), and worked herself up to a brilliant counterattack, "The Hue and Cry."

Arendt never publicly roused herself on McCarthy's behalf when the latter's books, after *The Group*, met with ever-frostier reviews, sometimes with critical silence (in the case of her Vietnam books, *Vietnam*, *Hanoi*, and *Medina*, and her book on Watergate, *The Mask of State*). I think Arendt's mentor status made it impossible for McCarthy to consciously expect that kind of reciprocity, but a shadow of resentment flashes out, a decade after the Eichmann furor, during their friendship's single (recorded) crisis of faith, which occurred over a trivial misunderstanding. After visiting the Wests in Maine, Arendt boarded her plane without "lingering over good-byes"—McCarthy believed Arendt had found her irritating, and in subsequent letters, plaintively, tried to coax Arendt into admitting it. She was less disturbed by Arendt's supposed irritation than by the possibility that her own perceptions were mistaken—and in a letter of September 1974 insists on her version of events: "As for Aberdeen, I *know* you were cross with me some times (for instance when I brought you some fruit paste candies from Paris). Then in Castine, feeling that I was on your nerves again, I wondered about that." This is followed by a rather devastating non-reproach:

> No, I am not suspicious of my friends. What an idea. It isn't a suspicion but a certainty, an objective fact, that when I got some

> very rough treatment in the press . . . not a soul came to my
> defense. . . . It is not that I think A or B should have come to my support; what astonishes me is that no one did. And I can't help feeling, though I shouldn't, that if one of my friends had been in *my* place, I would [have] raised my voice. This leads me to the conclusion that I am peculiar, in some way that I cannot make out; indefensible, at least for my friends. They are fond of me but with reservations. In any case, none of this involves you, because you were in the hospital and then recovering when it happened, because you weren't in the U.S. and didn't see those unpleasant pieces and because, finally, even if you had been on Riverside Drive and in the peak of condition, you couldn't have helped since people would have said that you were repaying the Eichmann debt, that we had dedicated books to each other, etc., etc.

This explosion of petulance is uncharacteristic and therefore notable; McCarthy detested self-pity in any form, though it must be said that Arendt was generally much quieter about her own complaints, or at least more stoic. (After a horrendous car crash in 1962—nine broken ribs, a concussion, hemorrhages in both eyes—she writes, "[W]hen I awoke in the car and became conscious of what had happened, I tried out my limbs, saw that I was not paralyzed and could see with both eyes; then tried out my memory—very carefully, decade by decade, poetry, Greek and German and English, then telephone numbers. Everything all right.") Arendt's side of the correspondence lapses for six months after the Maine episode, perhaps because she didn't wish to thrash out the misunderstanding on paper. It appears to have been mediated by publisher William Jovanovich, who crops up from time to time as a sympathetic, globe-trotting magus, gobbling up subsidiaries to keep his literary division afloat.

Between Friends owes much of its charm to an assortment of figures like Jovanovich, encountered on the trail, so to speak. While Arendt was mainly busy with academic work and domestic life, McCarthy, residing in Paris and much in transit, "the family" (Norman Podhoretz's derisive term) established in the '40s is ever with them. However exasperated or betrayed they feel by the old perennials—Lizzie, Cal, Philip, et al.—it is clear that people in the family will never be permanently banished to outer darkness, and that certain enemies will ever remain in focus. The political is often the personal. Arendt, who had a stake in postwar German intellectual life, had a bug in her brain against Adorno, and denounced him for trying to make himself interesting, on one occasion, to the Nazis in 1933; he had apparently blocked Arendt's graduate thesis way back when, and after the war led the attacks on Heidegger, one of Arendt's mentors.

McCarthy's circle of enemies was, of course, wider than Arendt's: Diana Trilling, Simone de Beauvoir, and Lillian Hellman were but a few, and she seems to have loathed them mostly on principle—though the campaign against Beauvoir, sustained over thirty years, had a quality of inexplicable excess. While it's always fun to read well-honed malice, both sides of this correspondence have their moments of cheap caricature and dishonesty, as well as egregious mutual flattery.

Like all good friends, they tactfully supported one another's prejudices, though not necessarily among other people. You will find, for instance, a much better opinion of Günter Grass's work from Arendt in her letters to Jaspers than in what she told McCarthy, and kinder words for Sartre from McCarthy, in a 1984 interview with Carol Brightman, than in what she told Arendt.

As this is an evolving record of two lives, inconsistencies, shifting attitudes and opinions, and sudden changes of heart are precisely what animate it. For two such eminent persons there are surprisingly few intractable hobbyhorses. The famous are often boringly fond of their own utterances, but in their letters, at least, Arendt and McCarthy were determined not to bore each other. Arendt was generous by nature, McCarthy by self-discipline (which finally mellowed into nature). They both had a moral commitment to truth telling, which meant being (or trying to be) fair-minded, which meant, finally, that they were willing to be surprised by people they did not expect much of. If a genuine idea emitted from a horse's ass, they felt honor-bound to consider it seriously.

This gives even their idle gossip a certain respectable texture, as when, for example, the certifiably crazy Robert Lowell appears to get saner on lithium, but then has an unfortunate lapse. McCarthy: "He is still taking his pills. And he spoke with horror of his old mania.... If one has known him so long, one is alert to the signs. There was one ominous note, I must admit, during the evening we spent together: he mentioned *Hitler*. In a guarded but somewhat commendatory way. I said: 'Cal, if I hear the word "Hitler" again, that finishes it.'"

They want poor Cal to be sane, and feel it's a pity he just isn't. Of course, it is also true that McCarthy hits her best stride, prosewise, when encountering stark raving eccentricity, and Arendt, too, surpasses herself when the people around her are plainly out of their minds. Earthbound by the obligation to make sense of reality, both writers take hilarious flight when reality repudiates sense: the correspondence positively sizzles in the period around May '68.

Between Friends is an exemplary dialogue of two astonishing minds, set against a background of progressive loss—the decay of the body, the disappearance of friends, the coarsening of the public sphere, the ruin of nature—that serves as an effective primer in what Arendt saw as the three activities of human consciousness: thinking, willing, and judging. Anchored in the data of the everyday, these letters reflect a shared search for a modern, godless transcendence, an ethics, a tolerable way to live in the world we have now. To soldier on while knowing this quest is doomed to failure is itself a quixotic triumph of mind over matter. "As a person and a writer, I seem to have had little effect on improving the world I came into," McCarthy told an audience at the MacDowell Colony in 1984. "Why should I care that I have lived my life as a person and as a writer in vain? Most of our lives are in vain. At best, we give pleasure to some."

(1995)

SOMEWHAT SLIGHTLY DAZED: ON THE ART OF RONI HORN

GIACOMETTI (THE RECOGNITION FACTOR)

Entities that are double in the world but not exactly double, but the same at different moments.

Things that are double in different minds. Viewed from behind or face to face or sidewards. No privileged viewpoint being that by which someone or thing is recognized.

People and things we recognize from behind, from a far distance, seeing only a motion, a manner of walking, a fragment, a color, or the beginning of a color.

THE GLOVE

In Breton's *Nadja*, among its strangenesses and inversions of what, at the time of its composition, were regarded as events and objects typifying quotidian reality, there is an anecdotal meditation gathered around a glove: I'm relying upon memory, as I haven't a copy of the book in front of me.

A woman's glove has a somewhat fetishistic interest for the narrator, who would like to possess it. (I may be inventing this from a defect of memory, but it doesn't matter.) Instead of the "real" glove (which he asks the owner for), the narrator receives (or finds in a flea market, or is given by the first glove's wearer) a replica made of lead, or brass, or some other heavy metal, which resembles in all or most of its details (stitching, the fold of the unoccupied fingers, the curvature of the hand it would enclose) the soft, feather-light glove that originally emanated a certain erotic magnetism. This heavier glove, a glove I prefer to imagine so materially dense that it would be impossible to pick up (a glove that would be a black hole), is both useless and invaluable: it can't be worn, instead serves a consolatory function; it exists not simply as an *objet trouvé* but a replacement, in a realm of utopian/dystopian substitutions, for the original object of Breton's attraction.

PERFORMANCE

Is Breton the narrator of *Nadja*, or only naming the narrator of a novel "André Breton"?

In *Pornografia*, a novel by Witold Gombrowicz, the narrator, a writer named Witold Gombrowicz, who (in reality) spent the years of the Second World War marooned in Buenos Aires, depicts himself during the war in Poland, trafficking on the black market, participating, in a dark way, in various operations of the Polish Resistance; in another novel, *Trans-Atlantyk*, the same Gombrowicz portrays Gombrowicz as a deserter, when in reality he made efforts to return to Poland to serve in the war, and was prevented from doing so by entirely innocent contingencies.

This kind of fictive self-representation is the literary equivalent of how an actor performs a role, despite the convention in which the portrayed character is given, for example, fictitious relationships, jobs, a different name, often a different nationality, a change of personality. (The subject of a still photograph is also performing herself, enacting herself.)

However, just as the characters of a dream are said to each be different facets of the dreamer, the actor can never entirely claim that the character she depicts is *not her*.

JOHN MALKOVICH

The actor who has most explicitly dissolved the tacitly agreed-upon disparity between "the character" and the actor playing the character is, of course, John Malkovich, in the Spike Jonze film *Being John Malkovich*: in this film, other characters discover a portal that allows anyone who enters it to *become John Malkovich* for fifteen minutes, before being ejected from Malkovich onto a fallow stretch of the New Jersey Turnpike.

As an ancillary tweak on this ("postmodern"?) demolition of the difference between identity and being (*en-soi/pour-soi*), Malkovich subsequently played, in a film called *Color Me Kubrick*, an alcoholic, escalatingly fruity homosexual conman named Alan Conway who, over a period of several months, impersonated Stanley Kubrick (whom he in no way resembled) to seduce gullible young men, obtain small loans and gifts, and to "be someone," rather than the nothing Alan Conway thought he was. The film's tag line: "They wanted something for nothing. He gave them nothing for something." *Color Me Kubrick* was directed by the (real) assistant to Stanley Kubrick, Brian W. Cook (who had during the period of Conway's impersonation been asked by Stanley Kubrick to follow Conway's activities as Kubrick). After Conway was caught and remanded for psychiatric care, he became "something," a celebrity in his own right, the subject of several television documentaries and, finally, the protagonist of a film directed by Stanley Kubrick's assistant.

MONTAGE, THE CUT

The substitution involving the glove has a close affinity to the psychological properties of images: the relative weight of one image in relation to another, regardless of their morphological similarity to each another. We know how this is achieved by montage in cinema: an actor eating dinner in one shot is, in the next, hanging from a cliff by his fingernails.

But this example of cutting, involving as it does a total shift of mise-en-scène, external forces operating on the portrayed character, exemplifies a narrative crudity that should not concern us, because the actions of life, the internal weather that informs our moods and perceptions, are only rarely precipitated by abrupt and dramatic upheavals in our sensory scanning pattern.

The monadic life within us evolves in time, not from era to era (although that too), but from second to second. And what we portray, what we show to the other(s) of this inner movement, constitutes a caesura between ourselves and ourselves: what we are *for the others* and what we are *to ourselves* is never the same, cannot be the same.

If we want to represent "the truth" of what transpires within us, or simply to convey "what we are," we must reckon with what we imagine (calculate?) to be the habits of reception that exist in what, for lack of a more apt term, we would call "the audience."

MONICA VITTI I

Exemplary, here, would be the opening ten minutes of the Antonioni film *L'Eclisse*: specifically, in the persona incarnated by the actress Monica Vitti. By some alchemical or magical procedure we "see" Monica Vitti even before she appears. We hear the whir of a small desk fan (which is shown) and a panning shot moves slowly across a table that contains a shaded lamp, a small marble obelisk, a row of books; see the figure of the actor Francisco Rabal (seated in a wing chair), whose gaze is directed across what we sense to be a middle-class "living room," and, finally, across the room, the standing figure of Vitti, pictured from behind.

In this counter-shot, Vitti stands before an expanse of closed window drapes. She turns. In the first moment when we see her face, it is, at least arguably, without expression: but to describe this scene properly, we would have to resort to the trope of slow motion, even though everything occurs in "real time." Vitti's eyes glance down for a split second, and a very slight motion of her lips conveys almost nothing more than the (faintly amused) fact that she has noticed something, that this something she's noticed is something inconsequential, a mere existential detail, the position of an object (an overfull ashtray) in proximity to a small glass sculpture on the floor.

Without proceeding any further in this scene, Vitti has already performed its entire significance with the smallest expenditure of expression. (We must, of course, include the atmospheric accoutrements of an incessantly whirring fan, the implicit presence of the other actor, the disconcertingly bright lighting of the room, etc.) We know it is roughly five in the morning, that two people have been awake all night, that their relationship is over (the full ashtray, the physical distance between them in the room, the sense of exhaustion conveyed by Vitti's initial, almost mask-like visage).

Are we looking at Monica Vitti? Yes, and no: we're looking at "Monica Vitti." Moreover, we're observing the *durée* of "Monica Vitti," the performative enactment of "Vitti" by Vitti within an increment of time, an enactment of sublime subtlety that all but obliterates the normative conventions of cinema: the idea that *nothing happens* in this fragment of *L'Eclisse* could not be further from the truth. In fact, *everything happens*, and happens with an economy of objects, movements, and expressions that is, when closely considered, absolutely baroque in its amplitude of meaning.

Admittedly, this synecdoche communicates anxiety, depression, exhaustion, psychic conflict, and therefore may be too facile an example of how two seemingly identical images (Vitti in one frame, Vitti in the next) invariably differ from each other. I haven't cited it because it's obvious, but because it's painful, and because watching this scene requires a quality of attention that contemporary cinema, and artistic culture in general, seems determined to eradicate in favor of velocity and spectacle.

If the emotions in *L'Eclisse* are painful, they're communicated by intensely pleasurable means: the materiality of the objects in the room, Vitti's deliberative yet aimless pacing, the soft click of her heels, her pauses, the way she first parts the curtains along their seams and later, as if closing an imaginary curtain on a night-long drama, opens the real ones using the cord pull.

Little is said between the two actors, each line is essential to our understanding (of what they have been to each other, of his inability to accept the end of something, of her confusion over how to draw a bead on their breakup)—the scene is highly stylized, but nothing in it's inauthentic; with all due credit to Rabal's portrayal of a lost, broken person, it must be said that Vitti carries all the truly onerous responsibility for their psychological debris.

MONICA VITTI II

Monica Vitti is a being in the world who has, in many different ways, exampled for me how I can remain human, while playing the role of a bored, intellectual heiress (in *La Notte*) or a neurotic on the edge of breakdown, or Modesty Blaise, or, for that matter, me. The *fixé* on Vitti is many-sided. Antonioni's Vitti is the legible register of anxiety in the confrontation with the void. The Vitti of Losey's *Modesty Blaise* is the existential actor par excellence—the (completely ironic) action heroine, who performs specific, daring feats to resolve the crisis.

Vitti is the visage of collapse and the visage of triumph.

But that isn't all of it, by any means. Within *L'Eclisse* itself, Vitti registers a formidable range of inner states which few actresses have ever approximated: spontaneous gaiety, for example, and unrestrained zaniness (in the scene where she performs a "native dance" while dressed in the Kenyan souvenir adornments of a neighbor); perhaps most pertinent, here, are the longueurs of "empty time" in which Vitti finds, in everyday things—the bar of an airfield, the prancing of the neighbor's poodle on a darkened street, the sudden jet of a lawn sprinkler—a fascinated delight to which she entirely abandons herself, forgets her "identity"—or, better put, *refuses the problematic in which her life continually attempts to trap her* (her mother's emotionally diseased relationship to the Stock Exchange, Rabal's importunities just after their breakup, et al.); moreover, it is abundantly clear that the woman Vitti portrays (and whom Vitti would certainly need to understand from within her own experience) possesses both a high emotional intelligence and a philosophical insight that she only articulates *when it's necessary*.

MONICA VITTI III

It was the goal of modernism to make machines for creating more anxiety (paraphrasing Paul Valéry). I realized, watching it again after a decade, that Antonioni's film *Red Desert* is this perfected modernist machine; that the "carefree" moments that Monica Vitti interjected into her earlier works with Antonioni, as well as the moments of idle curiosity, were utilized in *Red Desert* with a small but terrifying inflection toward the dire and irremediable, the laugh that sours into tears, the smile that freezes into a rictus of panic; *Red Desert* is a world where everything is toxic, and beautiful at the same time; everything toxic is beautiful; the industrial sludge, the flaming jets of chemical poison, the deafening, blinding emissions of turbine steam; the optimism of this world is "progress" instead of "emotion," but this progress entails the transformation of what human beings were before into something else.

Alexander Kluge's "science fiction" hypothesizes men and women bred to function on other planets, in different atmospheres. Parts of their bodies might be genetically altered so that, for instance, persons who have to perform certain functions would have elephantine legs, or massive arms, while other parts would atrophy or shrink. This could be a metaphor for our psychic adaptation to technology.

Guiliana, Vitti's character in *Red Desert*, cannot adapt. She's terrified of this future world that already surrounds her, she becomes both atavistic and helpless: and the others are incapable of helping her; even her son, whom she loves with normal maternal tenderness, torments her by pretending that he suddenly cannot walk and has no feeling in his legs: I have always interpreted this episode as an expression of extreme cruelty of the child "performing" his mother's distress as if puzzling out the psychic movements of a being from another species.

DORIS DAY, HER IMAGE

If images summon antitheses (as extreme, exemplary images do—as opposed, perhaps, to variations), the binary opposite of Antonioni's Vitti is unquestionably Doris Day. Day's thirty-eighth film, *Where Were You When the Lights Went Out?*, attempted to spoof Day's show business persona as the perpetually wholesome, "freckle-faced American sweetheart"; she plays an actress who tells an interviewer, "I was hoping Broadway would maybe give me a change of image. . . . What happens: I'm still The Constant Virgin." The film goes as far as having Day's character's husband tell the interviewer, "I knew her before she was a virgin," an aperçu that Oscar Levant had minted about Doris years earlier.

This effort to rehaul the Doris Day image flopped. Renata Adler, reviewing the film in the *New York Times*, wrote, "Doris Day's honor, from movie to movie, was becoming a kind of drag as she tumbled from euphemism to innuendo. The beginning of each movie asked the question whether Anything was going to Happen, the middle raised the desperate possibility that something Had Happened, and then . . . she was married . . . she seems doomed to exclaim in every movie some version of the 'Oh, Peter, I'm tarnished' line she has in this one—a perennial, uncertainly comic inspiration, by virtue of what doesn't happen to her."

DORIS DAY, HER REALITY

Yet according to an exhaustively researched biography by David Kaufman, Doris Day really didn't like her wholesome image, after its initial, fantastic popularity. She thought the scripts of nearly all her films were insufferably banal. She felt rueful in her marriage to a husband who invested all her money in preposterous losing schemes. She loathed being typecast as a kind of alluringly impenetrable Disney cartoon of a grown woman, and seized whatever chances to break this stereotype presented themselves (*The Man Who Knew Too Much*, *Midnight Lace*)—but had finally to accept, with a remarkably philosophic, sanguine embrace of show business as an approximation of "real life," that audiences simply didn't want to see anything really bad happen to "Doris Day."

If Doris Day had been afflicted with neuroticism, she would have driven every other day to Oscar Levant's house, as Judy Garland did, to pilfer barbiturates and amphetamines from his medicine cabinet.

The only thing that truly enraged Doris Day was cruelty to animals.

Now, here is something strange: when she was not incarnating modernist anxiety and existential nausea, Monica Vitti brought home the bacon as the queen of frothy Italian sex comedies. A little gamier than Doris Day, but even so, they have more in common than you might imagine.

"SOMETHING'S MISSING"

Bloch and Adorno have a famous dialogue on this statement of Brecht: "something's missing." Utopia is nowhere, but without the wish for it, life is pointless. It would be silly to ask if something is incomplete because there is something missing: the form of the question determines how seriously we ponder it. Bloch: "I believe utopia cannot be removed from the world in spite of everything, and even the technological, which must definitely emerge and will be in the great realm of the utopian, will form only small sectors."

FACES

Nothing intrinsic disqualifies a face from being a fetish. When the subject of androgyny arises, it presumes that *someone is confused* about the gender of a person seen, or someone is confused about his/her gender. The face, the gait, the posture of this *object* is supposed to be misleading, or mistaken: Why?

If I had a picture of a boy's face, and I liked boys, and then learned it was a girl's face, I'd feel a different relation to it (though I might not understand why); in that situation, the face would have been a fetish (substitution) for imagined genitalia, until I found out what it really was. There is something wrong, something missing, in this "faceness" business, something false in desire, with the suite of expectations and wishes that images trail in their wake; just as there is something missing in the anticipation that a glove will weigh almost nothing, rather than a thousand pounds: all right. I don't have an answer for what is missing, or if the thing is complete because there's something missing, or *incomplete because nothing's missing*. But neither did Bloch, neither did Adorno.

Bloch: "And when now there is nothing else? There is a picture by Voltaire of despair—the total despair of a shipwrecked man who is swimming in the waves and struggling and squirming for his life when he receives the message that this ocean in which he finds himself does not have a shore but that death is completely in the now in which the shipwrecked man finds himself. This is why the striving of the swimmer will lead to nothing, for he will never land. It will always remain the same. To be sure, this strongest counter-utopia exists, and that must be said to make things more difficult."

But further, Bloch again, quoting Oscar Wilde: "A map of the world that does not include Utopia is not even worth glancing at."

FROZEN SAILOR

I opened a magazine when I was thirteen. Some people exploring in the far north of Canada, Baffin Bay or some such place, found the remains of a seafarer from a shipwreck, perfectly frozen and preserved just the way he looked when his ship ran aground in the ice pack. I don't remember if his arms were folded on his chest, or simply lay straight out as if he were inside a coffin. You could be glib about it and say he had been freeze-dried. And there was the picture, him, whoever he had been, dead, but not really, not as we picture death, not like a corpse in a coffin (though it did, the box he happened to be found in, look like a coffin, I seem to recall), not wearing makeup and drained and eviscerated, but the whole him, albeit teeth bared, as if to gnaw some passing shard of blubber.

I AND I

"The cut carries all the information." (Kluge) (Or the space that separates two ostensibly identical objects in different rooms, the splice that reconnects two severed sections of a line.)

"I" am not "I," almost never: for this moment that's passing, already past, carries its specific weight and lightness. "I" am advancing beyond *here* and arriving *there* (but never arriving, never coming to a stop, until *it stops*); I am never clear, never wish to be clear, about the distinction between human and geological time; I am, I was, an atomic particle, a quark, a short-lived event within a continuum; something akin to an inscription, a crack or a streak or a reflection in a tonnage of glass or metal, a fractured line, a squiggle of ink, a suicide lost forever in the water, a frozen sailor preserved by permafrost.

(2010)

VIVA MANCHETTE!

Ivory Pearl is the lion's share of a book, which, sadly, Jean-Patrick Manchette—polymath, chess whiz, jazz super-enthusiast, comic-book lover, literary genius—didn't live to finish. Like Boris Vian, who also died young, Manchette was impossibly over-gifted, able to do anything supremely well with playful grace and intelligence. Like Vian, he's an artist whose work was matched by a beautiful personality, an artist one falls in love with.

After a seven-year break from novel writing, freshly inspired by the espionage thrillers of Ross Thomas and John le Carré, Manchette saw a way forward, envisioning stories spread across a wider terrain than the French settings of his other works. Starting with *Ivory Pearl*, the series would follow its characters far into the second half of the twentieth century, much the way the three finished volumes of Jean-Paul Sartre's planned tetralogy, *Roads of Freedom*, track diverse Parisians from prewar café society through the "phony war," the real war, and the German occupation.

The final chapters of *Ivory Pearl* exist only as notes left by the author, here edited by his son. Even in this incomplete state, however, the novel brilliantly manifests the simultaneities and expansive purview Manchette intended.

> Samuel Farakhan was not sleeping. In thrall to the dubious lucidity of insomnia, he was sitting in his private study smoking a Player's Navy Cut, both hands trembling slightly in the white light of a desk lamp wreathed in the fine smoke of the English cigarettes. In Budapest, Rákosi had resigned under pressure from the Russians

and János Kádár and the social democrat György Marosán, long imprisoned for fascist Titoism but recently rehabilitated, had entered the Party's Political Bureau, while certain spokespeople of the Petőfi Circle were calling for the reinstatement of Imre Nagy. This was why Lajos had said somewhat laughingly that afternoon that "Perhaps I should return to Hungary, perhaps things are really going to budge this time and I should ask my American friends to sneak me back in."

Manchette knew that we don't know the laws of history. But he believed *Ivory Pearl* and its sequels might illuminate, for himself and his readers, how the power tectonics and changing mores of the decades he'd lived through produced the global mess we live in now.

In the 1970s, Manchette reconstituted the *roman policier* as a sleek vehicle for social critique, producing eleven wildly original novels, their impact still being felt today. In Manchette's devising, the *néo-polar* has little to do with crime solving or the police (though he invented an existentially troubled detective, Eugene Tarpon, in *Que d'os!* and *Morgue pleine*). For Manchette, whatever justice the system dispenses is itself a predictable criminal enterprise, hardly worth a paragraph. His fictions play out in a more atavistic realm of private vendettas and mercenary slaughter, supervised by "higher-ups" with far more power than any police. The stupendous violence in *Three to Kill* issues from a paramilitary thug's decision to snuff a witness who doesn't know he is one. In *The Prone Gunman*, killer-for-hire Martin Terrier works for an organization so heavily veiled that it might very well be the government, but even he isn't sure.

Like his compatriot writers Didier Daeninckx and Patrick Modiano, Manchette was haunted by France's infamies during the German occupation and the independence struggles of French colonies (*L'Affaire N'Gustro*, one of his first novels, is based on the 1965 abduction and presumed torture-death of the Moroccan opposition leader Mehdi Ben Barka), though much of this happened during his childhood or before he was born. Disillusioned by the wane of radical energies after May 1968, taking cues from Dashiell Hammett and Guy Debord, Manchette depicted a demoralized, melancholic society where legal authority routinely delegates its monopoly of violence to syndicates and goons, crime pays very well, and the cops always get a cut of the take. Everyday life's banal surfaces seethe with ant-like humans dazzled by advertising and consumer products and deadened by jobs and television. The only interruption of the scanning pattern happens when violence slashes into an otherwise mediocre existence.

Manchette's view is bleak, matter-of-fact, risibly acerbic in its flat descriptions of carnage. Today it seems indisputably accurate as well. Derisive of reactionaries, the bourgeoisie, doctrinaire leftists, and anyone else with an answer for everything, Manchette never completely obscures his longing for better times, and better people, but his nose for emotional fatuity is too sharp to indulge it. The romance of revolutionary action fares no better. His farcical *Nada* illustrates the idea that if you're part of the solution, you're part of the problem. The Nada Gang's kidnapping of the US ambassador translates the backfiring strategies of the early 1970s Baader-Meinhof RAF and the Italian Red Brigades into asinine, bloody slapstick. A connoisseur of unintended consequences, Manchette surely would have scorned the resurgent folly that people living in the present can decide to be "on the right side of history"—as if the future, however often it arrives as a train wreck, inevitably starts up again in the direction of Utopia. The best we can do, Manchette implies, is to stay on the right side of our own sense of decency, or try to.

Despite their unrelieved violence, or perhaps because of its antic excess, Manchette's crime novels are wickedly cheerful, an inexhaustible pleasure to read. They sport characters so hollowed out and damaged that the adventures they embark on, often unwillingly and unwittingly, peel off whatever moral veneer and certainly whatever squeamishness they possess. If they finish up unimproved or destroyed, it must be noted that they were nothing special to begin with—sleepwalkers of capitalism, basically. But for a time they become compelling, forced to scramble for their lives against monstrous opponents. Frequently ripped from their urban comfort zones and hounded into wastelands of alien wilderness, isolated cabins, rural villages, and the like, reduced to eating berries and raw snake meat, they tap into a resourcefulness that suggests, at least to our imagination, different paths their lives might travel if they ever reach safety. When they're not dodging assassination, Manchette's personae listen to West Coast jazz, which indicates at least some dormant inner life.

Manchette's behaviorist style favors fractal glimpses of people rather than longueurs of subjectivity. Inner twaddle doesn't interest him. In prose so spare and precise it looks shaved with a straight razor, he brings people (and landscapes, buildings, ordinary objects) into vital clarity.

> The man could have been thirty or a little over. . . . His eyes were neither dark nor very pale. Ivy had a good close-up view of him through her 200 mm telephoto lens. He had a wide forehead beneath an unkempt shock of tow hair, strands of which fell over his ears. He was athletic, well built and deeply tanned. . . .
> Between his left nipple and his collarbone, a round scar was visible, absolutely white and roughly the size of a half dollar. When the hunter swung around with the black pig over his shoulders, Ivy could see his back, with on its left side a growth of gray and white scar tissue as big as a small tomato. Clearly the man had been run through by something.

His characters take shape through fleeting expressions, gestures, physical sensations (the weight of a holstered gun against an armpit, say, or, in *The Mad and the Bad*, the killer Thompson's churning gastritis), and dialogue as artlessly awkward as fumbling everyday speech. Everything in Manchette's novels is revealed through instability and menace. This is true of *Ivory Pearl* as well as the *néo-polars*, but *Ivory Pearl* differs from them in several interesting ways.

One striking difference is the immediate sympathy elicited for the principals—the famous war photographer Ivory Pearl; her mentor, the brewing heir and retired British army officer Samuel Farakhan; Farakhan's Hungarian boyfriend, Lajos Obersoxszki; the fugitives Ivory Pearl meets in Cuba, Victor Maurer and Negra. These are fleshed out with fuller backstories, and more appealing personal traits, than most of Manchette's earlier creatures, who often behave like panicking lab rats. Readers want *Fatale*'s Aimée Joubert or *The Prone Gunman*'s Martin Terrier to prevail mainly because their antagonists are even more twisted than they are. We root for Ivory Pearl, Farakhan, and the others, however, because they have clean hearts, despite the toxic secrets and agendas they conceal from one another. It can also be argued that the villains of the piece—not the hired psychopath Guido and his hit squad, but the casually murderous arms dealer Aaron Black, his streamlined assistant Julienne, and his son Simon, a moron—loom as avatars of their kind, giant pollinators of an ugly Zeitgeist, rather than merely evil as shit. Society needs such people. That is the problem Manchette is getting at.

Another difference is this novel's treatment of time. As already mentioned, Manchette's crime novels evoke a stagnant, reactionary period in France—the interminable 1970s, in which revolutionary violence was answered with repressive brutality, spreading a form of collective clinical depression. This despairing atmosphere is perfectly evoked in such films as Jacques Rivette's *Le Pont du Nord* and Robert Bresson's *The Devil, Probably*. Manchette's novels of the era note passing time by seasonal changes and alternations of night and day; exact months and years go unremarked, since the rotten state of things promises to drag on forever. In a way, this is slightly ameliorative; the minimal temporal mooring permits us to read *Fatale* or *Three to Kill* as hellish fairy tales floating in a vaguely familiar limbo: "And sometimes what used to happen was what is happening now: Georges Gerfaut is driving on Paris's outer ring road." When was then and when is now are equally fuzzy.

Ivory Pearl has its fairy-tale dimensions; timelessness isn't one of them. The novel begins on New Year's Day, 1956, and every significant action that follows is practically date-stamped and aligned with world events of that year, one of the frostiest of the early Cold War.

An inventory of pertinent milestones: In February, the British spies Guy Burgess and Donald Maclean, missing for five years, turn up in Moscow. In a closed session, Khrushchev denounces Stalin to the Twentieth Congress of the Soviet Communist Party, citing numerous crimes (in which Khrushchev and most of his audience have been loyally complicit).

In March, Morocco and then Tunisia declare independence from France. Pakistan becomes the first Islamic republic.

In May, Minister of State Pierre Mendès-France, having negotiated the French withdrawal from Indochina two years earlier, resigns from the government over its Algeria policy. Meanwhile, fighting between the Viet Cong and the US-backed ARVN enters its second year.

In June, the Algerian National Liberation Front commences guerrilla warfare with random shootings of civilians. Gamal Nasser becomes the second president of Egypt. Government troops crush a popular uprising in Poland.

In July, Nasser nationalizes the Suez Canal.

In August, at the Republican National Convention in San Francisco, a movement to replace Richard Nixon with the Massachusetts governor Christian Herter as the vice presidential candidate for Eisenhower's second term fails.

In October, the Hungarian Uprising, partly sparked by the Petőfi Circle of intellectuals led by Georg Lukács, precipitates the Soviet army's invasion of Hungary. Israel invades the Sinai, driving the Egyptian army back to Suez. The United Kingdom and France begin bombing Egypt to reopen the Suez Canal—France in retaliation for Egypt's support of the Algerian FLN. In early November, Dwight D. Eisenhower is reelected to the American presidency, with Richard Nixon as his vice president. In late November, Fidel Castro, Raúl Castro, Che Guevara, and seventy-nine other fighters set off on the yacht *Granma* from Tuxpan, Mexico, landing on December 2 at Playa Las Coloradas and taking refuge in the Sierra Maestra in Cuba.

Connections between the cast of *Ivory Pearl* and these distant happenings flash in and out of sight like livid tapestry threads under shifting light: Farakhan was at Cambridge with Burgess and Maclean; a progressive journal whose board he sits on, probably funded by the CIA, receives a leaked copy of Khrushchev's speech, which prompts the Hungarian revolt to go forward; Aaron Black sells weapons to all sides of the Algerian conflict, jets around sniffing out markets for the all-new AK-47, and presumably funnels money to Richard Nixon; photographs taken by Ivory Pearl in the Sierra Maestra, passed to French and American intelligence, trigger dire actions, separately, by Lajos Obersoxszki, Farakhan, and Aaron Black, etc., etc.

Manchette compels us to examine the stories we tell ourselves in light of the bigger, oppressive stories unfolding around us, to think about history as something we collectively make as well as something that makes us. Contingency and chance decide much of what happens in this novel, but the individual characters also make decisions of their own, and their actions ripple powerfully into the world at large. I've avoided discussing the actual plot of *Ivory Pearl*, in the outcome of which whole governments, waging proxy wars all over the planet, have a significant stake. That story is a Shakespearean drama of dynastic succession and inheritance. Its various loose threads, gathered from scattered sites where blood and capital run together, suddenly tighten into a garrote. The intrepidly calculated time scheme of this novel suggests either a world on the verge of transformation or an immutable process taking its fatal course, obscured by endless cover stories.

Since the question is still with us, we can only wish Manchette had lived to answer it to his own satisfaction. Instead, he left us this masterpiece.

(2018)